The Potteries Derbies

Jeff Kent

Witan Books

Jeff Kent was born in 1951 and educated at Hanley High School in Stoke-on-Trent. He gained a second-class honours degree in International Relations from London University in 1973 and has lectured at several colleges in North Staffordshire.

He is a prolific writer on a variety of subjects and has previously published eight books: "The Rise And Fall of Rock", "Principles Of Open Learning", "The Last Poet: The Story Of Eric Burdon" and a series of works on the history of Port Vale.

Jeff was a pioneer of Green music, has recorded two environmental concept albums and has performed benefit concerts for several environmental and humanitarian organisations. In addition, he is currently the co-ordinator of the radical political group, The Mercia Movement.

He has been a supporter of local football since 1956 when he was taken at the age of four to watch his cousin, Harry Poole, make his first team debut for Vale. Like many people, for a number of years, Jeff supported whichever Potteries team was at home and, although he gradually came to prefer the more tranquil atmosphere at Vale Park, he continued to watch Stoke occasionally, especially when they were in the old First Division. Not surprisingly, Jeff has been present at most of the Potteries Derbies played during the last forty years.

Witan Creations
1998 Main Catalogue

WTN 001   "Butcher's Tale"/"Annie, With The Dancing Eyes" – Jeff Kent & The Witan (animal rights protest single), 1981 – £1.50 including p & p.

WTN 002   "The Rise And Fall Of Rock" – Jeff Kent (484 page critical Rock music history, 56 photographs), 1983 – £8 including p & p.

WTN 025   "The Port Vale Record 1879-1993" – Jeff Kent (292 page statistical compilation, 60 photographs), 1993 – £4.75 including p & p.

WTN 027   "The Mercia Manifesto: A Blueprint For The Future Inspired By The Past" – The Mercia Movement (128 page radical political manifesto), 1997 – £7.80 including p & p.

WTN 028   "The Man Who Sank The Titanic?: The Life And Times Of Captain Edward J. Smith" – Gary Cooper (180 page biography of the merchant navy's most controversial captain, 70 photographs), 1998 – £13.10 including p & p.

The Potteries Derbies

First published in November 1998 by Witan Books, Cherry Tree House, 8 Nelson Crescent, Cotes Heath, via Stafford, ST21 6ST, England. Tel. (01782) 791673.

Copyright © 1998, Jeff Kent.

WTN 029

ISBN 0 9529152 3 5

A CIP record for this book is available from the British Library.

Cover concept: Jeff Kent.
Cover artwork: Ken Longmore.
Editorial adviser: Rosalind Kent.
Historical consultants: Pete Wyatt, Wade Martin, Phil Sherwin and Reg Edwards.
Main research: Jeff Kent, Cyril Kent, Pete Wyatt, Wade Martin, Phil Sherwin and Steve Carr.
Typeset, printed and bound by: PKA Print & Design, 5 & 7 Dunning Street, Tunstall, Stoke-on-Trent, ST6 5AP. Tel. (01782) 575280.

All rights reserved. No part of this publication may be reproduced, stored in a retrieval system or transmitted in any form or by any means, electronic, mechanical, photocopying, recording or otherwise without the prior permission in writing of the publisher.

This book is sold subject to the condition that it shall not, by way of trade or otherwise, be lent, resold, hired out or otherwise circulated without the publisher's prior written consent in any form of binding or cover other than that in which it is published and without a similar condition including this condition being imposed on the subsequent purchaser.

Dedicated to friendly rivalry

ACKNOWLEDGEMENTS

I should like to express my thanks to the following people and organisations for their invaluable assistance, not credited elsewhere, in the production of this book:

Colin Atkinson, Ian Bailey, Katherine Bailey, Paul Bailey, Ian Bayley, The British Newspaper Library, Andy Burgess, Jim Creasy, Alan Downs, Michael Featherstone, Peter Freeman, Kevin Frost, Terry Frost, Barry Hugman, Andy Jackson, Ken Longmore, Colin MacKenzie, Dave McPherson, Newcastle-under-Lyme Library, Lorna Parnell/The Football League Limited, Brian Pead, Dave Porter, Kevin Powell, Carole Reynolds/Manchester Central Library, Frank Rickerby/The British Library, Lindon Roberts, Jim Rushton, Dave Smith, Ray Spiller/The Association of Football Statisticians, Martin Spinks/Staffordshire Sentinel Newspapers Ltd, Allan Staples, Stoke-on-Trent City Central Library, Tony Tams, Graham Wilkes and Glen Wilmore.

ILLUSTRATION CREDITS

Illustrations were kindly supplied by the following:

Wade Martin – front cover, 9-11, 20, 21, 23, 41, 43; Smith Davis Press Agency – back cover, 45, 47, 48, 50-55, 57; Pete Wyatt – 1-3, 17; Norman Gosling – 4; Andrew Bowler/The Stoke City Memorabilia Collectors Club – 5, 8, 13, 14, 22, 24, 25, 27, 29, 39, 40, 44; Ian Johnson – 6, 31, 35, 37, 38, 49; Vera Mayland – 7; Don Briscoe – 12; Ray Johnson – 15; Phil Sherwin – 16, 19, 36, 42; Dave Porter – 18, 28; Brian Herbert – 26, 30, 32-34; Bob Wyper/Port Vale Football Club – 46; Paul Bradbury/Stoke City Football Club – 56.

Contents

Preface 1

The History 3

The Matches 18

The Statistics 199

    Stoke's Playing Record 200

    Vale's Playing Record 201

    Big Crowds 202

    Small Crowds 203

    Big Scores 204

    Hat Trick Heroes 205

    Most Appearances 206

    Top Goalscorers 208

Preface

At both Stoke and Vale, there is a long-standing tradition for the home fans to cheer loudly whenever it is announced on the scoreboard that their local rivals have conceded a goal. The more goals that they have conceded, the more enthusiastic the response! On occasions, long-suffering supporters lulled into silence through an uninspiring performance by their favourites on the pitch have been known to burst spontaneously and joyfully into life at the merest rumour that "the enemy" have gone behind! For most Vale and Stoke fans, it is almost as important that their arch rivals have lost a match as it is that their own team have won. Although, fortunately, few of the supporters are so passionate that they resort to violence when they encounter rival local fans, there are probably still fewer who genuinely and actively back both teams. Almost invariably, it is either Stoke or Vale. The clubs themselves have exhibited a variety of responses to each other throughout their history, but rarely have they been contented bed partners. Consequently, the rivalry between the two footballing giants of the Potteries is intense and little excites the emotions of local football supporters as much as a Potteries Derby match. It is the purpose of this book to encapsulate and record for posterity the events and emotions surrounding the fixture, which has dominated the sporting calendar in Stoke-on-Trent for well over a century.

The compilation and production of "The Potteries Derbies" proved a triumph for teamwork. More than in almost any of my previous works, the successful completion of this project relied upon the major input and kindness of several highly-respected football historians to such an extent that it is doubtful whether a satisfactory conclusion could have been reached without them. Pete Wyatt, a virtual walking encyclopedia on the history of Stoke City, loaned me for several months almost his entire collection of files and notebooks on the club, without once requesting any recompense for the provision of this absolutely invaluable information. Pete's extraordinary support was complemented by the watchful eye of Wade Martin, the celebrated author of "A Potter's Tale: The Story of Stoke City Football Club", whose painstaking constructive criticism of the text kept me on my toes throughout. It was also my privilege once more to work with Phil Sherwin and Reg Edwards, foremost authorities on the history of Port Vale, and, as ever, most of the few remaining gaps in information were filled by a number of other football statisticians only too eager to help at a moment's notice. In addition, my ageless father, Cyril Kent, acted as a major troubleshooter, eliminating a welter of problems and discrepancies through his diligent library research. Finally, my work, as always, had to run the gauntlet of my eagle-eyed and long-suffering wife and editor, Rosalind Kent.

As on previous occasions, I tried to exhaust all the sources in the quest for every shred of available information, but I am still unable to claim that this history is complete because a few details have not been traced and were almost certainly never recorded. I spent a vast number of hours on microfilm readers in the reference sections of both Stoke-on-Trent City Central Library and Newcastle-under-Lyme Library extracting vital facts from "The Staffordshire

PREFACE

Sentinel", the fundamental source for nearly all the match reports and of all the quotations used in this book unless otherwise stated. Nevertheless, it was essential to make further visits to the Football League to consult their dusty, but unique, records, whilst a trawl of "The Athletic News" at Manchester Central Library helped to fill several gaps.

The reader should also note that the majority of the crowds listed prior to the 1925-1926 season were newspaper estimates and primarily those of "The Sentinel", whilst all the Football League attendances from that time onwards were taken from the official sources (which then became available), as were the figures presented for the two F.A. Cup matches in 1951. Unfortunately, the crowds as reported by "The Sentinel" since 1925 have frequently been at odds with the returns as logged by the Football League and the situation has been further complicated in recent times by the inclusion of all Stoke's season ticket holders in their official gates, whilst, in contrast, the figures for Vale represent only the spectators who actually attend their games!

One additional point needs to be made for the benefit of vigilant readers who will notice that in a number of places where there are gaps in my information, the books written on Stoke City by Tony Matthews present specific data. It is no lapse on my part that I have not repeated this because my familiarity with the work of Matthews has unfortunately led me to regard him as being an unreliable source of historical detail.

I hope you will find "The Potteries Derbies" to be a valuable work of reference and I would be pleased to receive feedback from anyone who discovers any errors or has additional information which I can consider prior to publishing a future edition.

Jeff Kent,
Cotes Heath, October 1998.

The History

The History

Although it seems normal to football supporters in the Potteries that Stoke City and Port Vale, broadly representing the south and north of the city respectively, are the arch rivals in the area, this is the outcome of particular historical circumstances and there was nothing natural or inevitable about it. At the time of the foundation of Stoke and Vale, Hanley was the most populous town in the Potteries and later developed into a city centre, yet it has never spawned a Football League club, nor come remotely near doing so. Likewise, Tunstall, Fenton and Longton and neighbouring Newcastle-under-Lyme have remained backwaters of football. That Stoke-upon-Trent and Burslem became the local Meccas of the game is the result of very specific factors which came into play during the embryonic period of football in the area.

It was traditionally believed that Stoke were formed in 1863, but in 1988 Wade Martin produced persuasive evidence in his book, "A Potter's Tale", that the club was formally founded as Stoke Ramblers in 1868. This early origin was to prove an immense advantage and it gave the club at least an eight-year head start over Vale, whose establishment has been claimed as being in 1876, but was most probably in 1879. The Stoke founders were ex-public schoolboys who became apprentices at the North Staffordshire Railway Works, which was based in the town, and although their apparent leader, Henry John Almond, left the district after the initial match, the club had been born. Although Stoke's first games were played against relatively local teams, such as Congleton and Leek, they soon engaged opposition from further afield and within a few years were regularly pitched against sides from across the Midlands and the north-west of England. As football developed into a popular pastime and Stoke's opponents became increasingly attractive, so the crowds watching the matches grew and the club's takings burgeoned.

In 1879, Stoke were easily the premier team in the Potteries, having secured the Staffordshire Cup both times it had been contested, and were sufficiently powerful to achieve a magnificent 1-0 victory at Aston Villa in a friendly game on 11 October of that year. Cobridge and Talke Rangers were other strong local sides at that time, whilst "The Staffordshire Sentinel" recorded ten teams with "Burslem" in their names in 1879 alone. None of them was Port Vale, who were relative latecomers on the scene, almost certainly formed by a group of working-class breakaways from the moderately successful Porthill Victoria. The main objective of the Vale founders, led by Enoch Hood, was simply to play football closer to their work places and homes in the valley of ports on the Trent and Mersey Canal below.

On 15 March 1880, Teddy Johnson, a dashing centre-forward, played for England against Wales and thereby became Stoke's first international. Just over seven months later, "The Staffordshire Daily Sentinel" made the very first press reference to Port Vale, whose second team had won a friendly match 1-0 at Hot Lane on 16 October. Despite the continuation of Stoke's almost constant progress, the gap between the two clubs had narrowed considerably by 1882 when Vale finally moved out of the shadows and on to the full stage of Potteries

THE HISTORY

football history. That they did so was partly because they were paired with Stoke in the second round of the Staffordshire Cup on 2 December and, perhaps even more importantly, because they had the audacity to draw 1-1 with their mighty opponents before inevitably losing the replay at Stoke, which merited a sizable report in "The Sentinel". Vale were rapidly becoming the major footballing force, not only in Burslem, but also in the whole of the north of the Potteries. Their meteoric rise seems to have been a result of their early adoption of the novel passing game (as opposed to the traditional tactic of dribbling), their acquisition of a ground at Westport where they were able to charge admission and the consequent attractiveness of the club to better players in other nearby teams.

However, Stoke remained supreme in North Staffordshire and their 5-1 hammering of Vale in the Staffordshire Cup replay on 9 December 1882 was their first of thirteen successive victories against their new rivals. Nevertheless, Vale won their first trophy in 1883, the North Staffordshire Charity Challenge Cup, although they were twice beaten by Stoke in friendly matches during the 1883-1884 season. In the summer of 1884, Vale made further progress by constructing a new and larger ground in a more central location within Burslem, off Moorland Road, and added the name of the town as a prefix to their title. The following year, Vale became a limited company, with share capital to enable them to compete with other important clubs for the best players following the legalisation of professionalism, whilst Stoke also began to engage professional footballers.

After a two-year gap, the two teams met twice at the tail end of the 1885-1886 campaign, with the game on 1 May attracting a then record crowd to the Victoria Ground, whilst three weeks later, Stoke defeated their rivals to win the North Staffordshire Charity Challenge Cup. In the summer of 1886, Vale were once more on the move, to another newly-constructed stadium at Cobridge, whilst in November of that year they filed a case at Burslem County Court for breach of contract by two of their players, Billy Rowley and George Bateman, who had left to join Stoke. The court upheld Vale's case and Stoke consequently agreed to pay their costs, release the players and donate £20 to a charity. However, the incident served only to intensify the competition between the two clubs.

Stoke won all three of the friendly matches contested with their local rivals during the 1886-1887 season, that on 26 March being the first one staged at Vale's new Athletic Ground. Stoke continued their excellent Potteries Derbies form with three further victories during the following campaign, the most important of which was a 1-0 success at home in the first qualifying round of the English Cup on 15 October 1887. In 1888, Stoke became founder members of the prestigious Football League, whilst Vale joined the Football Combination, which was composed of strong clubs that had not gained admission to the premier competition. Thenceforth, the friendly games arranged between the Potteries teams increasingly declined in importance because there was little at stake except for local pride.

Although Stoke finished at the bottom of the initial Football League, they remained too powerful for their Cobridge rivals and put nine goals past them

THE HISTORY

in gaining two friendly victories in the late winter of 1889. However, on 20 May of that year, Vale at last ended their dismal sequence of Potteries Derbies results in securing a 1-1 draw at Cobridge and then followed up by sharing the spoils for the first time ever at the Victoria Ground on 30 November. Even better was to come for them because they gained their opening victory against Stoke in their seventeenth attempt, by 2-1 at home on 29 March 1890, and, to prove that this was no fluke, they won a further clash at Cobridge 3-1 six weeks later. That completed a dreadful year for Stoke, who dropped into the Football Alliance after once more ending up at the foot of the Football League and failing to gain re-election. At the same time, Vale became founder members of the new Midland League.

Stoke bounced back in the 1890-1891 season and won the championship of the Football Alliance, which helped them to obtain election to the Football League, whilst they recovered their footballing supremacy in the Potteries because Vale were unable to win any of the four Derbies played. Nevertheless, the most important of these, the final of the North Staffordshire Charity Challenge Cup, was drawn and the two clubs shared the trophy. The honours were even in three friendly games the following season, although Vale recorded their first ever victory away to Stoke (who included four England internationals), by 2-0 on 7 May 1892, to take the Staffordshire Charity Cup and finally achieve success in a competitive match against their rivals. That same month, Vale received a further boost by gaining inclusion in the Football League's newly-formed Second Division. Thereafter, the Potteries clubs concentrated their main efforts on the league and the English Cup and in consequence their friendly contests attracted diminishing numbers of spectators. One exception, however, was the game on 30 October 1893, which was advertised as 'the championship of the Potteries' and drew an impressive 5,000 fans to the Athletic Ground. Although Vale won on this occasion, they conceded eleven goals at home in two similarly billed encounters later that season, neither of which captured the public's imagination to the same extent.

The prospect of small crowds failed to dissuade the two clubs from organising three local Derby friendlies during the 1894-1895 campaign, which confirmed Stoke as the dominant team because they won two of them in spite of selecting a number of reserves, whilst the other was drawn. In addition, Stoke moved to the forefront as a club in March 1895 when they became a limited liability company, with a total value of £600. 1895-1896 was a particularly bad season for Vale because they were hammered 4-0 at home by Stoke in the first round of the Staffordshire Cup and, upon finishing third from the bottom of the Second Division, failed to gain re-election and were forced to return to the Midland League. In marked contrast, Stoke achieved their highest placing thus far in the First Division in finishing sixth. Vale's crowds fell alarmingly in their new tournament matches and their financial position became so desperate that they were only able to fulfil their league fixture at Heanor Town on 5 December 1896 because the home side lent them the required £5 expenses! Nevertheless, the club stabilised itself as a result of a resuscitation meeting and the team's confidence had sufficiently improved by 26 April 1897 for them to beat Stoke 2-0 in a friendly, although the latter actually selected their reserve side.

6

THE HISTORY

Vale kept up the good work the following season, remaining undefeated by their local rivals in three games, the most important of which was a Staffordshire Cup semi-final at Cobridge, which the home team won 3-1. Vale went on to secure the trophy for the first time and, more importantly, found themselves elected to the Second Division of the Football League in May 1898. A league clash with Stoke during the next campaign was prevented by a whisker because the latter retained their First Division status, after finishing bottom of the table, in the test matches which followed the season proper. Stoke took advantage of their reprieve to progress and reached the English Cup semi-finals in 1899, although their 1-0 home victory against Vale just over a month later attracted a mere 500 spectators. Nevertheless, the two clubs staged three further friendlies the following season, with Vale winning two and Stoke one, but the two recorded crowds sank to just 300 and 400!

In the autumn of 1900, the local rivals were drawn against each other in the first round of the Birmingham Cup and the Staffordshire Cup and Stoke took the honours in both cases before going on to win the former competition. However, Vale turned the tables in the spring when the two teams met in a benefit game for Vale's centre-half, Jim Beech. There were four Potteries Derbies in the 1901-1902 campaign and although Vale progressed in the Birmingham Cup after a replay, at the expense of their rivals, Stoke took the honours in a Staffordshire Cup tie and a friendly match. They gained further kudos the following March when the Wales international side fielded three Stoke players (Dickie Roose, Sam Meredith and Mart Watkins) in a goalless draw at home to England. The autumn of 1902 witnessed further local clashes in the Birmingham Cup and the Staffordshire Cup, both of which ended to Stoke's advantage, although the outcome in the latter was only decided in a replay. Indeed, Stoke produced particularly good form in the 1902-1903 season and finished just five points adrift of the First Division champions in sixth place.

Remarkably, the Potteries teams met in both the Birmingham Cup and the Staffordshire Cup for the fourth successive year in September 1903, with Stoke recording their sixth and seventh victories against their local rivals over that period in the two competitions. In addition, Stoke went on to share the Staffordshire Cup in 1904 as a result of two drawn games with Wolverhampton Wanderers in the final. For a change, Vale and Stoke were paired together only in the Birmingham Cup the following autumn and it was Vale who finally triumphed, after a replay. The Cobridge side kept up the good work by eliminating Stoke (who fielded their reserve team) from both the Birmingham Cup and the Staffordshire Cup within the space of seven days in September 1905, but were then thrashed at the next stage in both tournaments.

The 1906-1907 season proved an immense disappointment for Stoke because they finished at the foot of the First Division and were consequently relegated. This, therefore, should have led to their first Football League matches against Vale, which were scheduled for 7 September 1907 at the Victoria Ground and 4 January 1908 at Cobridge. However, the drawn local Derby of 29 April 1907, arranged for the benefit of Ted Holdcroft (an ex-player of both sides), was sadly the final one ever contested by Burslem Port Vale because a

THE HISTORY

decision to wind up the club was taken in the summer, following years of serious financial problems. Nevertheless, the spirit of the club was kept alive by Cobridge Church, a minor junior outfit, who took over the Athletic Ground, changed their name to "Port Vale" and stepped up into the North Staffordshire Federation League, but completed their first campaign in only fifth position out of nine teams before moving on to the North Staffordshire And District League.

Although Stoke stabilised their playing fortunes in the 1907-1908 season and reached the quarter-finals of the English Cup, the club unfortunately followed in Vale's footsteps and was likewise put into liquidation, in June 1908, because of a lack of funds. However, a surge of belated public interest enabled a new company to be formed almost immediately, although membership of the Football League could not be regained and Stoke subsequently found themselves in the Birmingham And District League. Although in their initial campaign in the new tournament they could only finish eighth, they were in immensely better shape than Vale, who were floundering at the bottom of the North Staffordshire And District League in December 1908 and were eliminated from the May Bank Cup on Boxing Day by Stoke Reserves. However, at this juncture, a group of former Burslem Port Vale officials bought themselves into the club, which gave fresh impetus.

Stoke continued to participate in the Birmingham And District League until 1911, when they won the championship, and also joined the Southern League, Division Two (West) in 1909. They topped this competition at the first attempt, winning every game in the process, and were promoted in second place from a combined second division the following season. At the same time, Vale remained in the North Staffordshire And District League where Stoke Reserves became amongst their main rivals. In the 1909-1910 season, Vale won the first clash, in the league, although Stoke Reserves turned the tables in the Hanley Cup final. However, Vale secured the locally prestigious Staffordshire Junior Cup, but the North Staffordshire And District League championship-deciding match at the Victoria Ground was abandoned following a pitch invasion with the visitors 2-0 ahead and the outcome of the tournament remained undecided because of an insoluble dispute which consequently developed! Nevertheless, the Staffordshire F.A. ordered the closure of Stoke's ground for the opening two weeks of the next campaign.

The 1910-1911 season was Vale's last as a junior club, but brought them four straight defeats by Stoke Reserves. As well as completing a league double, the latter knocked their rivals out of the North Staffordshire Nursing Society's Cup and the Hanley Cup, both of which they went on to win. The last of these games, played on 14 January 1911, proved to be the final Potteries Derby to be hosted at the Athletic Ground.

In the summer of 1911, Vale formed a new limited liability company and gained admission to the Central League, which consisted of Football League reserve sides with a smattering of other strong teams. Vale took a liking to this competition and, in four seasons as members, never finished outside the top four, whilst additionally they won the Staffordshire Cup in 1912 and the Birmingham Cup in 1913. At the same time as Vale's fortunes were waxing, those of Stoke were on the wane and they were relegated in bottom position

THE HISTORY

from the First Division of the Southern League in 1913. However, they won the Staffordshire Cup during the following campaign and on 4 April 1914 drew 0-0 at Vale's new stadium (the Old Recreation Ground) in Hanley in the final of the Birmingham Cup. The replay, which attracted a new record local Derby crowd to the Victoria Ground, ended 2-1 in favour of Stoke, who swept their opponents out of the same competition for good measure the next autumn also. Nevertheless, Vale gained revenge by eliminating Stoke from the North Staffordshire Infirmary Cup in January 1915 and went on to win the tournament, although their rivals turned the tables in a friendly two months later and then secured the championship of the Second Division of the Southern League.

Stoke recovered their Football League status on 19 July 1915 when they were elected to the Second Division, but their participation in the competition was delayed until 1919 because of the suspension of normal footballing activities as a result of the impact of the First World War. In the meantime, they operated in the Lancashire Regional Section of the wartime league, which Vale joined in 1916 after a year of inactivity. The two teams met four times in each of the following three seasons, being grouped in the same mini-section of a subsidiary tournament as well as clashing in the main competition. Stoke edged the honours in the 1916-1917 campaign, winning two of the local contests compared with Vale's one victory, and also triumphed in a further Derby arranged as a benefit for the North Staffordshire Regiment Prisoners of War Fund.

Stoke produced magnificent form in the 1917-1918 season to take the Lancashire Regional Section championship and beat Vale on six separate occasions, which included two Christmas friendly matches. Stoke fared almost as well in the final wartime competition in finishing as the runners-up and recorded three further successive victories (including one in a friendly) against their old rivals. Their triumph on 12 October 1918, by the remarkable score of 8-1 in the league at Hanley, still stands as a record for a Potteries Derby. However, Vale bounced back to gain a draw at the Victoria Ground in the final Subsidiary Tournament before surprisingly winning the return 4-1.

The Football League resumed its competitions proper in August 1919 and Stoke finally took their place in the Second Division, whilst Vale reverted to the Central League. On 6 October 1919, the Hanley side equalled their record local Derby score in winning a benefit game for their centre-half, Harry Pearson, by 5-0 and were sensationally elected to the Football League a week later after Leeds City had been expelled for their failure to answer allegations of illegal payments during the war period. The following Monday, Vale celebrated their good fortune in style by overcoming Stoke 1-0 in the first round of the Staffordshire Cup and went on to lift the trophy. The first ever full Football League Potteries Derby, which drew an all-time record crowd to the Old Recreation Ground on 6 March 1920, ended in a 3-0 victory to Stoke, whilst the return match finished goalless and proved even more popular with the public. The local rivals met for a fifth time that season, to contest the North Staffordshire Infirmary Cup, which was shared following a goalless draw.

Vale achieved a league double over their neighbours in the 1920-1921 campaign, with a still higher attendance being recorded at the Victoria Ground

9

THE HISTORY

on 2 October 1920, although Stoke gained revenge by winning the North Staffordshire Infirmary Cup. The balance of success was reversed the next season because Stoke, who achieved promotion in second place, took three points from the league Derbies, defeated their rivals in the first round of the English Cup and battled strongly to earn a 0-0 draw in the North Staffordshire Infirmary Cup. With Stoke's elevation to the top flight, the only local contest staged during the 1922-1923 campaign was in the almost annual hospital competition, which the premier team won 3-1. This victory, however, did little to ease Stoke's disappointment at their relegation from the First Division after just one season. Consequently, the league Derbies resumed in the autumn of 1923 and Stoke were triumphant in both games, whilst they reinforced their dominance by securing the North Staffordshire Infirmary Cup in addition. However, the positions were reversed in the 1924-1925 campaign when Vale achieved a league double over their old rivals.

In August 1925, Stoke added the suffix of "City" to their name in order to harmonise with Stoke-on-Trent's new title, but Vale confirmed their new-found status as the top side in the Potteries by winning both of the league Derbies 3-0 in the early stages of the 1925-1926 season. However, there was an extraordinary development the following April when the Vale directors agreed in principle to amalgamate the club with that of their arch rivals. Although the Vale supporters threatened to establish a new team at Cobridge, delegates of the two clubs met to discuss the proposal, but it was turned down by the Stoke board in May, even though their side had been relegated from the Second Division.

Stoke bounced back with a vengeance and took the Third Division (North) championship in 1927, with five points to spare, before trouncing Vale 5-0 to secure the North Staffordshire Royal Infirmary Cup. The next season, Vale picked up three points from the league Derbies, with that on 5 November attracting a new record crowd for the fixture to the Victoria Ground, but Stoke reached the quarter-finals of the F.A. Cup and finished only five points adrift of a second successive promotion. It was Vale's turn to taste relegation in penultimate position in the 1928-1929 campaign and, to add to their discomfiture, Stoke gained a league double over them. Even worse, financial pressures forced them to sell their leading scorer, Wilf Kirkham, to their dreaded rivals. However, like Stoke before them, Vale won the Third Division (North) championship at the first attempt, with a then record 67 points, although the former secured the North Staffordshire Royal Infirmary Cup by beating their local rivals 2-1.

Despite gaining just one point from the two Derbies during the 1930-1931 season, Vale finished in their highest ever Football League position, fifth in the Second Division, although the contest at Hanley on 18 April 1931 attracted the fixture's all-time lowest league gate. However, Vale's overall progress was not maintained and they were hammered 4-0 in the local clash on 26 September 1931, although the two points they picked up from the return the following February proved vital in helping them to maintain their divisional status on goal average. Nevertheless, they were acutely embarrassed in May when Stoke won what turned out to be the final North Staffordshire Royal Infirmary Cup match by 7-0! Indeed, Stoke hit excellent form during the next

THE HISTORY

campaign, gaining a league double over their old rivals and taking the Second Division championship with a point in hand. It subsequently transpired that the game at the Old Recreation Ground on 4 March 1933, which Stoke won 3-1, was the last local Derby to be contested in the Football League proper for over twenty-one years.

Because Vale and Stoke essentially operated in different spheres from 1933, the spate of Potteries Derbies was at an end and there were only two more prior to the Second World War. Stoke quickly stabilised themselves in the First Division and reached the quarter-finals of the F.A. Cup in 1934 before being eliminated by 1-0 at Manchester City in front of a remarkable crowd of 84,569! Vale largely continued to hold their own in the Second Division, but the quality gap which had developed between the two teams was perfectly illustrated on 20 September 1935 when Stoke won a benefit match for Vale's right-back, George Shenton, by 6-2 at Hanley. Although Vale played magnificently to beat the eventual First Division champions, Sunderland, 2-0 in an F.A. Cup third round replay on 13 January 1936, they were relegated that same season in penultimate place to the Third Division (North). In stark contrast, Stoke, who had assembled a fine side, attained their highest ever position in the top flight— fourth. It was at the tail end of that campaign that Stoke benevolently hosted a local Derby game in aid of Vale's 40,000 Shillings Fund, which had been launched to try to combat a severe financial crisis. Stoke's players were less kind and won the match 3-2.

On 18 November 1936, the Victoria Ground was the venue for an England international game against Northern Ireland, whilst three Stoke players, Stanley Matthews, Freddie Steele and Joe Johnson, constituted sixty per cent of England's forward line in a 3-1 defeat at Hampden Park in front of a then world record crowd of 149,547. Although Stoke's performances gradually fell away during the 1936-1937 and 1937-1938 seasons, they recovered to finish seventh in 1939. On the other hand, Vale achieved little of note in the three years before the Second World War and drifted further down the table each time, so that they ended the 1938-1939 campaign fifth from the bottom of the Third Division (South), to which they had been transferred the previous summer.

Vale were spared any further embarrassment by the intervention of the war against Germany, which led to the abandonment of the Football League programme at the beginning of September 1939. The Potteries teams met for the first time in over three years in a friendly match at Stoke on 23 September, which the home side surprisingly only won 3-2. The two clubs were then paired together in the same Football League wartime competition, the Western Regional Tournament, of which Stoke became the initial champions, after defeating Vale twice en route. Because of the prohibitive cost of maintaining senior operations, Vale went into abeyance for four years from 1940, apart from running an amateur junior team, although Stoke continued to operate fully throughout the whole of the war period.

During the war, Vale's financial problems escalated, especially with a large ground to maintain and little income, and came to a head in 1943 with the death of their president, Major William Huntbach. Unfortunately, his debentures had to be called in and the club were forced to sell the Old Recreation Ground

THE HISTORY

to Stoke-on-Trent City Council in order to survive the ensuing crisis. Happily, Vale were able to obtain a short-term lease on the stadium whilst they found alternative accommodation. In addition, they joined the Football League North in 1944 and consequently resumed senior activities in a tournament which included Stoke. Although Vale lost the initial local clash 2-0 on 18 November, a week later they defeated their old rivals, by 3-0, for the first time since 1932. However, this proved the prelude to their complete humiliation because they were annihilated 8-1 and 6-2 by Stoke within the space of a week in two Football League North Cup, Qualifying Competition, matches in February 1945. Vale were embarrassed still further that May when Stoke scored ten times against them within four days in two Football League North, Second Championship, games, the second of which doubled up as a contest for the Staffordshire Victory Cup to celebrate the end of the war in Europe and turned out to be the final local Derby staged at the Old Recreation Ground.

Fortunately for Vale, the pre-season friendly match to celebrate V-J Day, on 16 August 1945, in which Stoke trounced them 6-0, was the last time the two teams met for over five years. Stoke competed without any great success in the Football League North, which comprised First and Second Division sides, in the 1945-1946 season, whilst Vale played in the Third Division (South) North Region tournament. Stoke fought their way to the quarter-finals of the F.A. Cup in 1946, but were eliminated from the competition on a tragic day at Burnden Park, Bolton, where thirty-three spectators were killed in a crush. The Football League proper recommenced in 1946 and Stoke resumed their activities in the First Division, whilst Vale continued to operate in the Third Division (South). Stoke made a magnificent attempt to become the First Division champions in the 1946-1947 campaign, despite selling their star right winger, Stanley Matthews, to Blackpool, but a 2-1 defeat at Sheffield United in their final game cost them the title and they finished fourth. They were unable to repeat anywhere near this kind of form during the following three campaigns, whilst Vale's postwar efforts were largely nondescript.

In the summer of 1950, Vale opened their new ground, off Hamil Road in Burslem, which was initially sadly lacking in cover, but they quickly had an opportunity to stage a Potteries Derby. The two teams fought out a 2-2 draw at Stoke in the third round of the F.A. Cup on 6 January 1951 in front of an all-time record local Derby crowd of 49,500, but major drainage problems at Vale Park led to the replay also being contested at the Victoria Ground and the Potters won 1-0. The next clash between the two sides was in a benefit match for the dependants of the ex-Vale manager, Gordon Hodgson, on 1 October 1951, which Stoke won 2-1 despite fielding a line-up composed almost entirely of reserves. When the next Potteries Derby was contested on 4 May 1953, in celebration of the impending coronation of Elizabeth II, Stoke had just been relegated from the First Division in penultimate position, whilst Vale had missed out on the Third Division (North) championship and consequent promotion by a single point in their first season in this section. Nevertheless, Stoke proved too strong for their opponents and won 2-0.

In 1954, Vale remarkably reached the F.A. Cup semi-finals before being beaten 2-1 in controversial circumstances by the eventual winners and then

THE HISTORY

First Division leaders, West Bromwich Albion. Also, Vale secured the Third Division (North) championship with ease, a full eleven points clear of their nearest rivals, whilst their "Iron Curtain" defence conceded just 21 goals in the league. Vale's success set up a long-awaited clash with Stoke in the Football League at the Victoria Ground on 4 September 1954, which was drawn 0-0 in front of an all-time record Potteries Derby league gate of 46,777. The return match, on 25 April 1955, was the first local contest played at Vale Park and a record crowd for a Derby game staged by Vale of 41,674 saw the visitors win 1-0 to intensify their promotion challenge, which finally fell short of success by a mere two points. The following season, Vale beat their arch rivals, by 1-0, for the first time in twelve attempts and nearly eleven years and took a further point from the return game for good measure. However, they finished at the foot of the division and were relegated in the 1956-1957 campaign, suffering a 3-1 defeat in the first league match to be played under floodlights at the Victoria Ground, although they bade farewell with a 2-2 draw at home to the Potters in their final game on 29 April.

Vale had the misfortune to be demoted for the second successive season in 1958 as they ended up fifteenth in the Third Division (South) in the very year when the clubs in the bottom half of the table were detached to help form a new Fourth Division. However, Vale were boosted by a 2-1 home win against Stoke in a friendly the following autumn, although their opponents gained more than ample revenge three weeks later when they hammered the Valiants 4-0 in the return. Nevertheless, Vale exhibited tremendous form during most of the rest of the campaign to become the first champions of the Fourth Division and scored 110 league goals to boot. The Supporters' Clubs' Trophy, a new two-legged competition contested purely by Stoke and Vale, was introduced in October 1959 and the Potters triumphed in the first tournament by 5-3 on aggregate. However, this proved the prelude to a storming F.A. Cup run by Vale, which ended in a 2-1 home defeat by Aston Villa in the fifth round in front of an all-time ground record gate of 49,768. The Supporters' Clubs' Trophy went to a deciding tie in the 1960-1961 season after both teams had won their home matches 1-0 and this time it was Vale who were successful, in achieving a 1-0 victory at the Victoria Ground. However, it turned out to be the final game in this competition and the last local Derby of any kind for more than nine years.

In October 1961, Stoke's manager, Tony Waddington, produced a master-stroke and signed their former star outside-right, the forty-six-year old Stanley Matthews, from Blackpool for just £3,000. A remarkable crowd of 35,974 assembled to watch the former international make his return debut and the interest generated by "the wizard of the dribble" was such that Stoke were able to buy several class players, the result of which was their promotion from the Second Division as the champions in 1963. That same year, Vale finished third in the division below and failed to progress to the next flight by just one place. In the summer of 1963, they spent heavily in a determined attempt to achieve success, but fell back to midtable at the end of that season, whilst Stoke, reinforced by further notable signings, reached the two-legged final of the League Cup, in which they were beaten 4-3 on aggregate by Leicester City.

THE HISTORY

The huge gap in standard that had developed between the Potteries teams became a chasm in 1965 when Vale were relegated to the Fourth Division and a new era dawned as the club pinned their future hopes on a youth policy under the supervision of a general manager, Sir Stanley Matthews. However, Vale's first team found even the Fourth Division a struggle and disaster struck in 1968 when the club were fined £4,000 and expelled from the Football League for making illegal payments to players, although they were subsequently re-elected. The youth policy was then scrapped and a new team manager, Gordon Lee, whose ideas were based on fitness and effort, was appointed. For most of this time, Stoke had held their own in the First Division and had earned the reputation of being a good side to watch.

In 1970, Stoke finished ninth, their highest position since rejoining the top flight, whilst Vale gained promotion to the Third Division. At this juncture, on 1 May, the two teams finally clashed again, in a friendly at the Victoria Ground to launch the Stoke-on-Trent Festival, with Vale surprisingly running out 3-2 winners, although the home side were a little under full strength. The clubs then parted company for nearly another six years, during which time Stoke enjoyed the most successful spell in their history. In 1971 and 1972, they fought their way to the F.A. Cup semi-finals, only to be eliminated by Arsenal, after replays in both cases, and won their only major tournament on 4 March 1972 when they defeated much-fancied Chelsea 2-1 at Wembley in the final of the League Cup. In addition, Stoke ended up fifth in the First Division in both 1974 and 1975, in the latter year finishing just four points behind the champions. Over most of this period, Vale battled on gamely in the Third Division, almost entirely in Stoke's shadow, although they flirted with promotion in 1973 and 1975, despite drawing poor crowds.

The picture began to change somewhat in January 1976 when a gale caused so much damage to the Butler Street Stand that Stoke were forced to stage their following home game, against Middlesbrough on the 17th, at Vale Park and foot the bulk of a £250,000 repair bill, which in turn prompted the sale of players. Nevertheless, the Potteries teams drew 1-1 in a friendly on 26 April to celebrate Vale's centenary and Stoke kindly allowed their rivals to keep the entire proceeds of the gate. The following season, Stoke were relegated in penultimate place to the Second Division, but were good enough to beat the Valiants 3-2 in a friendly at the Victoria Ground on 18 October 1977. Vale were then having a difficult time and were demoted to the Fourth Division at the end of that campaign. The balance of footballing power in the Potteries was fully restored in Stoke's favour in 1979 when they regained their top flight status and they warmed up for the task ahead by winning 2-0 in a friendly at Vale on 30 July. However, in the 1979-1980 season, Vale reached their nadir and avoided finishing in the re-election zone only because of their superior number of goals scored.

Vale achieved a creditable 1-1 home draw in the next local Derby, on 5 August 1980, in what was becoming an annual pre-season friendly, although they still ended up sixth from the bottom of the Fourth Division that campaign. The following summer, Stoke trounced their rivals 6-1 at Burslem and on 21 April 1982 defeated Vale 3-2 to take the new Wedgwood Trophy in a match

THE HISTORY

which had also been arranged as a testimonial for the Potters' stalwart defender, Alan Dodd. Stoke were victorious once more, by 1-0, that August, in the last local Derby to be played for almost three years, and thereby retained the Wedgwood Trophy. In addition, Stoke's manager, Richie Barker, was so impressed with the performances of their opponents' goalkeeper, Mark Harrison, and outside-left, Mark Chamberlain, that he paid Vale a £181,000 combined fee for their signatures a week afterwards. As it transpired, the Burslem club not only banked the cash, but also gained promotion to the Third Division in 1983, although their stay lasted just the one season. As a consequence, a new manager was appointed—John Rudge.

Stoke suffered great misfortune in the 1984-1985 campaign in finishing bottom of the First Division with an all-time record low haul of points (17) since the introduction of three points for a win. In addition, they were only able to draw 1-1 with Vale at the Victoria Ground on 6 August 1985 and therefore shared the Wedgwood Trophy. However, Stoke reasserted their local dominance the following April, winning a testimonial match for Vale's long-serving left-back, Russell Bromage, 1-0 in front of the lowest Potteries Derby crowd since 1945. However, Vale more than amply made up for their defeat by gaining promotion to the Third Division later that month. By August 1986, the Wedgwood Trophy had receded into history, so that the pre-season friendly between the local rivals had no extra purpose attached to it, which was unfortunate for Stoke, who won 3-1 at Burslem. It was business as usual a year to the day afterwards when the Potters were once more successful in a pre-season Derby, this time by 2-0, but Vale's star was rising.

30 January 1988 marked a turning point in Vale's history because that day they beat First Division Tottenham Hotspur 2-1 in a pulsating fourth round F.A. Cup tie and the funds generated before they were knocked out of the competition enabled them to strengthen their team into a Third Division force to be reckoned with. Vale's new-found impetus was well-indicated less than two months later when they held Stoke to a 1-1 draw in the Phil Sproson testimonial game and more specifically on 16 August when they won their first Potteries Derby since 1970, by 1-0. Vale continued the good work by drawing 1-1 at Stoke in a benefit match for the Potters' former midfielder, Chris Maskery, the following October and in 1989 they finally succeeded in returning to the Second Division, via the play-offs, after an absence of thirty-two years. The long-awaited league clash between the two sides took place on 23 September at the Victoria Ground in front of a fine crowd of 27,004 and Vale showed how much recent progress they had made by drawing 1-1. However, Stoke's form went from bad to worse that season and by the time of the return game in February 1990, they were adrift at the foot of the division. Although they succeeded in gaining a point at Vale Park, Stoke duly finished at the bottom of the table and were relegated.

For two seasons, Vale remained a division ahead of their arch rivals, but the balance was gradually redressed. Stoke regained some pride by winning a pre-season Derby 1-0 in August 1990 and although they ended the 1990-1991 campaign in their lowest ever league position, fourteenth in the Third Division, the appointment of Lou Macari as their new manager transformed the

THE HISTORY

situation. Whilst Vale were relegated in last place from the Second Division in 1992, Stoke reached their divisional play-offs and won the Autoglass Trophy at Wembley. Consequently, the 1992-1993 season saw both Potteries teams in the new Second Division and no fewer than five local Derbies were played during that campaign, with both sides achieving two victories, whilst one game was drawn. However, Stoke won arguably the two most important matches, those in the league, on their way to the championship, whilst Vale finished third, four points behind. The Valiants therefore entered the play-offs, but were beaten 3-0 by West Bromwich Albion in the final at Wembley. Nevertheless, they gained some compensation in knocking Stoke out of the F.A. Cup after a replay and by eliminating their rivals from the Autoglass Trophy en route to winning the tournament.

Although Stoke had surged ahead of the Burslem club into a higher grade of football, Vale caught up in 1994 when they too gained promotion to the First Division, so that the Football League Derbies resumed after a one-year interlude. Vale took four points from the initial two local clashes in the spring of 1995 and by winning 1-0 on 22 April, achieved a victory at the Victoria Ground for the first time in the league since 1927. Vale repeated their triumph the following August and completed the double over their arch rivals on 12 March 1996. Nevertheless, Stoke finished fourth in the division and thus qualified for the play-offs, but lost 1-0 on aggregate to Leicester City in a two-legged semi-final.

The balance of fortune in the Potteries Derbies swung back in Stoke's favour in the 1996-1997 season when they gained four points at the expense of the Valiants, with their 2-0 win on 20 April 1997 being the final local contest held at the Victoria Ground. Stoke's victory also struck a serious blow to their rivals' promotion aspirations and Vale tailed off to end up eighth, which nevertheless was a position they had not bettered since 1931. The next local Derby was played at Stoke's recently-completed Britannia Stadium on 12 October 1997 and finished in a 2-1 win for the home side, who also took a point from the return in the spring, although this was insufficient to prevent them from being relegated in penultimate place to the Second Division.

Therefore, no Potteries Derbies were scheduled for the 1998-1999 season, but after 180 local clashes in under 116 years, it did not require the services of a seer to predict that the next meeting of the two clubs would be sooner rather than later. Nevertheless, in response to the gloomy "Deloitte & Touche Annual Review of Football Finance", "The Sentinel", on 26 August 1998, carried a two-page article on the feasibility of a merger between Stoke and Vale, possibly under the name of "Potteries United".

It is certainly true that ultimate footballing success requires massive applications of capital in the modern age, whilst in contrast Stoke-on-Trent remains the least populous city in England to support two professional football clubs. In addition, Stoke have rarely had large sums of money to throw around, whilst almost Vale's entire existence seems to have been spent in a struggle to survive financially. However, because local football was born from and largely remains rooted in specific communities in and around the Potteries, it is inconceivable that the two clubs will not continue virtually indefinitely to loom

THE HISTORY

large as separate entities, irrespective of modern financial and commercial pressures impelling them to amalgamate. And if a merger did occur, it is highly likely that supporters of at least the smaller, more absorbed, club would establish a new team under the old name to keep the flag flying, just as the Vale fans threatened to do in such a situation in 1926.

Long live the Potteries Derbies! For excitement, there's nothing quite like them.

The Matches

1: SATURDAY 2 DECEMBER 1882, STAFFORD-SHIRE CUP, SECOND ROUND

PORT VALE (?) 1 (unknown), STOKE (?) 1 (unknown).

VALE: The team is entirely unknown.
STOKE: The team is entirely unknown.

Venue: Westport Meadows, Westport.
Attendance: Unknown.
Referee: Unknown.

THE SETTING

This was the first ever meeting between the two clubs, which were destined to become extremely familiar to one another through their continuous battle for football supremacy within the Potteries. The clash was highly significant for Vale because it was their very first match in an organised tournament and they had been pitched against the local giants of football. Indeed, the fact that Vale were playing Stoke was almost certainly the very reason why their first team finally came to the attention of "The Staffordshire Sentinel". In contrast, Stoke were a club of some repute in the Midlands and the north of England, competed mainly against strong teams from outside the area and had had one of their players, Teddy Johnson, become an English international nearly three years previously. Therefore, they cannot have been unduly excited or alarmed at the prospect of meeting Port Vale. Indeed, Vale had only joined the Staffordshire Football Association on 6 September and had progressed to the second round of the Staffordshire Cup as a result of their initial opponents, Cliffe Vale, scratching from the competition. However, Stoke had already stamped their mark on the tournament by annihilating Mow Cop 24-0 in the first round! In addition, they remained unbeaten that season, as far as is known, and had hammered Wirral Birkenhead 6-0 away in a friendly a fortnight before the Derby. Unfortunately, the names of none of the players who participated in the historic first local clash are known and no doubt never will be.

THE MATCH

Sadly, no details of the match have been traced and it is almost certain that there is no written report of it in existence. "The Sentinel" gave the score only in its Monday 11 December edition and stated merely that the contest had been 'a spirited game'. Nevertheless, many people must have been extremely surprised that mighty Stoke had not convincingly dispatched the minnows from the competition.

THE AFTERMATH

The replay was scheduled for the following Saturday, at the Victoria Ground in Stoke, and Vale's heroic efforts in the initial match did much to capture the public's attention for the occasion, particularly because an exciting struggle appeared to be on the cards.

2: SATURDAY 9 DECEMBER 1882, STAFFORD-SHIRE CUP, SECOND ROUND REPLAY

STOKE (4) 5 (Shutt 4, Johnson), PORT VALE (0) 1 (E. Hood).

STOKE: Wildin, Ringland, Mellor, Cox, Bettany, Myatt, Fennell, Johnson, Brown, Shutt, Shufflebotham.
VALE: Baskerville, Dain, Poulson, Simpson, Bateman, Boulton, E. Hood, Davies, Alcock, Reynolds, H. Hood.

Venue: The Victoria Ground, Stoke-upon-Trent.
Attendance: A large number.
Referee: R. Green (Goldenhill).

THE SETTING
This cup replay was the first ever game played between the two sides at Stoke and only the second recorded first team match in Vale's history. Although Vale had held their illustrious opponents to a 1-1 draw in the initial match at Westport on the previous Saturday, they still faced a monumental task in the replay. Stoke were determined to progress further in the competition, as is illustrated by the fact that they fielded their strongest available side, as naturally did Vale. Amongst the players to note in Stoke's team were Teddy Johnson, the proud possessor of an England cap; George Shutt, a future English international, and Percy Fennell, who had scored four goals in a 6-0 thrashing of Wirral Birkenhead three weeks earlier. Vale's line-up included Enoch Hood, a founder member of the club and its first captain, and Billy Poulson and George Bateman, who were other pioneers.

THE MATCH
Vale won the toss and chose to kick off. The match began at 3.05 p.m. and was evenly contested for the first quarter of an hour. Then Stoke started to get on top and Johnson scored the first goal from a centre by Fennell, who almost immediately set up Shutt for the second. After this, the home side took complete command, won a series of corners and rained shots on Vale's goal. The visitors seemed to lose heart and Shutt scored again, following some fine passing by Brown and Myatt. Although Vale then held firm for a while, Shutt completed his hat trick before half-time from a Shufflebotham cross.

Vale improved in the second half and finally began to exert some pressure on Stoke's defence, but Johnson and Brown carved out the chance for Shutt to notch his fourth goal. The game then lost impetus as it was clear that the home team would emerge as the victors. Nevertheless, as the light faded, a throw-in by Bateman resulted in a 'determined rush' by Vale, as a result of which Enoch Hood scored a consolation goal shortly before full-time.

THE AFTERMATH
Stoke fought their way through two further rounds of the tournament, but were beaten 3-2 at home by West Bromwich Albion in the final the following April. Despite being defeated in the local Derby, Vale had finally entered recorded history as a club to note and furthered their progress by overcoming powerful Leek 4-2 to secure the North Staffordshire Charity Challenge Cup on 28 April.

3: SATURDAY 26 JANUARY 1884, FRIENDLY

STOKE 3 (Wilson, Bennett, Shutt), PORT VALE 0 (match abandoned after 30 minutes).

STOKE: Wilson, Bennett and Shutt played, but the team is otherwise unknown.
VALE: The team is entirely unknown.

Venue: The Victoria Ground, Stoke-upon-Trent.
Attendance: Unknown.
Referee: Unknown.

THE SETTING

The prospect of the game raised much excitement in North Staffordshire, especially as the rivalry between the two clubs had intensified since their previous meeting. Both teams had already reached the semi-finals of the Staffordshire Cup and Vale had continued to make great strides during the previous autumn, beating both Aston Unity and Everton in friendly matches. In addition, they had won 4-0 at Goldenhill in the third round of the Staffordshire Cup in their previous game on the Saturday before the local Derby. Stoke had also generally performed well during the season, although they had lost 2-1 at home to Manchester in the first round of the English Cup and had been defeated by the same score at Oswestry in a friendly match a week prior to the Derby. Although the line-ups for the local clash were not recorded, Stoke were without their captain, Johnson, who had been selected for an England trial.

THE MATCH

The game was played during a 'hurricane' and Stoke had an immense initial advantage attacking with the wind at their backs. Driving sleet added to the discomfort of their opponents and the home side were 3-0 up within half an hour thanks to successful shots by Wilson, Bennett and Shutt. Because of the ferocity of the storm, Vale had the greatest difficulty in getting anywhere near to Stoke's goal and after thirty minutes, with the rain falling in torrents, both captains decided that the conditions made it impossible to continue. The match was therefore stopped and the captains left the ground, but other members of both teams persisted in arguing as to whether play should be resumed! Nevertheless, the existing scoreline was generally accepted as the final result, especially by "The Staffordshire Sentinel" and "The Athletic News", although the Vale players remained convinced that they would have won the game with the 'hurricane' in their favour in the second half. Thus the issue was never fully settled and the actual result was still argued about years later!

THE AFTERMATH

Stoke continued their goalscoring form the following Saturday when they trounced Small Heath Alliance 9-1 at home in another friendly match, although they were knocked out of the Staffordshire Cup by West Bromwich Albion. Vale quickly put their local Derby misfortunes behind them and annihilated Middlewich 16-0 at home in a friendly a week afterwards to record their all-time club record best score. Nevertheless, their quest for Staffordshire Cup honours came to an end when they were dispatched 7-1 by Birmingham St. George's.

4: SATURDAY 22 MARCH 1884, FRIENDLY

PORT VALE (0) 3 (Payne, Hood, Reynolds), STOKE (4) 5 (Stanford 2, Johnson 2, Hodgkinson o.g.).

VALE: Morris, Dain, Bateman, Moss, Clare, Hodgkinson, Payne, Simpson, Reynolds, Hood, Davies.
STOKE: Birch, Stanford, Mellor, Bettany, Shutt, Smith, Wilson, Bennett, Johnson, Yates, Lawton.

Venue: Westport Meadows, Westport.
Attendance: 2-3,000.
Referee: Mr. Wheatley.

THE SETTING
Vale had exhibited variable form prior to the local Derby, but were still recovering from their 7-1 thrashing by Birmingham St. George's in a semi-final of the Staffordshire Cup three weeks earlier. Neither had their confidence for the Stoke clash been helped by a 2-1 home defeat by Notts Rangers in a friendly match two weeks beforehand. Although Stoke had annihilated Small Heath Alliance 9-1 at home the previous month, their recent results also had been rather inconsistent and they too were suffering from the disappointment of having been eliminated from the Staffordshire Cup by 2-0 by West Bromwich Albion in the other semi-final a week before the Derby. With local pride at stake, both clubs fielded their strongest available line-ups.

THE MATCH
Stoke won the toss and elected to kick off on a rather 'spongy' surface, though the weather was fine. The game did not start until 3.40 p.m., but Stoke quickly took control. Although Yates' effectiveness was soon limited through an injury, the visitors remained on top and Smith struck the bar with a long shot. Shortly afterwards, Stoke took the lead when Hodgkinson, trying to clear a Wilson corner, steered the ball between his own posts. The visitors added two goals in quick succession, both being scored by Stanford, firstly from a centre by Wilson and then from a fine pass by the same player. Afterwards, Vale came more into the game and had a goal disallowed for offside, but another Wilson centre enabled Johnson to extend Stoke's lead.

The home side initially took command in the second half, but a magnificent solo run by Johnson put Stoke 5-0 up. Remarkably, Vale were then transformed and Payne reduced the arrears from a Simpson pass. Hood added a second, following some exciting attacking play, and Reynolds the third, but, with Stoke on the ropes, the home side ran out of time to complete their comeback.

THE AFTERMATH
Vale experienced mixed fortunes in their two further recorded friendly games that season, beating Wednesbury Town 6-1 at home on 5 April, but then being thrashed 6-0 at Westport by West Bromwich Albion a fortnight later. In contrast, Stoke won three of their four remaining friendlies and scored nine goals in the process. The highlight was their 4-0 victory at Shrewsbury Castle Blues two weeks after the local Derby.

5: SATURDAY 1 MAY 1886, FRIENDLY

STOKE (2) 3 (Sayer, Holford, Rowley o.g.), BURSLEM PORT VALE (0) 1 (Lawton).

STOKE: Birch, Clare, E. Montford, Brown, Shutt, Farmer, Sayer, Edge, Bennett, Holford, Ballham.
VALE: Rowley, Bateman, Powell, Hodgkinson, Bettany, Ramsey, Lawton, Owen, Reynolds, C. Simpson, Davies.

Venue: The Victoria Ground, Stoke-upon-Trent.
Attendance: No less than 10,000.
Referee: R.J. Smith (secretary, Derbyshire Association).

THE SETTING
The local rivals had not met for over two years and during that time there had been much discussion as to which team was the better. Stoke had produced mixed form during the 1885-1886 season, but had drawn 0-0 with West Bromwich Albion in the final of the Staffordshire Cup at the Victoria Ground a week before the local Derby. Vale had generally fared well and had fought their way to the fifth round of the English Cup before withdrawing from the competition. However, they had lost their last game, a friendly at home to Walsall Swifts, by 1-0, a fortnight before the Derby. Both clubs selected their strongest available sides for the clash and in response to the interest that the match had generated, special trains were put on to carry spectators from Leek and Crewe as well as from the north of the Potteries, which helped to generate a then ground record crowd.

THE MATCH
Because both teams had put on white shirts, the Vale players wore a scarlet sash to distinguish them. The visitors won the toss and chose to defend the Boothen goal, but Stoke rapidly showed their superiority and only five minutes had elapsed when Sayer opened the scoring with a wonderful shot. Holford added a second goal for the home side following a foul by Reynolds, but Vale roughed up the play and came more into contention.

In the second half, the visitors began to get on top and Lawton reduced the arrears with a superb goal, which was greeted with a tremendous roar by the Vale supporters. The visitors then pressed strongly for an equaliser, but Stoke responded, stimulated by the encouragement of their fans, and only some brilliant goalkeeping by Rowley prevented them from increasing their lead. Nevertheless, shortly before the end, the home side's pressure finally paid off when Rowley fell into his own goal, clutching the ball. Unfortunately, the goalkeeper broke a rib in his fall and was led from the pitch in some pain.

THE AFTERMATH
The gate receipts amounted to over £230, although the excellence of this figure did not help Vale's keeper, Billy Rowley, who was unable to work for four months because of his injury. Unfortunately, the Derby victory did not inspire Stoke to Staffordshire Cup success because they lost the replayed final 4-2 ten days afterwards, although Vale qualified to meet their local rivals in the final of the North Staffordshire Charity Challenge Cup.

6: SATURDAY 22 MAY 1886, NORTH STAFFORD-SHIRE CHARITY CHALLENGE CUP, FINAL

STOKE (0) 1 (Bennett), BURSLEM PORT VALE (0) 0.

STOKE: Birch, Clare, E. Montford, Brown, Shutt, E. Smith, Sayer, Edge, Bennett, Holford, Gladwin.
VALE: Horne, Bateman, Powell, Poulson, Ramsey, Hodgkinson, C. Simpson, Owen, J.A. Smith, Reynolds, Davies.

Venue: The Victoria Ground, Stoke-upon-Trent.
Attendance: One of the best recorded in the area up till then.
Referee: C.W. Cramp (president, Birmingham Association).

THE SETTING

Just three weeks after their previous encounter, the leading clubs in the Potteries met once more, with Vale having thrashed Stoke Free Wanderers 5-0 in a semi-final of the competition on the Saturday beforehand, although the means of Stoke's passage to the final is unknown. The teams were at their fullest available strength, though Vale were still without the services of their injured goalkeeper, Rowley. It was noted that members of the 'fair sex' were present at the match in large numbers.

THE MATCH

The game kicked off late at 3.45 p.m. and, although Stoke had more of the play, the match was rough and largely lacking in skill. It appeared that the stalemate had been broken when the visitors scrambled the ball over the line, but the goal was disallowed because of offside, much to the displeasure of the Vale supporters. Nevertheless, the visitors dominated the rest of the half, although they were unable to take the lead.

Stoke came more into the game after the interval and, in the seventieth minute, Bennett put them in front from a Holford centre. The goal inspired Stoke to greater efforts and Bennett increasingly caused the visitors problems by running at their defence. After the home side had hit the bar, Vale finally forced their first corner, but they were unable to level in a thrilling finish.

THE AFTERMATH

Stoke therefore won the trophy against the co-holders in what was the final match of the season for both sides. Whilst Stoke assembled their squad over the summer of 1886 for the following campaign, Vale were involved in much greater activity because they were forced to relocate their ground as they were only able to extend the lease on their current headquarters at Moorland Road, Burslem, by six years. Consequently, they moved to a seven-acre waste site off Waterloo Road, Cobridge, which was soon 'the best ground in the district', with a cinder track for athletics and cycling, a grandstand to accommodate a thousand spectators, three shower baths for the players and a gymnasium.

7: SATURDAY 5 FEBRUARY 1887, FRIENDLY

STOKE (0) 2 (Edge, Shutt), BURSLEM PORT VALE (0) 1 (Aston).

STOKE: Hassall, Clare, Bateman, Holford, Shutt, Smith, Ballham, Lawton, Bennett, Edge, Owen.
VALE: Heath, Powell, Ramsey, Poulson, Shields, Hodgkinson, Aston, Ditchfield, Reynolds, Rhodes, May.

Venue: The Victoria Ground, Stoke-upon-Trent.
Attendance: 6,000.
Referee: Mr. Cooper.

THE SETTING

Stoke had annihilated Biddulph 14-0 at home in the first round of the Staffordshire Cup on 23 October and Caernarvon Wanderers 10-1 at home in the first qualifying round of the English Cup a week later, but had then been eliminated from the latter competition by 6-4 at Crewe Alexandra. However, they had warmed up for the local Derby by defeating Notts Jardines 4-2 at home in a friendly match five days beforehand. Although Vale had also been knocked out of the English Cup, they were in a confident mood, having beaten Bolton Wanderers 3-2 at home in a friendly the previous Saturday. For the local clash, Stoke were without Sayer, who was on England international duty, and the ex-Vale goalkeeper, Rowley, who had fractured his collarbone a week earlier. However, the only alterations in their line-up from their previous game were the replacement of the full-backs, Edgar Montford and Lowe, by the former Vale players, Clare and Bateman. In contrast, Vale were entirely unchanged.

THE MATCH

Vale kicked off against a strong breeze and on a slippery surface, but were unable to produce their fine form of the previous week. Although Stoke initially gained the advantage, the contest soon became even and neither goal came under much threat. However, shortly before half-time, the ball burst, which greatly amused the crowd.

Soon after the interval, Vale claimed the ball had crossed the line for a goal following a centre, but it was not given and a tremendous melee ensued in the home goalmouth, as a result of which Aston scored. Vale began to scent their first victory against their illustrious opponents, especially as Heath brilliantly withstood everything Stoke could throw at him. Nevertheless, the home side's relentless pressure eventually told and Edge equalised. Finally, marvellous work by Ballham allowed Shutt to snatch victory for Stoke near to the final whistle.

THE AFTERMATH

The continuation of their team's supremacy proved insufficient satisfaction for a number of the Stoke supporters, who 'hooted' some of the Vale players after the game and followed them, 'howling and yelling like a pack of wolves', to the players' hotel! The result itself did not provide a springboard for the fortunes of the home side, who lost their following four matches, although, in contrast, Vale gained four straight victories immediately afterwards!

8: SATURDAY 26 MARCH 1887, FRIENDLY

BURSLEM PORT VALE (0) 0, STOKE (1) 1 (Heath o.g.).

VALE: Heath, Ramsey, Powell, Poulson, Shields, Bettany, Aston, J.A. Smith, Reynolds, Ditchfield, Hodgkinson.
STOKE: Rowley, Bateman, Clare, Holford, Shutt, E. Smith, Sayer, Lawton, Bennett, Ballham, Owen.

Venue: The Athletic Ground, Cobridge.
Attendance: 6,000.
Referee: Mr. Brownlow (Halliwell).

THE SETTING

Vale's recent form had been poor with four defeats and a draw resulting from their five games played earlier that month and they had lost 2-1 to Walsall Swifts in a semi-final of the Staffordshire Cup a week before the local Derby. Stoke had fared little better, losing six of their last seven matches and likewise being eliminated from the Staffordshire Cup. They had also been beaten 3-0 at West Bromwich Albion in the fourth round of the Birmingham Cup on the Saturday prior to the Derby. Vale made four alterations in their line-up from their previous game, with Ramsey, Shields, Bettany and Ditchfield replacing Martin, Elson, Rhodes and Randles, whilst Stoke were unchanged for the first clash between the two rivals at Vale's new ground at Cobridge.

THE MATCH

Stoke won the toss and decided to play with a strong breeze to their advantage. Only eight minutes had passed when Heath put the ball over his own line from a corner by Holford to give the visitors the lead, but shortly afterwards the Vale goalkeeper made amends by producing a magnificent save from a goal-bound effort by Owen. Stoke continued to press strongly, but were unable to add to their score.

After the interval, the game became more evenly contested and Vale gradually gained command, but the visiting defence stood firm. Nevertheless, Heath made a splendid save from Holford and Vale survived a furious melee in front of their own goal before Ditchfield hit the visitors' post with a screw-shot. Immediately afterwards, Reynolds headed over from a good position and a minute before the end, in a final effort, Hodgkinson just failed to equalise by shooting over the bar.

THE AFTERMATH

Following their failure in the local Derby, Vale's poor form continued with three defeats in their next four matches, which included a 5-1 hammering by West Bromwich Albion in a Birmingham Cup semi-final on 30 April. In contrast, Stoke thrashed Leek 5-0 in a semi-final of the North Staffordshire Charity Challenge Cup two days after the local Derby and then followed up by beating Queen's Park 1-0 and Edinburgh Hibernians 2-0 in friendly games.

9: SATURDAY 7 MAY 1887, FRIENDLY

BURSLEM PORT VALE (0) 0, STOKE (1) 4 (Ballham 3, Bennett).

VALE: Heath, Ramsey, Powell, Poulson, Shields, Hodgkinson, Sproston, Aston, Reynolds, Ditchfield, J.A. Smith.
STOKE: Rowley, Clare, Bateman, Holford, Shutt, E. Smith, Sayer, Lawton, Bennett, Ballham, Owen.

Venue: The Athletic Ground, Cobridge.
Attendance: Unknown.
Referee: Mr. Moore.

THE SETTING

This match should have been the final of the North Staffordshire Charity Challenge Cup, but was actually played as a friendly following an argument about the eligibility of several of the Vale players. Although Ditchfield, Powell and Shields had not been registered for competitive games, the charity committee's promotional handbill described both teams as being at 'full strength' and the Vale committee were reluctant to select a weakened side. An agreement was eventually reached whereby Vale would field their full team, but the visitors would receive the cup regardless of the result. Vale had won just one of their last ten matches and had lost 5-1 to West Bromwich Albion in a semi-final of the Birmingham Cup a week before the local Derby. In contrast, Stoke's form had been much better and in their previous game, on 16 April, they had held Corinthians to a 1-1 draw at the Victoria Ground. Stoke had qualified for the final of the Charity Challenge Cup by trouncing Leek 5-0 in the previous round on 28 March, whilst Vale had overcome Staffordshire Zingari at the same stage.

THE MATCH

Vale won the toss, kicked off and put the visitors under early pressure, but Stoke took the lead through a magnificent shot by Ballham. The rest of the first half was evenly contested, with neither side being able to make a further breakthrough.

A few minutes into the second half, Ballham took advantage of Heath being blinded by the sun to add to his tally and Stoke took command. Ditchfield received a bad knock, which required some attention, and the home team became overrun. Bennett scored Stoke's third goal and shortly afterwards Ballham completed his hat trick. However, the pressure on the Vale defence was eased ten minutes from the end when Holford was kicked on the knee and forced to retire, so that no further goals were added.

THE AFTERMATH

Vale ended their season on a high note by beating Walsall Swifts 1-0 at home in a friendly match on the Saturday after the local Derby, although Stoke completed their programme with a 1-0 defeat at West Bromwich Albion a week after that.

10: SATURDAY 15 OCTOBER 1887, ENGLISH CUP, FIRST QUALIFYING ROUND

STOKE (0) 1 (Lawton), BURSLEM PORT VALE (0) 0.

STOKE: Rowley, Clare, Underwood, Smith, Shutt, Meakin, Sayer, Lawton, Ballham, Edge, Owen.
VALE: Morgan, Bateman, Powell, Bettany, Elson, Poulson, Simpson, Sproston, Reynolds, Randles, May.

Venue: The Victoria Ground, Stoke-upon-Trent.
Attendance: At least 3,000.
Referee: J.J. Bentley (Bolton).

THE SETTING

Stoke had won four and lost three of their matches played thus far in the 1887-1888 season and had made it through safely to the second round of the Birmingham Cup. However, they had been defeated 1-0 at Nottingham Forest in a friendly a week before the local Derby. Vale had won four and lost five of their opening nine games and, although they had progressed to the second round of the Staffordshire Cup, they had been beaten 4-1 at Burnley in a friendly in their last match a fortnight prior to the Derby. Vale were forced to field five reserves in the local contest as their regular forwards, Cookson, Ditchfield and Elston, and their defenders, Ramsey and Shields, were all ineligible to play, whilst Stoke were missing only Holford, through illness.

THE MATCH

The match started late, as had become usual, at 3.25 p.m. and Stoke, who lost the toss, kicked into a slight wind, but were encouraged by the large numbers of their assembled supporters. Vale were the first to make a serious threat on goal when Randles forced Rowley into a desperate fisted clearance and the visitors then took control, but most of the play was individual in nature and rather disjointed. Although Stoke eventually came more into the game, both defences were resolute.

A marvellous save by Rowley prevented Vale from taking the lead at the very start of the second half, but the home side adopted a more aggressive approach and started to dominate the game. Stoke's pressure paid off fifteen minutes into the period when Lawton opened the scoring with a fast, long shot and brilliant wing play by Sayer caused the visiting defence constant problems. As Vale's goal came under siege, Shutt struck the bar, but the home team were unable to add to their lead, although, remarkably, the ball crossed the visitors' goal line once more, straight from a throw-in!

THE AFTERMATH

Stoke progressed through two further qualifying rounds of the competition before being eliminated by West Bromwich Albion, the eventual winners, and also made it into the semi-finals of the Birmingham Cup. In contrast, Vale's form was generally poor and they were knocked out of the Birmingham Cup in the second round, although a 7-0 home triumph against Tunstall at the same stage of the Staffordshire Cup set up a second local Derby with Stoke in the next round.

11: SATURDAY 31 DECEMBER 1887, STAFFORD-SHIRE CUP, THIRD ROUND

STOKE (1) 1 (Millward), BURSLEM PORT VALE (0) 0.

STOKE: Rowley, Clare, Underwood, Broadhurst, Shutt, E. Smith, Ballham, Lawton, Millward, Edge, Owen.
VALE: Morgan, Bateman, Powell, Poulson, Surtees, Elson, Rhodes, J.A. Smith, Reynolds, Randles, May.

Venue: The Victoria Ground, Stoke-upon-Trent.
Attendance: Very large.
Referee: J.J. Bentley (Bolton).

THE SETTING

Stoke had generally performed well recently and had won seven matches in total in the English Cup and the Birmingham Cup to remain in contention in both competitions. In addition, they had beaten Leek 2-1 at home in a friendly game five days before the local Derby. Although Vale's form had been poor, they had drawn 0-0 at Newton Heath in a friendly on the same day and had reached this stage of the Staffordshire Cup with fine home victories against Market Drayton (4-0) and Tunstall (7-0) in the earlier rounds. However, they were once again handicapped by the ineligibility of Ramsey, Shields, Cookson, Ditchfield and Elston for the local clash and had to select five reserves in their stead. In contrast, Stoke were strengthened by the return to the team of Lawton, who replaced Farmer.

THE MATCH

The match was initially fairly evenly contested, but Stoke gradually became more dangerous and Edge, Ballham and Lawton all went close before Owen missed a golden opportunity by shooting wildly. Nevertheless, the home side took the lead seven minutes before the interval when Millward ran through from the halfway line to score. Stoke continued to press and were very unlucky not to add to their lead.

Stoke began the second period where they had left off, but Ballham shot wide with the goal at his mercy and then lofted the ball over the bar with only Morgan to beat. Stoke remained in control and on the rare occasions that the vistors threatened their opponents' goal, the shooting of the Vale forwards was poor. The visitors finally gained their first corner ten minutes from the end, but this only resulted in a quick breakaway by Broadhurst, which almost led to a deserved second goal for Stoke.

THE AFTERMATH

Although they had the satisfaction of beating their Potteries rivals yet again, Stoke were eliminated from the competition in the next round, the semi-finals, by West Bromwich Albion. Stoke were also dispatched by Albion from the English Cup a week after the local Derby, whilst their Birmingham Cup aspirations ended at home to Aston Villa later the same month. Vale's defeat finished their cup hopes for the season and their form became even more dismal as they recorded only two victories in their following ten matches.

12: SATURDAY 5 MAY 1888, FRIENDLY

BURSLEM PORT VALE (1) 2 (Ditchfield, Reynolds), STOKE (1) 4 (Ballham 2, Shaw, Goodall).

VALE: Morgan, Ramsey, Powell, Poulson, Shields, Elson, Sproston, Danks, Reynolds, Ditchfield, May.
STOKE: Rowley, Clare, Underwood, Holford, Shutt, Smith, Sayer, Goodall, Shaw, Ballham, Owen.

Venue: The Athletic Ground, Cobridge.
Attendance: Upwards of 4,000.
Referee: J.J. Bentley (Bolton).

THE SETTING
The two teams met for the third time this season in a match which was promoted as 'the championship of the Potteries', especially as both clubs were able to field their strongest available sides. Vale included Dick Danks, of Wolverhampton Wanderers, in their team, while Stoke's line-up contained two guests – "Shiner" Shaw, from Walsall, and Archie Goodall. Vale had shown excellent recent form with seven victories and two draws in their previous nine games, which had included a 10-0 annihilation of Derby Junction and a 7-2 drubbing of Nottingham Forest a fortnight before the local Derby. In contrast, Stoke had performed steadily since the turn of the year, with their 7-3 crushing of East Stirling in a friendly match a highlight, but they had been knocked out of both the Birmingham Cup and the Staffordshire Cup at the semi-final stage.

THE MATCH
Stoke won the toss and elected to play from the Grange goal with the wind and sun in their favour. At first, there was little to choose between the two teams, but, after fifteen minutes, Ballham dribbled right through the Vale defence to open the scoring. Immediately from the restart, Danks surged up the wing and centred low and fast for Ditchfield to touch the ball in for the equaliser, to the great delight of the home crowd. The match proceeded at a furious pace, but unfortunately, shortly before half-time, Owen broke his collarbone in a collision with Powell and had to leave the pitch.

Although they had been reduced to ten men and faced the wind, Stoke soon put paid to the home side's hopes of securing their first Derby victory. Ballham restored Stoke's lead after a solo run and Shaw netted in a goalmouth scramble before Goodall sealed the victory with a fourth goal. Ballham then had to retire with an injury, which finally enabled Reynolds to reduce the arrears for Vale from a scrimmage.

THE AFTERMATH
The local Derby was the final game of the season for both teams, although Vale held a gala and athletic sports event at their ground a fortnight later. They strengthened their side for the 1888-1889 campaign by signing Lewis Ballham from Stoke in August, although he was ineligible to play until October. Stoke's close season was more momentous in that the club prepared to take its place in the newly-formed Football League, which commenced the following September.

13: SATURDAY 16 FEBRUARY 1889, FRIENDLY

BURSLEM PORT VALE (0) 1 (Vessey), STOKE (3) 5 (Edge, Underwood, McSkimming, Hendry, Milarvie).

VALE: Millward, Bateman, Skinner, Poulson, Shields, Elson, Ballham, Danks, Ditchfield, Vessey, Locker.
STOKE: Rowley, Clare, Underwood, Ramsey, Shutt, Smith, Sayer, McSkimming, Hendry, Edge, Milarvie.

Venue: The Athletic Ground, Cobridge.
Attendance: Upwards of 5,000.
Referee: S. Ormerod (Accrington).

THE SETTING

Neither side had fared particularly well during the campaign and Stoke were occupying the penultimate position in the Football League in its initial season. They had played seven league games without gaining a victory, had been eliminated from the English Cup and had been hammered 5-1 at Northwich Victoria in a friendly a week before the local Derby. Vale were competing in the Football Combination, which had been established for important teams that had failed to be selected for the Football League, but they had won only five of their twenty-three matches. Indeed, they had been beaten 2-1 at Northwich Victoria in their most recent fixture a fortnight before the Derby. Vale brought in the guest services of Vessey and Billy Locker from Long Eaton Rangers to enhance their chances in the local clash, whilst Stoke borrowed Billy Hendry from West Bromwich Albion. An overnight frost, followed by rain and snow on the morning of the game, had made the pitch greasy and treacherous.

THE MATCH

Stoke won the toss and decided to defend the Grange goal with the wind at their backs. They quickly got into their stride and in the eighth minute Edge scored the opener from a pass by Sayer. Although Vessey and Locker impressed for Vale, the visitors remained on top and Edge hit the outside of a post. Shortly before the interval, Underwood tried a speculative shot from the halfway line, but Bateman and Millward allowed the ball to pass between them and into the goal amidst 'considerable laughter'! A minute later, Stoke were three up as McSkimming shot home.

Early in the second half, Vessey gave Vale hope with a hard, low shot which passed across the line because Ditchfield knocked Rowley over as he tried to make a save. The home side then applied considerable pressure, although McSkimming scored from a breakaway, only to find the effort ruled out because of offside. Nevertheless, Hendry added a fourth goal for Stoke from a Sayer cross and Milarvie completed the victory following some fine inter-passing.

THE AFTERMATH

Vale had no match arranged for the following Saturday and so had no opportunity to get the psychological effects of this crushing defeat out of their system before the local rivals clashed again on 2 March. Stoke, however, gained a satisfactory 2-2 draw at Leek in a friendly game on 23 February in preparation.

14: SATURDAY 2 MARCH 1889, FRIENDLY

STOKE (2) 4 (Edge 2, Milarvie 2), BURSLEM PORT VALE (1) 2 (unknown).

STOKE: Rose, E. Montford, Underwood, Ramsey, Shutt, Smith, Hutchinson, McSkimming, Hendry, Edge, Milarvie.
VALE: Broomhall, Bateman, Shields, Poulson, Surtees, Elson, Ditchfield, Stokes, Ballham, unknown, unknown.

Venue: The Victoria Ground, Stoke-upon-Trent.
Attendance: Large.
Referee: F. Norris.

THE SETTING
Stoke had warmed up for the return Derby (following their 5-1 victory a fortnight earlier) by drawing 2-2 at Leek in a friendly match a week before the clash. However, they were weakened by the loss of their goalkeeper, Rowley, and right-back, Clare, to England international duty, but secured the guest services of the illustrious William Rose, of Wolverhampton Wanderers. Vale had not played since the Derby and fielded an under-strength team because of injuries.

THE MATCH
Hutchinson received the ball from the kickoff, ran down the wing and centred for Edge to shoot Stoke ahead in under a minute. Shortly afterwards, the home team put the ball over the line again, following a scrimmage, but offside was given. The play then became more even, but, during a bout of sustained pressure, Vale equalised. This was the signal for the home side to press once more and Milarvie had a goal disallowed for offside before Edge headed Stoke back in front from a Hutchinson cross.

In the second half, Vale began to look more dangerous and Ballham scored, only to find his effort ruled out by offside. However, Stoke extended their lead in controversial fashion from a disputed throw-in, which was awarded to the home team. As the Vale players protested, Stoke took the throw, from which Milarvie scored, but the goal was not accepted by the visitors who walked off the pitch in disgust! After about seven minutes, they were persuaded to return and the play then moved rapidly from one end to the other before Milarvie added his second goal. However, Vale then pressured the home rearguard and were rewarded with another consolation goal towards the end of the match. Nevertheless, they had failed to prevent Stoke from recording their thirteenth consecutive Derby victory.

THE AFTERMATH
Stoke did not win either of their remaining two Football League games and consequently finished at the foot of the first ever table. As a result, they had to apply for re-election. They were further disappointed by being eliminated from the Birmingham Cup in the semi-finals and from the Staffordshire Cup in the fourth round. Vale also exited from the latter competition at the same stage and, although they won two out of their three final Football Combination matches, the tournament was dissolved before its completion!

15: MONDAY 20 MAY 1889, FRIENDLY

BURSLEM PORT VALE (?) 1 (unknown), STOKE (?) 1 (unknown).

VALE: The team is entirely unknown.
STOKE: The team is entirely unknown.

Venue: The Athletic Ground, Cobridge.
Attendance: Unknown.
Referee: Unknown.

THE SETTING

This match was played as a benefit for the North Staffordshire Charity Association and was the final outing for both teams that season. Vale had not fared at all well during the campaign, having been eliminated from the English Cup, the Staffordshire Cup and the North Staffordshire Charity Challenge Cup at the first hurdle and having won only seven of their twenty-six games in the ill-fated Football Combination, a competition for non-Football League clubs. They had also lost three of their previous four fixtures and had been annihilated 7-1 at Bootle in a friendly match six days before the local Derby. It was debatable whether Stoke's experience during the season had been any happier as they had ended up at the bottom of the inaugural Football League and had been knocked out of the English Cup in the first round by 2-1 at home to non-league Warwick County. However, they had at least won one tie in both the Birmingham Cup and the Staffordshire Cup before being eliminated, whilst they had secured the North Staffordshire Charity Challenge Cup by beating Leek, the holders, 1-0 in the final, nine days prior to the Derby. Also, to Stoke's relief, they had been re-elected to the Football League with the most votes of the thirteen clubs contesting the four available places. Unfortunately, none of the names of the players who took part in the local clash have been traced, so that the relative strengths of the two sides are entirely unknown, although it was stated that the game would kick off at 6.15 p.m.

THE MATCH

Although "The Staffordshire Sentinel" drew attention to the fixture in advance, it neglected to report the outcome of the match until 30 November and even then did not give the score! However, this was revealed by "The Athletic News", whose reporter merely commented that Vale would have won 3-1 had 'fair play' taken place. Nevertheless, Vale must have been relatively satisfied with the outcome after suffering thirteen successive defeats by their local rivals.

THE AFTERMATH

The Vale committee were determined to improve their team's performances in the following season and therefore appointed a professional trainer, Joey Law, during the summer, as well as engaging the services of Stoke's top marksmen, Bob McSkimming and Bob Milarvie. Stoke also bolstered their squad for the next campaign by signing five new players from Scotland, who included the international forward, Bob McCormick.

16: SATURDAY 30 NOVEMBER 1889, FRIENDLY

STOKE (0) 1 (Baker), BURSLEM PORT VALE (0) 1 (Ditchfield).

STOKE: Rowley, Clare, Underwood, Gee, Hendry, Ramsey, Sayer, McCormick, Baker, McReddie, Dunn.
VALE: Davis, Barr, Bateman, Poulson, McCrindle, Elson, Ballham, Reynolds, McGinnis, Ditchfield, Law.

Venue: The Victoria Ground, Stoke-upon-Trent.
Attendance: About 8,000.
Referee: Mr. Brownlow (Halliwell).

THE SETTING

Stoke were at the bottom of the Football League and had won just once in eleven outings. Even worse, they had been annihilated 10-0 at Preston North End (their equal heaviest ever league defeat) and 8-0 at Everton, but they were drawing 2-2 at home to Notts County a week before the local Derby when the match was abandoned. Vale's form had been remarkably erratic and the team had already recorded two 9-0 victories and two 9-0 defeats in friendly games, although immediately prior to the Derby, they had achieved four straight wins which had yielded twenty-three goals! Stoke made one alteration in their line-up from their previous match, with Sayer replacing Simpson, whilst Vale did likewise and Law stood in for McSkimming.

THE MATCH

Vale won the toss and chose to attack the Town goal in the presence of a following which matched the size of the home crowd. Although the play was fast and furious from the outset, both teams had difficulty in passing the ball on a greasy surface. Vale were the first to threaten seriously when Rowley scooped a Law shot off the line and the Stoke custodian then saved a tremendous shot from Ballham. However, towards the end of the first half, Baker looked certain to open the scoring for the home side, but instead ballooned the ball way over the bar.

Nevertheless, three minutes after the interval, Stoke did go in front when Baker made amends with a marvellous shot after sprinting clear. As Vale replied, McGinnis shot fractionally over the bar and then twice lost out in a one-on-one with Rowley. The contest continued to be intensely fought and Ditchfield finally equalised for the visitors with a fine shot, which was greeted by a tremendous cheer. However, Stoke thought they had sneaked a victory in the latter stages when Baker put the ball over the Vale line following a scrimmage, but the goal was disallowed for offside. Thus, for the first time ever, in nine encounters, Vale had avoided defeat at Stoke.

THE AFTERMATH

There was no initial improvement in Stoke's form and their following four Football League games all resulted in defeat, with nineteen goals conceded! Vale's efforts remained rather inconsistent and whilst their forwards scored with considerable regularity, their defence was too easily prised open.

17: SATURDAY 29 MARCH 1890, FRIENDLY

BURSLEM PORT VALE (1) 2 (Ditchfield, rush), STOKE (1) 1 (Edge).

VALE: Davis, Bateman, Coyle, Barr, McCrindle, Elson, Ballham, Reynolds, McGinnis, Ditchfield, Connolly.
STOKE: Rowley, Clare, Eccles, Ramsey, Christie, Brodie, Sayer, Gee, Baker, Edge, Dunn.

Venue: The Athletic Ground, Cobridge.
Attendance: Over 7,000.
Referee: T. Bryan (Birmingham).

THE SETTING
Vale were very confident of finally getting the better of their local rivals and the committee selected what they believed was the best team they had ever fielded. Five days earlier, Vale had won 2-1 at mighty Wolverhampton Wanderers in a Staffordshire Cup fourth round replay, but their overall record since the turn of the year had been rather erratic. Stoke were in dire straits, having drawn their final Football League fixture 1-1 at home to struggling Notts County on the Monday before the Derby, and had again finished at the bottom of the table. Remarkably, the side had reached the quarter-finals of the English Cup, but had then been trounced 8-0 at Wolverhampton Wanderers! They made two changes from their previous match with Clare and Dunn replacing Underwood and Owen.

THE MATCH
Despite the presence of a large crowd, the atmosphere was unusually quiet when the game finally kicked off at 4.20 p.m. Much of the play was end to end and both teams came close to scoring, with Ballham shooting just over for Vale and Dunn heading against the home bar from a superb cross by Sayer. It was indeed the visitors' right winger who was largely responsible for the breaking of the deadlock when he produced another fine centre for Edge to prod the ball in after forty minutes. Stoke almost extended their lead shortly afterwards when Baker hit the bar, but Ditchfield equalised just before the interval with a high shot in the corner of the goal.

Although Stoke took the initiative at the start of the second half, Ballham broke away and centred for Ditchfield and McGinnis to rush the ball in between them, amidst loud cheering. This had the effect of further increasing the tempo and, although both sides exhibited plenty of open, attacking play, Stoke's pressure mounted towards the end, but they were unable to prevent Vale from finally registering their first Derby victory in seventeen attempts! At the final whistle, the home supporters were unable to contain themselves and surged on to the pitch to celebrate.

THE AFTERMATH
Although Vale were knocked out of the Staffordshire Cup in the semi-finals, their local Derby success seemed to inspire them so that they gained four straight wins in their programme of friendlies. Stoke regained some pride with several favourable results in friendly matches, but were eliminated from the Staffordshire Cup by West Bromwich Albion two days after the Derby.

18: SATURDAY 10 MAY 1890, FRIENDLY

BURSLEM PORT VALE (3) 3 (McGinnis, Ballham, Barr), STOKE (1) 1 (Baker).

VALE: Davis, Bateman, Coyle, Barr, McCrindle, Elson, Ballham, Lowe, McGinnis, Ditchfield, Connolly.
STOKE: Rose, Clare, Underwood, Christie, Allen, Brodie, Sayer, Edge, Baker, Simpson, Dunn.

Venue: The Athletic Ground, Cobridge.
Attendance: About 4,000.
Referee: Mr. Jope (Wednesbury).

THE SETTING

Vale entered the local Derby with a run of five consecutive victories in friendly games under their belt and their most recent success had been a 5-1 home beating of Walsall Town Swifts the previous Saturday. They were effectively at full strength for the local clash and included a new forward, Lowe, in their team. However, Stoke were without their English international goalkeeper, Rowley, who preferred to play in a cricket match instead! For a second time, William Rose of Wolverhampton Wanderers guested in his place and Harry Allen, another star player from the same club, was drafted in at centre-half. Although Stoke boasted a strong line-up, they were labouring under the ignominy of having finished bottom of the Football League for the second year in succession. Nevertheless, they had annihilated Hanley Town 7-0 at home in the final of the North Staffordshire Charity Challenge Cup a week before the local Derby.

THE MATCH

Stoke made most of the initial running, but the play soon became more even and McGinnis opened the scoring for the home side with a twenty-yard 'daisy-cutter'. The visitors then pressed hard for an equaliser, but there was an outburst of laughter when Allen hit a close-in free kick both well above and wide of the Vale goal. Almost immediately afterwards, Ballham gave the home team the comfort of a two-goal lead with a rising shot following a solo run. Nevertheless, Stoke reduced the deficit through a Baker shot from Sayer's centre and an abundance of goalmouth action followed, with Edge hitting a Vale post and Barr striking the custodian's legs at the opposite end. Then, shortly before half-time, Barr shot the home side further ahead from a throw-in.

After the interval, Stoke exerted immense pressure on the home goal, but Edge twice shot wildly over the bar and Davis performed heroics to keep the visitors at bay. Although the excitement continued unabated, the nearest either team came to adding to the score was when Lowe had a goal disallowed for offside and Baker hit the Vale bar.

THE AFTERMATH

Although this was the final match of the season for both clubs, significant changes were afoot. Vale joined the Midland League for the following campaign, whilst Stoke failed to be re-elected to the Football League and consequently dropped down into the Football Alliance.

19: SATURDAY 20 DECEMBER 1890, FRIENDLY

BURSLEM PORT VALE (0) 0, STOKE (3) 3 (Dunn 2, Baker).

VALE: Davis, Barr, McAlpine, Poulson, McCrindle, Elson, Coyle, Davies, McGinnis, Ditchfield, Jones.
STOKE: Brookes, Clare, Underwood, Brodie, Clifford, Christie, Naughton, Baker, Turner, Ballham, Dunn.

Venue: The Athletic Ground, Cobridge.
Attendance: Under 3,000.
Referee: Mr. Mcintyre (Manchester).

THE SETTING
Although Vale had already been eliminated from the English Cup, they were coping quite well in the Midland League and had beaten the bottom club, Rotherham Town, 3-0 at home a week before the local Derby. Stoke were at the top of their new league, the Football Alliance, and had won 4-2 at Sheffield Wednesday on the same day. Both sides were at full strength for the local clash and both included debutants from Scotland, with Naughton (recently signed from Celtic) representing Stoke and McAlpine the home team. Although the weather was bitterly cold, the worst of the snow had been removed from the pitch and the partisanship of the crowd was such that their feelings 'often could be heard expressed in language not fit for publication'.

THE MATCH
Both sides had difficulty in adapting to the bone-hard pitch and the game was littered with fouls. Baker missed an excellent opportunity to open the scoring and Dunn struck a post before he put Stoke in front from a pass by the former in the thirty-fifth minute. The visitors then took complete control and Dunn added a second goal seven minutes later from a Naughton cross. Just before half-time, Baker extended Stoke's lead and the home team were being so overrun that they pulled Coyle back to reinforce their defence.

Vale came more into the match after the interval, although Baker missed a golden opportunity to pile on the agony by shooting straight at the home keeper. The play became increasingly rough, especially after McGinnis had been cautioned twice for fouling, and this whipped up the crowd into great excitement. As the game wore on, the light began to fade and the efforts of both sides became very disjointed. Although McGinnis forced Brookes to make a great save from a tremendous long shot, neither team posed any serious threat to their opponents' goal in the closing stages.

THE AFTERMATH
Vale's local Derby defeat was the prelude to a disastrous Christmas period in which they lost three Midland League matches in consecutive days. The 11-0 annihilation at Gainsborough Trinity on Boxing Day was an all-time club record league defeat, but this was surpassed the following month by a 12-0 trouncing at Aston Villa in the second round of the Staffordshire Cup! In contrast, Stoke continued their excellent form in the Football Alliance and, by the end of the season, had extended their unbeaten run in the competition to fourteen games.

20: MONDAY 30 MARCH 1891, FRIENDLY

STOKE (0) 1 (Slater o.g.), BURSLEM PORT VALE (0) 1 (McGinnis).

STOKE: Brookes, Brodie, Underwood, Christie, Clifford, Coupar, Ballham, Naughton, Turner, Edge, Dunn.
VALE: Higginson, McAlpine, Clutton, Elson, McCrindle, Slater, Davies, Dean, McGinnis, Keeling, Ditchfield.

Venue: The Victoria Ground, Stoke-upon-Trent.
Attendance: About 3,000.
Referee: W.H. Gough.

THE SETTING
Stoke were the clear leaders of the Football Alliance and therefore very well placed in their bid to return to the Football League. They were undefeated in thirteen league matches, had reached the quarter-finals of the English Cup before being eliminated and had held Football League Notts County to a 1-1 draw at home in a friendly game two days before the local Derby. Vale were holding their own in the Midland League, but had lost 3-1 at home to Gainsborough Trinity on the Saturday prior to the Derby. For the local clash, Stoke were without their regular right-back, Clare, who was injured, whilst Barr and Poulson were absent from the Vale defence.

THE MATCH
Stoke kicked off into a strong and bitterly cold wind, but were soon forced back by the visitors and hard-pressed not to go behind. McCrindle sent in a pile-driver, which was well saved by Brookes, and then twice hit the bar, whilst in addition a dangerous Vale free kick was cleared with difficulty for a corner. The play was almost entirely in the home half and Vale rained in a series of shots, but Stoke held on and went close to taking the lead through Turner and then Naughton in two rare breakaways.

At half-time, hundreds of spectators ran across the pitch to get behind the Vale goal in anticipation of a wind-assisted home onslaught, but the visitors continued their pressure after the interval and forced three corners in succession. Vale's persistence was finally rewarded when McGinnis scored from a terrific shot and a minute later he almost doubled his tally. Although Ditchfield was forced to retire for some time after being badly kicked, Stoke were unable to take advantage, even though a tremendous roar from their supporters urged them on. The clever passing of McGinnis ensured that the visitors remained a threat, but four minutes from the end Slater turned a Ballham centre into his own goal for the equaliser.

THE AFTERMATH
Stoke hammered Sheffield Wednesday, the bottom club, 5-1 at home in their final Football Alliance match five days after the local Derby and thus secured the championship. However, they were knocked out of the Birmingham Cup in the semi-finals and were then beaten 4-1 by Football League Aston Villa in the final of the Staffordshire Cup. Vale continued their reasonable but unexceptional form and took five points from their last four Midland League games.

21: MONDAY 27 APRIL 1891, FRIENDLY

STOKE (0) 1 (Higginson o.g.), BURSLEM PORT VALE (0) 0.

STOKE: Rowley, Clare, Eccles, Christie, Brodie, Clifford, Dunn, Edge, Schofield, Naughton, Coupar.
VALE: Higginson, Clutton, McAlpine, Elson, McCrindle, Barr, Davies, Dean, McGinnis, Ditchfield, Jones.

Venue: The Victoria Ground, Stoke-upon-Trent.
Attendance: Not more than 1,500.
Referee: W. Heath (Hanley).

THE SETTING

Stoke approached the clash on a relative high, having secured the championship of the Football Alliance, although nine days earlier they had been beaten 4-1 in the final of the Staffordshire Cup by Football League Aston Villa and had lost 3-2 at home to Middlesbrough in a friendly match the following Saturday. Despite securing five points from their final three games in the Midland League, Vale were still only in eighth place out of eleven teams as the competition drew to a close. However, they had won 3-0 at second from the bottom Staveley two days before the Derby. For the local contest, Stoke were without three regulars: their left-back, Underwood; outside-right, Ballham, and centre-forward, Turner, whilst Schofield made his debut. In contrast, Vale were entirely unchanged from their previous match.

THE MATCH

The teams did not take the field until 5.20 p.m., despite a five o'clock kickoff being scheduled, and then there was a further delay while a dispute about the referee was resolved, with Vale refusing to play under the official selected by the home club! Although Stoke had the advantage of the wind at their backs in the first half, the contest was evenly fought, but the play became very rough. When Barr, who was lying on the ground, was deliberately kicked in the back by Dunn, a number of Vale fans invaded the pitch to protest, but order was quickly restored. However, the same degree of excitement was not witnessed in terms of goalmouth action, although McGinnis hit the Stoke bar with a pile-driver.

After the interval, Vale took command, but a long, looping shot by Brodie was deflected in by Higginson for the opening goal, although the custodian unsuccessfully claimed he had been obstructed by Dunn. The passing of the Vale half-backs then became extremely wayward, which led to a furious row between McGinnis and Elson as the visitors' frustration mounted. Nevertheless, Vale exerted intense pressure as the game entered its final stages and Elson came within a whisker of an equaliser with a shot which crept just outside a post.

THE AFTERMATH

Stoke's victory put them in good heart for their friendly match at home against the Football League runners-up, Preston North End, the following Thursday, which in the event was lost 1-0. Nevertheless, this was ideal preparation for the forthcoming North Staffordshire Charity Challenge Cup competition, which had also been entered by Vale.

22: SATURDAY 9 MAY 1891, NORTH STAFFORD-SHIRE CHARITY CHALLENGE CUP, FINAL

BURSLEM PORT VALE (0) 1 (unknown), STOKE (1) 1 (unknown).

VALE: Higginson, Clutton, McAlpine, Elson, McCrindle, Barr, Davies, Dean, McGinnis, Ditchfield, Draycott.
STOKE: Rowley, Clare, Underwood, Christie, Clifford, Brodie, Ballham, Naughton, Schofield, Dunn, Edge.

Venue: The County Ground, Shelton.
Attendance: A fair gathering.
Referee: Unknown.

THE SETTING
Stoke were the holders of the trophy and as such may have been exempt until the final of this season's competition. Although this was not normal practice for the tournament, no semi-final match involving Stoke has been traced. Vale had set up a local Derby final by annihilating Burton Wanderers 7-0 away a week beforehand in a semi-final, but they cannot have been too hopeful of success as they had already failed to beat Stoke on three previous occasions during the campaign, had finished third from the bottom of the Midland League (out of ten teams) and had progressed no further in the English Cup than the second qualifying round. In contrast, Stoke approached the Derby on the crest of a wave as the champions of the Football Alliance, quarter-finalists in the English Cup, semi-finalists in the Birmingham Cup and the runners-up in the Staffordshire Cup, whilst they had been rewarded for their sterling efforts by being elected to the Football League five days earlier. Prior to the local clash, there was a dispute about the venue and so the charity committee decided upon a neutral ground. Although both clubs fielded their strongest available sides and a reasonable-sized crowd assembled, "The Athletic News" commented that 'anything like the old interest was conspicuously absent'.

THE MATCH
Unfortunately, only one extremely sparse report of the match, by "The Staffordshire Sentinel", has been traced, according to which, Jimmy Ditchfield, the Vale captain, won the toss and chose to kick with the wind in the first half. However, this ploy seemed to have backfired because Stoke 'forced the leather through' in only the seventh minute and still held the lead at the interval. Nevertheless, the game was hard fought, with 'a vast amount of feeling being manifested by both players and spectators'. Rather surprisingly, in view of the adverse conditions, Vale equalised in the second half to earn a replay.

THE AFTERMATH
In the event, the replay did not take place and the trophy was shared, probably because of a lack of impetus to arrange a further match so late in the season. The Vale committee decided to adopt a local players policy for the following campaign and offered contracts of up to five years for the most impressive ones they could find. Neither did Stoke sign any new players of reputation for the difficult task ahead in the Football League.

23: MONDAY 28 SEPTEMBER 1891, FRIENDLY

BURSLEM PORT VALE (?) 2 (unknown), STOKE (?) 3 (unknown).

VALE: Higginson, Clutton, McAlpine, McCrindle, Shutt, Slater, McHarg, Dean, McGinnis, Ditchfield, Scarratt.

STOKE: Rowley, Clare, Underwood, Smith, Clifford, Christie, Ballham, Naughton, Turner, Draycott, Schofield.

Venue: The Athletic Ground, Cobridge.
Attendance: Capital.
Referee: T. Armitt (Leek).

THE SETTING

Vale had opened the 1891-1892 season quite brightly, with only one defeat in their first eight games, and had hammered Doncaster Rovers 4-0 at home in the Midland League on the Saturday before the local Derby, whilst their centre-forward, McGinnis, had already scored 13 goals! Although Stoke had begun their first season back in the Football League with a home victory, they had gained only one point from their three matches since, a 1-1 draw at struggling Notts County two days prior to the Derby. Vale fielded an unchanged team for the local clash, but Smith, Draycott (who made his debut) and Schofield replaced Brodie, Cameron and Dunn for Stoke.

THE MATCH

Unfortunately, no report of the match with much specific detail has been discovered. However, the clash was extremely exciting and both sides fought hard for victory, loudly encouraged by their supporters. Nevertheless, the game was played in a good spirit, although Underwood annoyed the Vale fans with his over-zealous tackling. 'Few were to be found who did not declare that Vale were the better team', but an inept display by their keeper led to their defeat. Indeed, Higginson was guilty of an astonishing blunder when he wandered up the pitch to join in the general play, which Vale were controlling, only to miskick the ball and enable Stoke to score from a breakaway! The visiting custodian also gifted a goal to the opposition, whilst Vale had vigorous appeals for a penalty ignored. Nevertheless, the brilliance of Schofield and the resilience of the Stoke defence proved sufficient to clinch the victory.

THE AFTERMATH

An excellent sum of £92 17s. 6d. was taken at the gate, but Vale subsequently struck a poor run of form, in which they lost five of their next seven Midland League games and were knocked out of the English Cup at home in the first qualifying round. Stoke fared even worse, being annihilated 9-3 at Darwen, the penultimate team, in the league on the Saturday after the local Derby and picking up only four points from their nine matches to the end of November, which left them second from the bottom of the table. Even worse, their financial position became so difficult that the use of season tickets for the home fixture against Sunderland on 28 November was suspended, whilst three of their players, Hugh Clifford, Billy Fraser and John Cameron, returned to Scotland in December following a dispute with the Stoke committee!

24: SATURDAY 26 DECEMBER 1891, FRIENDLY

STOKE (1) 2 (Ballham, Evans), BURSLEM PORT VALE (2) 2 (McGinnis, Walker).

STOKE: Brookes, Clare, Underwood, Christie, Proctor, Brodie, Ballham, Evans, Turner, Schofield, Dunn.
VALE: Nixon, Clutton, McAlpine, McCrindle, Ditchfield, Elson, Walker, Dean, McGinnis, Scarratt, Reynolds.

Venue: The Victoria Ground, Stoke-upon-Trent.
Attendance: About 2,000.
Referee: A. Cooper (Wolverhampton).

THE SETTING
Although Stoke were struggling in the Football League at third from the bottom of the table, they had at least won two matches earlier in the month. However, they had been beaten 3-2 at second-placed Preston North End the day before the local Derby. Vale were in fifth position in the Midland League, but had lost six of their eleven games and had also been eliminated from the English Cup in the first qualifying round. However, they had won 3-1 at Burton Swifts in a friendly a week prior to the Derby. Stoke were at full strength for the local clash, apart from Brookes standing in for Rowley in goal, whilst Vale also fielded a strong team, although the veteran Reynolds had to be included at the last minute because the visitors were a man short.

THE MATCH
Stoke kicked off with the wind to their advantage on an extremely slippery surface resulting from drizzle falling onto a thick frost. Although the play was not surprisingly disjointed, the home side pressed strongly and after fifteen minutes Ballham opened the scoring with a fine shot which sailed past Nixon, who was stuck in the mud! Just under twenty minutes later, Walker missed a golden opportunity to equalise for Vale following a stylish run up the wing by Scarratt and shortly afterwards, to the relief of the players, the referee blew for half-time some ten minutes early.

Scientific football was no more in evidence during the second period and the players were hard pushed to stay on their feet. Nevertheless, Stoke extended their lead through a marvellous strike by Evans after some intricate interplay between him and Ballham. However, Vale were not finished and McGinnis reduced the arrears almost immediately with a tremendous shot, which was loudly applauded. Finally, another strong effort from the same player led to the equaliser as the ball was only parried by Brookes and Walker tapped it home.

THE AFTERMATH
Stoke's Football League form fell apart after the Derby and the team lost their following seven matches, although once more they fought their way into the quarter-finals of the English Cup. Holding their local rivals to a draw seemed to act like a tonic to Vale who won four of their next five league games, scoring eighteen goals in the process, and battled their way into the semi-finals of the Staffordshire Cup.

25: MONDAY 18 APRIL 1892, FRIENDLY

BURSLEM PORT VALE (1) 1 (Dean), STOKE (0) 0.

VALE: Higginson, Clutton, McAlpine, Farrington, McCrindle, Elson, Beats, Dean, McGinnis, Jones, Walker.
STOKE: Rowley, Clare, Underwood, Christie, Proctor, Brodie, Evans, Naughton, Turner, Ballham, Dunn.

Venue: The Athletic Ground, Cobridge.
Attendance: 2,000.
Referee: T. Armitt (Leek).

THE SETTING

Although Vale had been eliminated from the Staffordshire Cup in the semi-finals on 4 April, they had moved into the top half of the Midland League following four victories in their last five matches, the most recent of which had been a 1-0 win at Derby Junction nine days before the local clash. Stoke were struggling in penultimate position in the Football League, but had at least ended a row of eight successive defeats by drawing 2-2 at struggling West Bromwich Albion a week prior to the Derby. Also, they had reached the quarter-finals of the English Cup before being knocked out of the competition. For the local contest, Vale were without Scarratt and Ditchfield, their normal left-forward pairing, although Stoke named the same team which had performed creditably at West Bromwich.

THE MATCH

Stoke kicked off in front of a small crowd, but more than matched their opponents. However, after around fifteen minutes, McGinnis tricked the visiting defenders by arguing about the distance they were standing from a free kick and he then quickly touched the ball to Dean who shot home. Rowley, the Stoke keeper, stood in amazement and never moved! The incident seemed to rattle the visitors whose goal then had several narrow escapes, but Vale were unable to extend their lead.

After the interval, the match was more evenly contested, although the play was largely scrappy and mainly concentrated in the middle of the pitch. Naughton went close for Stoke with an overhead kick, whilst Turner headed just over the bar, but these threats stirred the home team back into action and Jones forced Rowley to produce a fine save from a hard, long shot. Nevertheless, neither side was able to add to the score and the Vale supporters 'hooted loudly' at several of the visiting players whom they deemed to have been guilty of rough tactics.

THE AFTERMATH

Vale completed their Midland League fixtures with two victories, which finally put them in a highly satisfactory third place out of eleven teams. Although Stoke won their remaining game in the Football League, it did not prevent them from finishing second from the bottom of the table and having once again to apply for re-election.

26: SATURDAY 7 MAY 1892, STAFFORDSHIRE CHARITY CUP

STOKE (0) 0, BURSLEM PORT VALE (0) 2 (Walker, other).

STOKE: Rowley, Clare, Underwood, Christie, Proctor, Brodie, Evans, Naughton, Turner, Schofield, Dunn.
VALE: Higginson, Clutton, McAlpine, Farrington, McCrindle, Jones, Walker, Dean, McGinnis, unknown, Scarratt.

Venue: The Victoria Ground, Stoke-upon-Trent.
Attendance: About 1,000.
Referee: Mr. Jefferies (Derby).

THE SETTING
Stoke had finished second to the bottom of the Football League and therefore were having to seek re-election for the third time in four seasons! Also, they had been hammered 5-1 in a friendly match at Ardwick a week before the local Derby. However, Vale had ended their Midland League programme with three straight victories in April, which had secured third place for them. Unfortunately, they had been thrashed 6-1 at Northwich Victoria in a friendly on the Saturday prior to the Derby. Stoke were at full strength for the clash and included their four England internationals, whilst Vale also fielded a very strong line-up.

THE MATCH
Although Vale kicked off, the home side nearly went in front almost immediately as Dunn found himself with only the goalkeeper to beat, but shot weakly straight at him. The play became fast and furious and the Stoke forwards peppered the visitors' goal with shots, but it remained intact. Towards half-time, the home team increased the pressure even further and forced three corners in quick succession, but Vale hung on and survived close calls from excellent efforts by both Naughton and Schofield.

After the interval, Vale got back into the match and Walker soon shot them into the lead. A minute later they doubled their score with the Stoke defence in utter confusion, but soon afterwards Dunn missed a second great chance for the home side by shooting wildly across the pitch. After Schofield had put another effort over the bar, McGinnis was cautioned for frequent foul play and was subsequently ordered off for attempting to trip Christie. However, he refused to depart and two minutes passed before he was finally persuaded to leave the pitch, to the accompaniment of 'loud groans'. The game then became very bad tempered and Naughton used his fists against an opponent, but was not spotted by the referee. The outcome was that the match petered out amidst considerable ill feeling, which was unfortunate as Vale's victory was their historic first at Stoke in thirteen attempts and their first in a competitive Derby.

THE AFTERMATH
Stoke were re-elected to the Football League with a single vote to spare, whilst Vale became founder members of a new Second Division which was formed for the 1892-1893 season. Sadly, they took their place without their star centre-forward, Frank McGinnis, who died from kidney disease on 25 June.

27: MONDAY 30 OCTOBER 1893, FRIENDLY

BURSLEM PORT VALE (1) 3 (scrimmage, other, Scarratt), STOKE (1) 1 (Smith).

VALE: Baddeley, Ramsey, Youds, Farrington, McCrindle, Elson, Scarratt, Dean, Beats, Wood, Campbell.

STOKE: A. Evans, Clare, Brodie, Christie, Proctor, Dowds, Naughton, Dickson, Robertson, McReddie, Smith.

Venue: The Athletic Ground, Cobridge.
Attendance: 5,000.
Referee: J. Lewis (Blackburn).

THE SETTING

Vale had begun the season like a hurricane, winning all their opening seven matches in the Second Division, but had then suffered three successive defeats. They had also been eliminated from the English Cup in the first qualifying round, although they had won 1-0 at fourth from the bottom Rotherham Town two days before the local Derby to hold on to third place in the league. Stoke were eleventh in the First Division out of sixteen teams, but had beaten fourth-placed Blackburn Rovers 3-1 at home on the Saturday prior to the Derby. Both clubs fielded strong line-ups for the local clash and Stoke included a trialist from Rangers on the left wing called Smith, although his real name was Tom Hyslop! The game was billed as 'the championship of the Potteries' and created such interest that crowds swarmed around the entrances and hundreds of people got in free by climbing over the turnstiles.

THE MATCH

Vale had only got nine men on the pitch at the kickoff, but the visitors were unable to take advantage of the absence of Farrington and Beats, who entered the fray after a few minutes. Thus heartened, the home side went close with Beats firing just wide and Dean landing the ball on the top of the net. The play was unsophisticated, but switched from end to end until Smith rammed the ball home to put Stoke into the lead. The visitors then took command and kept the Vale keeper well occupied, but eventually the home team broke away and equalised through a scrimmage.

After the interval, Vale dominated the play through meticulous passing and although the visitors showed some fine individual skill, they did not combine at all well together. Vale displayed great determination to win and, after they'd taken the lead, Scarratt sewed up the victory with a wonderful swerving shot.

THE AFTERMATH

Vale's perilous financial position was eased by the £105 gate money taken and by the Stoke committee's donation of their share of the proceeds to the cause. Vale won three of their next five league matches, but their promotion hopes took a serious jolt as a result of three consecutive defeats which followed. Stoke steadied their own position in the First Division by gaining four victories in their following seven games, although the local Derby proved to be the final match for their centre-half, Jack Proctor, who died of pneumonia on 8 November.

28: SATURDAY 17 FEBRUARY 1894, FRIENDLY

BURSLEM PORT VALE (0) 0, STOKE (3) 7 (Robertson 2, Schofield 2, Brodie, Dickson, Naughton).

VALE: Mackay, Rhodes, Ramsey, Boughey, McCrindle, Elson, Scarratt, Dean, Edwards, Wood, Campbell.
STOKE: Cain, Clare, Eccles, Christie, Dowds, Brodie, Naughton, Dickson, Robertson, McReddie, Schofield.

Venue: The Athletic Ground, Cobridge.
Attendance: Never more than 800 or 1,000.
Referee: S. Ormerod (Accrington).

THE SETTING
Vale stood in fourth place in the Second Division, but their hopes of promotion were slipping away as a result of having achieved only a single victory in their last seven league matches. Even worse, they had lost 2-1 at home to second from the bottom Walsall Town Swifts a week before the local Derby and had then been eliminated from the Birmingham Cup. Stoke were comfortably positioned in the First Division, but had been knocked out of the Birmingham Cup five days prior to the Derby. The local clash was loosely referred to as 'the championship of the Potteries', but there was considerable doubt as to whether it would be played because water lay several inches deep on part of the pitch and snow continued to fall as the kickoff time approached. Indeed, only the hardiest spectators turned up to watch and Vale's centre-forward, Beats, was told that the match had been postponed and returned home to Wolstanton! Nevertheless, both clubs fielded very strong line-ups.

THE MATCH
Vale kicked off, playing into the snow and wind, and quickly came under pressure in a contest reduced to half an hour each way. Stoke peppered the home goal and Brodie shot them in front. Robertson added a second by deflecting in a drive by Schofield and Dickson extended the visitors' lead by stroking the ball home following a solo run.

After the interval, Mackay, who had been injured, did not reappear and he was replaced in the Vale goal by Wood. This made the task even tougher for the home team and Robertson put the ball in the net almost immediately, but had the effort ruled offside. Nevertheless, the same player scored a fourth goal for Stoke from a corner and Naughton added a fifth with a long shot just after the restart, at a time when the home side were temporarily down to nine men with Scarratt having treatment for a knee injury. Schofield registered a sixth goal with a deceptive shot and then completed the rout almost on time after Stoke had missed several good chances.

THE AFTERMATH
Not surprisingly, in view of their severe local Derby mauling, Vale won only one of their three following Second Division games, which killed their promotion hopes. However, Stoke gained two victories in their next three league matches to keep them well clear of the relegation zone.

29: TUESDAY 27 MARCH 1894, FRIENDLY

BURSLEM PORT VALE (2) 2 (Wood, McCrindle), **STOKE** (2) 4 (Naughton, Dickson, others).

VALE: Baddeley, G. Eccles, Ramsey, Edwards, McCrindle, Elson, Scarratt, Dean, Beats, Wood, Campbell.
STOKE: Cain, Meston, J. Eccles, Morrell, Dowds, Brodie, Naughton, Dickson, Robertson, McReddie, Schofield.

Venue: The Athletic Ground, Cobridge.
Attendance: Between 1,000 and 1,500 when the game started.
Referee: J. Lewis (Blackburn).

THE SETTING

Although Vale were sixth in the Second Division, their promotion chances had been finally ended by a 6-0 defeat at third-placed Small Heath three days before the local Derby. In addition, earlier in the month, they had been eliminated from the Staffordshire Cup. Stoke had also been knocked out of this competition, in the semi-finals, but had guaranteed the retention of their First Division status by beating second-placed Sunderland 2-0 at home on the Saturday prior to the Derby. Apart from including their reserve goalkeeper, Vale were at full strength, but Stoke fielded a somewhat makeshift defence for a match described as deciding 'the championship of North Staffordshire'.

THE MATCH

Vale kicked off towards the Wolstanton end and immediately almost took the lead with a determined rush on the visitors' goal. The home team remained on top and Wood hit a post following a free kick, but the play gradually slowed down and became more even. Eventually, Wood put Vale in front after knocking the ball out of the Stoke keeper's hands, but shortly afterwards, a beautiful centre by Naughton drifted into the net to equalise the score. However, the home side quickly went back in front through a rising shot from McCrindle who dug the ball out of a scrimmage. The goalmouth action continued to be fast and furious and Stoke drew level once more on the stroke of half-time when Dickson headed in from a brilliant McReddie overhead kick.

After the interval, Stoke controlled the game and showed greater stamina and strength in a very physical contest. Although Vale fought hard to stay in the match, Stoke had an extra 'bit up their sleeves' and ran out comfortable winners. Unfortunately, the scorers of the visitors' two second half goals are unknown because the only report which has been traced covered the play just to half-time.

THE AFTERMATH

Vale ended their Second Division campaign with only one point from two of their best performances of the season against the undefeated champions, Liverpool, and finished a disappointing seventh. Although Stoke lost two of their remaining three league games and conceded twelve goals in the process, they finished in eleventh place, six points clear of the relegation zone.

30: MONDAY 10 SEPTEMBER 1894, FRIENDLY

STOKE (0) 0, BURSLEM PORT VALE (0) 0.

STOKE: Clawley, Walker, Boardman, Morrell, Christie, Turner, Sandland, Brookfield, Grewer, T. Eccles, Schofield.
VALE: Baddeley, Eccles, Ray, Regan, Edwards, Haslam, Scarratt, Dean, Beats, Wood, unknown.

Venue: The Victoria Ground, Stoke-upon-Trent.
Attendance: Unknown.
Referee: Unknown.

THE SETTING
Stoke had opened their First Division programme with a creditable 2-2 draw at Bolton Wanderers before going down 3-1 at home to Everton two days before the local Derby. Vale had commenced the season with a 1-0 home victory against Walsall Town Swifts in the Second Division, but had sustained a 4-1 defeat at Manchester City on the Saturday before the Derby, which was eagerly anticipated. Vale were at their fullest available strength, but the Stoke committee decided to rest most of their star players and Schofield was the only regular first-teamer selected, although Jim Turner, a recent acquisition from Bolton Wanderers, made his debut. Because the full admission prices were still charged, there was a lot of grumbling amongst the crowd and there was some discussion in the Vale camp as to whether they should refuse to play the match.

THE MATCH
The Vale players were so disgusted that they were not meeting their old rivals' first team that they treated the game as a practice match and made only a token effort. The Vale custodian was never seriously tested as the visitors put together a series of intricate passing moves and toyed with their opponents. Beats caused the Stoke centre-half considerable problems and Scarratt ran riot on the right flank, but on two separate occasions deliberately thumped the ball straight at the Stoke keeper when he only needed to tap it in to score. Also, Scarratt further showed his contempt for the affair by lofting the ball into the adjoining tennis court when he was presented with an open goal! The match was therefore a fiasco, much to the chagrin of the spectators, and ended goalless.

THE AFTERMATH
The respite that the Stoke first-teamers had gained from their non-involvement in the local Derby did not seem to do them a great deal of good because they lost three of their following four league games and conceded thirteen goals in the process! However, Vale fared even worse and suffered four consecutive defeats before the tide was finally stemmed by a draw at home.

31: MONDAY 8 OCTOBER 1894, FRIENDLY

BURSLEM PORT VALE (0) 1 (Scarratt), STOKE (1) 3 (Dickson 3).

VALE: Baddeley, G. Eccles, Ray, Edwards, Beech, Regan, Scarratt, Dean, Beats, Wood, J. Smith.
STOKE: Clawley, Foster, J. Eccles, unknown, T. Robertson, Brodie, Schofield, T. Eccles, Dickson, Sandland, Heames.

Venue: The Athletic Ground, Cobridge.
Attendance: 2-3,000.
Referee: W. Maddocks (Longton).

THE SETTING
Vale were having a torrid time in the Second Division, having lost five matches in a row before finally stopping the rot with a 4-4 home draw against fifth from the bottom Newcastle United two days before the local Derby. As a result, they were third from the bottom of the table. Stoke were faring little better and stood second from the bottom of the First Division. They had been beaten 3-1 at second-placed Sunderland on the Saturday prior to the Derby. Vale selected their strongest available line-up for the local clash, but Stoke were without four regulars.

THE MATCH
Unfortunately, the appointed match referee missed his train and failed to arrive at the ground. The consequent search for a replacement procured the reluctant services of Wilfred Maddocks of Dresden United, but, according to the Vale reporter for "The Staffordshire Sentinel", the game was then marred by the most 'woeful exhibition' of refereeing ever seen on the home team's ground! Dickson put Stoke 2-0 up by the interval, although Vale and their fans claimed that both goals were offside and that the referee, who was well behind the play, was in no position to judge. Their viewpoint was supported by "The Athletic News" correspondent in the first instance, but the newspaper vindicated Mr. Maddocks in the second.

Shortly after half-time, Scarratt scored 'a beauty' to bring Vale back into contention, but Dickson secured the victory for the visitors by completing his hat trick. Stoke produced a particularly energetic performance and Schofield caused the home defence considerable problems. The robust Dickson was kept well in check by Beech, but the Vale forwards found the visiting keeper to be in excellent form, which was instrumental in Stoke gaining the victory.

THE AFTERMATH
Although Vale recovered to win their next Second Division game, they took only three points from their following fifteen matches to plunge deep into the re-election zone. They also exited rapidly from all the three major cup competitions they had entered. Stoke lost their first two league games after the local Derby and gradually sank to the foot of the table following a run of further poor results from the middle of November. They too made little impact on the three major cup tournaments and were dispatched from all of them within the space of three weeks in the new year.

32: MONDAY 15 APRIL 1895, FRIENDLY

BURSLEM PORT VALE (?) 2 (J. Mason, Evans), STOKE (?) 4 (Schofield Hyslop, Dickson, Grewer).

VALE: Evans and J. Mason played, but the team is otherwise unknown.
STOKE: Grewer, Dickson, Hyslop (inside-left) and Schofield played, but the team is otherwise unknown.

Venue: The Athletic Ground, Cobridge.
Attendance: Unknown.
Referee: H. Brown (Cobridge).

THE SETTING
Vale were third from the bottom of the Second Division, but were making a heroic attempt to escape from the re-election places with four victories in their last six league matches after more than four months without a single win! Their most recent success had been a 2-1 victory at Newcastle United three days before the local Derby. Stoke were also in dire straits in the First Division, being in penultimate position, but likewise had begun a late recovery, with successive 5-1 home victories in their last two games, against Burnley and fourth-placed Blackburn Rovers. Stoke did not field all of their first team players for the Derby, but no report commenting upon the Vale line-up has been discovered.

THE MATCH
Stoke dominated the match, but there was little excitement after the first twenty minutes because both teams 'seemed out for a holiday'. The best football was exhibited in that opening spell, but the visitors' inside-left, Hyslop, produced a marvellous display throughout and was instrumental in all Stoke's four goals. He notched one himself and set up others for Schofield, Dickson and Grewer. Mason and Evans replied for Vale. The visitors' impressive revival therefore continued, although "The Staffordshire Sentinel" made it clear that this owed nothing to the refereeing of the former Stoke player, Harry Brown, who was 'prompt, accurate and fair', despite receiving 'plenty of instruction' from the home supporters!

THE AFTERMATH
Although Vale hammered the bottom side, Crewe Alexandra, 4-0 at home in their final Second Division fixture five days after the local Derby, the result was insufficient to prevent them from finishing in penultimate position and having to apply for re-election. Stoke won their last two league games of the season to extend their successive victories to four, although they still ended up third from the bottom of the table. Consequently, they were obliged to play off in a test match against the Second Division's third-placed team, Newton Heath, to try to preserve their status, which they did by winning 3-0 at Vale's ground twelve days after the local Derby.

33: SATURDAY 8 FEBRUARY 1896, STAFFORD-SHIRE CUP, FIRST ROUND

BURSLEM PORT VALE (0) 0, STOKE (1) 4 (Schofield 2, Wood, Dickson).

VALE: Baddeley, G. Eccles, Youds, Fallows, Barlow, McDonald, Downie, Beckett, Sandham, Evans, J. Mason.
STOKE: Clawley, Clare, J. Eccles, Robertson, Grewer, Brodie, W. Maxwell, Dickson, A. Maxwell, Wood, Schofield.

Venue: The Athletic Ground, Cobridge.
Attendance: Close upon 4,000.
Referee: G.H. Dale (Manchester).

THE SETTING
Vale were fifth from the bottom of the Second Division and had been eliminated from the English Cup and the Birmingham Cup, but had hammered struggling Rotherham Town 4-0 at home in the league a fortnight before the local Derby. However, Stoke were fifth in the First Division and had thrashed non-league Tottenham Hotspur 5-0 at home in the first round of the English Cup on the Saturday prior to the Derby. Although both clubs selected strong teams for the local clash, the occasion was affected by a dispute which had followed Stoke's unsuccessful demand for a £20 guarantee from the gate.

THE MATCH
Vale attacked with a very stiff wind in their favour, but quickly found their goal under siege and then lost George Eccles, who broke his collarbone in a collision. Schofield notched the first goal for Stoke after sixteen minutes with a remarkable shot from an acute angle following a brilliant solo run, whilst the home keeper stood and watched in amazement, thinking that the ball was going out! Schofield ran riot on the wing as a result of Eccles' absence, but Vale stood firm, although Clare put the ball straight in the net from an indirect free kick.

After the interval, Vale were reduced to nine men because Evans, who had been limping badly, did not reappear. Two minutes into the second half, Wood extended Stoke's lead after Baddeley had dropped the ball, following a charge by Dickson, and the visiting goalkeeper decided to put on an overcoat because he had so little to do! Although Baddeley performed wonders to keep Stoke at bay, Dickson hit a post and then struck a ten-yard shot high into the corner of the net to add a third goal. Vale had to work overtime to withstand the pressure and Clare hit the bar before Schofield completed the scoring with a 'grand' shot.

THE AFTERMATH
Vale received £85 1s. 8d. as their share of the £115 4s. 9d. match receipts, which helped to soften the blow of their heavy defeat. However, the team produced a dire series of results to the end of the season, which left them third from the bottom of the Second Division. They subsequently failed to gain re-election and dropped into the Midland League. In contrast, Stoke progressed to the final of the Staffordshire Cup before being beaten in a replay, made it into the quarter-finals of the English Cup and finished sixth in the First Division.

34: MONDAY 26 APRIL 1897, FRIENDLY

BURSLEM PORT VALE (0) 2 (Peake, D. Simpson), STOKE (0) 0.

VALE: Lawton, Morse, Platt, Smith, Beech, Holdcroft, R. Evans, Hewitt, D. Simpson, Peake, Belfield.
STOKE: Sheldon, Peacock, Durber, Ferns, H. Simpson, Capewell, Eardley, Bentley, Wood, Woods, Boullemier.

Venue: The Athletic Ground, Cobridge.
Attendance: A few hundred.
Referee: J. Tunnicliffe (Longton).

THE SETTING
Vale had completed their Midland League programme with two home victories to finish in seventh place, but had experienced a very mediocre season overall, as they attempted to stabilise their fortunes following their drop out of the Football League. Their level of performance was well illustrated by the 3-1 defeat suffered at Wellingborough Town in a semi-final of the Wellingborough Cup six days before the local Derby. Only three consecutive wins had enabled Stoke to climb to fourth from the bottom of the First Division and thereby escape the threat of relegation, but they had drawn 0-0 at home to Wolverhampton Wanderers in the final of the Staffordshire Cup on the Saturday prior to the Derby. Because the replay had been arranged to take place three days after the local clash, Stoke fielded their reserve team in the Derby, although Vale put out a strong line-up.

THE MATCH
Vale attacked the Church end of the ground and, although they were playing into the wind, they quickly applied pressure to their opponents' goal. However, Stoke came back into the game and Capewell had a tremendous shot well saved before Bentley hit the bar. Vale found it difficult to exert their authority and the play eventually became bogged down in the midfield.

With the wind at their backs, Vale seized the initiative after the interval and struck the bar from a corner, but soon had better fortune. Sheldon could only parry a shot from Evans and Peake was perfectly placed to steer the rebound into the net. The home side then pressed strongly, but tended to over-hit their shots which were frequently carried over the Stoke goal by the wind. Nevertheless, Evans netted, only to find himself ruled offside, and Danny Simpson made the game safe with a second goal five minutes from the end. Although Vale had had the lion's share of the possession, it was believed by "The Staffordshire Sentinel" reporter that they had not overexerted themselves because they were due to contest the final of the Staffordshire Senior Charity Cup two days later.

THE AFTERMATH
Vale duly won the Staffordshire Senior Charity Cup by beating Dresden United 3-0 at the Victoria Ground, Stoke, but missed out on being elected to the Football League by two votes, whilst Stoke's season ended on a disappointing note because they lost the Staffordshire Cup final replay 2-0.

35: SATURDAY 27 NOVEMBER 1897, FRIENDLY

BURSLEM PORT VALE (1) 1 (R. Evans), STOKE (0) 0.

VALE: Lawton, Clare, Spilsbury, Boullemier, Beech, McDonald, R. Evans, J. Evans, Simpson, Peake, Belfield.
STOKE: Johnston, Robertson, Eccles, Murphy, Grewer, Parsons, Johnson, Pugh, Wood, Mellor, Shaffery.

Venue: The Athletic Ground, Cobridge.
Attendance: 1,600 'besides ticket-holders and supernumeraries'.
Referee: J.B. Brodie (Brewood).

THE SETTING
Vale had found life very difficult in the Midland League, starting with just one win in their initial eight matches, but had redeemed themselves with back-to-back home victories against the top two sides, Ilkeston Town and Rushden. Also, they had progressed through the fourth qualifying round of the English Cup on the Saturday before the local Derby because their opponents, Kidderminster, had scratched from the competition. Stoke were second from the bottom of the First Division and had lost nine of their opening fourteen games. Their most recent failure had been a 2-1 home defeat by Nottingham Forest a week prior to the Derby. Vale were at full strength for the local clash, whilst Stoke were also well-represented, but the size of the crowd was seriously affected by heavy rain which had threatened a postponement.

THE MATCH
Although Vale chose to attack with a strong breeze after winning the toss, it soon became obvious that the muddy pitch would enable little constructive football as the players had the greatest difficulty in staying on their feet. Nevertheless, the home team had the better of the initial exchanges and, after thirteen minutes, Dick Evans put them into the lead with a fine shot following some clever inter-passing. Vale remained on top, but Belfield was carried off with a broken leg as a result of a collision with Robertson after about half an hour and Peake then received a nasty kick from the same opponent following a scuffle.

Stoke were also reduced to ten men after the interval because Parsons had suffered a serious leg injury, but neither side was able to make much headway in the second period. However, there was considerable excitement when Simpson and Robertson clashed and a spectator ran on to the pitch and threatened the latter with his fists. A number of other fans gathered round, but order was eventually restored by the referee, although the play became extremely rough as Stoke desperately, but unsuccessfully, pressed for an equaliser.

THE AFTERMATH
Although the match receipts amounted to little over £40, which was barely sufficient for the payment of the players' wages, the Stoke team offered to take part in a benefit game for the injured Fred Belfield. Vale's recent improvement continued and they lost just one of their next seven league and cup matches. In contrast, Stoke won only two of their following seven First Division games, although they did battle through to the semi-finals of the Staffordshire Cup.

36: MONDAY 10 JANUARY 1898, STAFFORDSHIRE CUP, SEMI-FINAL

BURSLEM PORT VALE (2) 3 (J. Evans, others), STOKE (0) 1 (unknown).

VALE: Birchenough, Clare, Spilsbury, Boullemier, Beech, Bayley, J. Evans, R. Evans, Simpson, Peake, Heames.

STOKE: Sheldon, Robertson, Eccles, Murphy, Wood, Durber, Maxwell, Mellor, T. Hill, J. Hill, Schofield.

Venue: The Athletic Ground, Cobridge.
Attendance: 7,000.
Referee: T. Armitt Leek).

THE SETTING

Remarkably, Vale were second in the Midland League, despite having lost more matches than they'd won, but they had settled into a spell of good form with five victories in their last seven league games. However, they had only managed a 0-0 draw at struggling Doncaster Rovers two days before the local Derby. Stoke, on the other hand, were third from the bottom of the First Division, with a single win in their previous five league matches, and had lost 1-0 at home to Sunderland on the Saturday prior to the Derby. Both clubs fielded very strong line-ups for the local clash, although Vale were without their usual left-half, McDonald, who was injured, and Tom Hill deputised as Stoke's centre-forward for the unavailable Hingerty. A dense morning fog gave way to beautiful sunshine, which helped to attract an unusually large crowd for a local Derby at that time.

THE MATCH

Although Stoke won the toss, the conditions offered no significant advantage, but the visitors were not deterred and attacked vigorously. Nevertheless, they were unable to find a way through the Vale defence and the home side gradually got back into the game through great determination and some fine, flowing football. Eventually, a mistake by Sheldon gave Vale the lead, which they extended before half-time.

Shortly after the interval, Vale went three up when "Jammer" Evans put in a superb header following fine interplay by their forwards and the Stoke players started to look rather despondent. Nevertheless, the visitors pulled a goal back about ten minutes later, although they were never able to exert sufficient pressure to make a real fight of it. Consequently, Vale ran out comfortable winners to reach the final of the Staffordshire Cup for the first time and well merited the enthusiastic reception they received upon leaving the pitch.

THE AFTERMATH

The receipts of £170 were the largest amount taken at the Athletic Ground for several seasons. Vale's team continued to prosper and took nine points from their next five league matches to climb into second place, whilst they also beat the eventual First Division champions, Sheffield United, in the first round of the English Cup before being eliminated. Stoke also discovered some fighting spirit and lost only three of their following eight league and cup games.

37: SATURDAY 19 MARCH 1898, FRIENDLY

STOKE (0) 0, BURSLEM PORT VALE (0) 0.

STOKE: Wilkes, Ponsonby, Rowley, Murphy, Raisbeck, Wood, Schofield, Kennedy, Molyneux, Mellor, J. Hill.
VALE: Birchenough, Clare, Hulme, Boullemier, Beech, McDonald, Hodgkinson, R. Evans, Simpson, Price, Heames.

Venue: The Victoria Ground, Stoke-upon-Trent.
Attendance: Not more than 3,000.
Referee: J.B. Brodie (Brewood).

THE SETTING
Stoke were third from the bottom of the First Division and had not won in the league for over two months. Although they had also been knocked out of the English Cup, they had at least drawn 0-0 at fellow strugglers Preston North End in their previous league match two weeks before the local Derby. In contrast, Vale were in third place in the Midland League as a result of nine victories in their last twelve games; they had had an excellent run in the English Cup and, a fortnight earlier, had defeated First Division West Bromwich Albion 1-0 in the final of the Staffordshire Cup at the Victoria Ground, Stoke. In a desperate attempt to preserve their status, Stoke had recently signed four new players (Tom Wilkes, Alex Raisbeck, Jack Kennedy and Fred Molyneux) and all were selected for the Derby. Like their opponents, Vale fielded a strong line-up.

THE MATCH
Stoke kicked off, playing against a strong breeze and on a soft pitch. The contest was fast from the outset and Vale pressed strongly, despite initially having only ten men. After five minutes, McDonald appeared and brought the visitors up to the full complement, which confirmed their superiority, and Hodgkinson then had a goal-bound effort deflected wide before hitting the bar with a fine shot. Vale remained mostly on top, but were unable to break the deadlock.

After the interval, Stoke came right back into the game and only two minutes had passed before Birchenough brilliantly fisted out a misdirected headed clearance by McDonald. Shortly afterwards, Molyneux netted for the home side from a Mellor pass, but was ruled offside, much to the annoyance of the Stoke supporters. Nevertheless, Vale became increasingly pinned in their own half, although the nearest that the home team came to taking the lead was when Murphy hit a post.

THE AFTERMATH
Despite their vastly superior status, this was the first time in three local Derbies that season that Stoke had been able to prevent Vale from winning. Although Stoke gained six points from their final four matches, the haul was insufficient to prevent them from ending up at the foot of the First Division. However, their status was preserved by their successful participation in the test match play-offs which were subsequently staged. Vale completed their Midland League campaign with two defeats and finished a disappointing fifth, although they were later elected to the Second Division of the Football League.

38: MONDAY 24 APRIL 1899, FRIENDLY

STOKE (1) 1 (Farrell), BURSLEM PORT VALE (0) 0.

STOKE: Clawley, Robertson, Eccles, Parsons, Holford, Bradley, Johnson, Kennedy, Farrell, Maxwell, J. Turner.
VALE: Birchenough, McFarlane, Spilsbury, Boullemier, Beech, Lander, Hodgkinson, Beckett, Harvey, McDonald, Heames.

Venue: The Victoria Ground, Stoke-upon-Trent.
Attendance: About 500.
Referee: A.J. Barker (Hanley).

THE SETTING
Stoke had completed their league season with a 1-1 home draw against Bury the previous Saturday and had finished twelfth in the First Division, well clear of the relegation places. They had additionally reached the semi-finals of the English Cup before being defeated 3-1 by Derby County. Vale had also wound up their league campaign and had ended in a disappointing ninth position in the Second Division after heading the table until the middle of the previous November. Furthermore, they had fought their way to the final of the Birmingham Cup for the first time, but had then been beaten 4-0 by the eventual First Division champions, Aston Villa. Both clubs selected very strong sides for the Derby, even though the outcome was of little importance.

THE MATCH
For a second time, McDonald failed to make the kickoff of a local Derby and, taking advantage of his absence, Stoke attacked strongly. They opened the scoring in the third minute when a Bradley header rolled down the back of Farrell, who had bent down, and into the net! McDonald then arrived, but Vale were unable to stem the tide of home pressure. Maxwell hit the bar as Stoke peppered the visitors' goal and Holford did likewise just before half-time.

Although Stoke continued to press after the interval, the visitors at last began to show and Beckett just failed to head in a long punt from Lander. Shortly afterwards, the home side missed a golden opportunity to extend their lead when Kennedy and Farrell got in each other's way at the vital moment and Maxwell then squandered two open goals. Further easy chances were missed by Turner, Maxwell and Kennedy (twice) and the best entertainment was provided by a dog which cleverly tackled Boullemier in a rare Vale breakaway and then threatened to bite Bradley's legs!

THE AFTERMATH
The match was described in "The Staffordshire Sentinel" as 'a complete fiasco' and 'another nail in the coffin of friendlies' because of 'the disgraceful show made by the Vale', which received widespread criticism. A return local Derby had been arranged for the following Saturday at Cobridge, but the pitch was so 'utterly unfit' for play that the game was cancelled, even though spectators had already been admitted to the ground!

56

39: MONDAY 25 SEPTEMBER 1899, FRIENDLY

BURSLEM PORT VALE (?) 3 (unknown), STOKE (0) 0.

VALE: Birchenough, Stokes, McFarlane, Boullemier, Beech, McDonald, Grassam, Reid, Simpson, Harvey, Leech.
STOKE: Robertson and Jones played, but the team is otherwise unknown.

Venue: The Athletic Ground, Cobridge.
Attendance: Very satisfactory.
Referee: Unknown.

THE SETTING

Stoke were in a comfortable eighth place in the First Division, despite having been defeated 1-0 at Nottingham Forest on the Saturday before the local Derby. Vale were one rung lower in the Second Division and a 3-1 home win against Barnsley on the same day had produced some joy after the team had been beaten in three of their opening four league games. They fielded their strongest available side for the Derby, but Stoke decided to rest a number of their first-choice players and selected six reserves, which did not commend them to the spectators nor to the reporters.

THE MATCH

Stoke were well beaten, even though they possessed quite a strong defence on paper. Although Robertson in particular defended stoutly and bottled up Vale's left wing, the home side scored three times without producing any exceptionally inventive play. Nevertheless, Vale displayed some neat football and were as solid as a rock in defence, with Stokes, McFarlane and Birchenough especially outstanding. In contrast, the Stoke forwards indulged themselves in fine skills suitable for an exhibition game, but, Jones apart, rarely threatened the home goal. Consequently, both sets of supporters were left to argue about what the outcome might have been had Stoke fielded their entire first team.

THE AFTERMATH

Although Vale took only £51 in gate money, during the following month they began an excellent sequence of six successive league victories, which pushed them up into fourth position. However, their promotion hopes gradually faded as they then fell apart and managed to win just one of their next thirteen matches! Nevertheless, they progressed through two qualifying rounds of the English Cup before being eliminated and fought their way to the finals of both the Birmingham Cup and the Staffordshire Cup. Stoke won four of their following six First Division games to move up to fourth place, although they then gradually slipped down the table. Also, they exited at the first hurdle in all the three major cup competitions which they had entered.

40: MONDAY 9 APRIL 1900, FRIENDLY

STOKE (0) 0, BURSLEM PORT VALE (0) 1 (Grassam).

STOKE: Wilkes, Robertson, Eccles, Bowman, Wood, Bradley, Whittaker, Kennedy, Higginson, Jones, Turner.
VALE: Poole, Stokes, McFarlane, Boullemier, Beech, Leech, Grassam, Whitehouse, Walters, Price, Heames.

Venue: The Victoria Ground, Stoke-upon-Trent.
Attendance: Perhaps 300.
Referee: A. Pennington (Fenton).

THE SETTING
Stoke were relatively safely placed in ninth position in the First Division, but had been quickly dispatched from all the major cup competitions. In addition, they had been beaten 1-0 at Manchester City on the Saturday before the local Derby. Vale were also in ninth place, in the Second Division, but had lost 2-1 to top flight Wolverhampton Wanderers in the final of the Birmingham Cup a week prior to the Derby. Stoke fielded their strongest available line-up for the local clash, apart from experimenting with Whittaker on the right wing, whilst Vale also included just one reserve, Walters. Although local supremacy was being tested, there was very little interest in the outcome because fewer than fifty spectators were present at the kickoff!

THE MATCH
Stoke set the match in motion and, although the play was generally initially uneventful, Poole made an excellent save from a shot by Jones to prevent the home side taking the lead. The Vale custodian then surpassed himself and made a series of remarkable saves in quick succession from Higginson, Jones and Kennedy. Also, Bradley fired a curving shot over the bar as Stoke continued to dominate, but the visitors hung on.

After the interval, Stoke continued to press, although gradually the visitors came back into contention and eventually took the lead in controversial fashion. Wilkes ran out from the left side of his goal and caught the ball from a Vale attack, but Grassam succeeded in robbing him and shot into the empty net. Not surprisingly, the goal was strongly disputed and it seemed to demoralise the Stoke players. Nevertheless, the home team twice went near to saving the game in the closing stages. Firstly, a nifty move between Jones and Turner presented the latter with a golden opportunity to score, but the referee ruined the chance by deciding to blow for a foul in Stoke's favour and then an exciting but unproductive melee in the Vale goalmouth followed.

THE AFTERMATH
Stoke completed their First Division programme by taking six points from their final four matches, which temporarily lifted them into eighth position. In contrast, Vale lost two of their remaining league games and were consequently left in tenth place in the Second Division, although some of the rival teams had still to finish their fixtures.

41: SATURDAY 28 APRIL 1900, FRIENDLY

BURSLEM PORT VALE (0) 1 (Heames), **STOKE** (1) 2 (Wood, Higginson).

VALE: Poole, Stokes, McFarlane, Lander, Beech, Leech, Grassam, Walters, Simpson, Price, Heames.
STOKE: Wilkes, Davenport, Eccles, Parsons, Baddeley, Bradley, Johnson, Kennedy, Higginson, Wood, Jones.

Venue: The Athletic Ground, Cobridge.
Attendance: 400.
Referee: J. Ditchfield.

THE SETTING
Vale had completed their league programme and were tenth in the Second Division, but had been trounced 5-0 by First Division West Bromwich Albion in the replayed final of the Staffordshire Cup two days before the local Derby. Stoke had likewise finished their league campaign and were in a creditable eighth position in the First Division, owing particularly to a fine run-in, which had included a 2-2 draw at sixth-placed Newcastle United on the Saturday prior to the Derby. Although it was a bright, sunny day and both sides were strongly represented, there was little public interest in the encounter, which was referred to as the 'local championship'. Billy Leech made his final appearance for Vale because his transfer to Stoke had been arranged.

THE MATCH
Stoke attacked vigorously from the outset and quickly put the home goal under pressure. McFarlane kicked a goal-bound effort off the line, but after eighteen minutes Wood gave Stoke the lead following some fine inter-passing. Then Johnson put in a brilliant shot, which the Vale keeper had the greatest difficulty in saving, and from the resulting corner, the home goal had 'a miraculous escape'. However, Vale came strongly back into contention, especially inspired by the dazzling wing play of Price, but Simpson twice failed to get the ball on target when well placed.

Almost immediately after half-time, Stoke extended their lead when Higginson touched the ball in from a fine centre by Johnson and the visitors then bombarded the Vale goal with tremendous determination. Poole kept the home side in the game with a marvellous double save, but Vale then exerted some sustained pressure, although Heames shot well wide when presented with a clear-cut opportunity. However, he atoned for this miss fifteen minutes from the end and Vale subsequently pressed hard for an equaliser, with both Walters and Price going close before the final whistle.

THE AFTERMATH
Vale finished the season in eleventh place in the Second Division and Stoke ended up ninth in the division above. There was quite an exodus of players from Vale during the close season, but they were replaced by only two signings of note, Tommy Clare and James Peake, whilst Stoke similarly reduced the quality of their playing staff.

42: MONDAY 24 SEPTEMBER 1900, BIRMINGHAM CUP, FIRST ROUND

STOKE (1) 1 (Wood), BURSLEM PORT VALE (0) 0.

STOKE: Holford, Wood, Johnson and J. Jones (outside-left) played, but the team is otherwise unknown.
VALE: Maybury, Stokes, Davies, Boullemier, Beech, Seaton, Eardley, Henshall, Price, Peake, Heames.

Venue: The Victoria Ground, Stoke-upon-Trent.
Attendance: 1,500.
Referee: Unknown.

THE SETTING
Stoke had got off to a very bad start in the 1900-1901 season and were bottom of the First Division, with only one point from their opening five matches. Their most recent defeat had been by 1-0 at home to fellow strugglers, Sheffield United, two days before the local Derby. Vale were faring little better and were third from the bottom in the Second Division, with just a single victory to their credit. Also, they had already suffered two heavy away defeats, 6-1 at Grimsby Town on 8 September and 4-0 at struggling Newton Heath on the Saturday prior to the Derby. Therefore the prospect of a regional cup clash between the Potteries rivals did little to encourage the attendance of a large crowd. Nevertheless, Vale were at full strength, with Davies being selected in preference to Clare, but Stoke's line-up has not been traced.

THE MATCH
The play was mainly scrappy throughout, which made the match a rather dull affair. Nevertheless, Vale began well and pinned their opponents back, but the home side eventually got into their stride. As the pressure mounted, Maybury proved equal to the task and Seaton was a tower of strength for Vale, completely dominating everything that was thrown near him in the air. However, Davies was a weak link in the visitors' defence and consistently struck his clearances into the crowd. Although Eardley and Henshall caused Stoke's defenders some problems, the home team's full-backs were frequently able to join in with their attacks. Most of the game was dominated by Stoke, who took the lead through a header by Wood in the twentieth minute, but they missed numerous opportunities to extend their lead, many of which were created by Jones. After the interval, the players seemed somewhat lethargic, but in the last quarter of an hour Vale pressed strongly, though in vain, for an equaliser, which they finally deserved.

THE AFTERMATH
A mere £50 was taken at the gate and Stoke's local Derby success did not act as a tonic because they lost their next two league matches and extended their sequence without a victory to eight games. Nevertheless, they put themselves in serious contention for a trophy by winning 2-0 at West Bromwich Albion in a semi-final of the Birmingham Cup three weeks after the Derby. Vale gained four points from their following four Second Division matches and consequently hauled themselves clear of the re-election zone.

43: MONDAY 22 OCTOBER 1900, STAFFORDSHIRE CUP, FIRST ROUND

STOKE (2) 2 (Watkins, Wood), BURSLEM PORT VALE (0) 0.

STOKE: Wilkes, Capewell, Durber, Leech, Wood, Bradley, Johnson, Watkins, Higginson, Maxwell, Jones.
VALE: Maybury, Stokes, Davies, Boullemier, Beech, Seaton, Eardley, Price, Simpson, Peake, Heames.

Venue: The Victoria Ground, Stoke-upon-Trent.
Attendance: About 2,000.
Referee: T. Armitt (Leek).

THE SETTING

Stoke were anchored to the foot of the First Division with a single victory in their opening nine league matches, gained by 2-0 at the expense of sixth from the bottom Blackburn Rovers just two days before the local Derby. However, they had reached the final of the Birmingham Cup, by beating West Bromwich Albion in the previous round. Vale were also in difficulties in the league, but were at least positioned fifth from the bottom in the Second Division, with two wins to their credit, and had drawn 1-1 at struggling Chesterfield on the Saturday prior to the Derby. Both clubs fielded very strong teams for the local clash in dry, windless conditions much conducive to the production of good football.

THE MATCH

Although Vale kicked off, the home side were soon in the ascendancy and, after seven minutes, gained the lead through a swerving low shot from Watkins which took a slight deflection off Stokes. Vale gradually hauled themselves back into the match and Heames had a rocket shot well saved during a spell of pressure by the visitors. Stoke weathered the storm and then regained control, with Maxwell skimming the bar before Wood extended their lead shortly before half-time with a nicely-placed ground shot.

The second half was not reported in any detail, but Stoke generally continued to exert their superiority, although the visitors worked hard to get back into contention and occasionally threatened danger to the home goal. Nevertheless, the Stoke defence was highly resilient and no further goals were added, so that the home team deservedly ran out the winners.

THE AFTERMATH

Stoke continued to struggle against relegation for the rest of the season and only preserved their First Division status with two points to spare as they finished third from the bottom. However, they progressed to the final of the Staffordshire Cup before losing 3-1 at Wolverhampton Wanderers and then lifted the Birmingham Cup by beating Aston Villa 4-3 in a thrilling replayed final. Although Vale exited from the English Cup at the first hurdle, a marked improvement in form enabled them to end up in ninth place in the Second Division.

44: MONDAY 15 APRIL 1901, FRIENDLY

BURSLEM PORT VALE (1) 2 (Peake pen., Eardley), STOKE (1) 1 (Lockett).

VALE: Chadwick, Stokes, Davies, Boullemier, Beech, Wainwright, Eardley, Price, Capes, Peake, Heames.
STOKE: Wilkes, Capewell, Durber, Leech, Holford, Bradley, Johnson, Higginson, Watkins, Maxwell, Lockett.

Venue: The Athletic Ground, Cobridge.
Attendance: Fair.
Referee: Unknown.

THE SETTING
This game was played as a benefit for Vale's long-serving centre-half, Jim Beech, and both sides were at full strength, except that Chadwick was tried in the home goal instead of Maybury. Vale had completed their Second Division programme and three victories in their final four matches had secured them a respectable ninth position. Their parting shot had been a 1-0 home win against fifth-placed Woolwich Arsenal on the Saturday before the local Derby. Stoke had remarkably escaped relegation from the First Division by taking four points from their last two games, both away from home, to scramble to third from the bottom. In contrast, they had fared well in cup competitions and had reached the final of the Staffordshire Cup before securing the Birmingham Cup on 11 March. They had also been boosted by winning 4-2 at second-placed Notts County in their final league match two days prior to the Derby.

THE MATCH
Vale won the toss and chose to attack with the wind and sun in their favour, but it soon became apparent that the contest was going to be a rather tame affair. Stoke exerted most of the initial pressure, although Wainwright missed the target when only a few yards from goal and Capes squandered a further opportunity for Vale shortly afterwards. However, the visitors took the lead in the tenth minute with a curving shot from the dangerous Lockett, but Maxwell then wasted a golden opportunity to double their score. This mistake proved costly because Peake equalised from a penalty in the thirty-fifth minute after Price had been tripped.

After the interval, Stoke took control, but on the hour Capes broke away and shot against a post. Although the ball bounced out, Eardley was on hand to stroke it home and put Vale into the lead. Subsequently, the visitors pressed strongly and Maxwell was unlucky when he hit an upright, but Stoke's efforts were often too individual in nature to threaten seriously an equaliser.

THE AFTERMATH
In the close season, Vale continued their local players policy which had proved successful, so that no new signings of note were made to replace the outgoing A.E. Maybury, Frank Stokes and James Peake. Financial difficulties led to Stoke selling Willie Maxwell to Third Lanark for £250, although they spent a portion of the fee on securing the services of Andy Clark, a promising left-back from Heart of Midlothian.

45: MONDAY 30 SEPTEMBER 1901, BIRMINGHAM CUP, FIRST ROUND

STOKE (0) 2 (Watkins, Lockett), BURSLEM PORT VALE (1) 2 (a 'cluster' of Vale players, Price).

STOKE: Wilkes, Meredith, Clark, Leech, Baddeley, Capewell, Whitehouse, Watkins, Higginson, Harris, Lockett.
VALE: Cotton, Mullineux, Davies, Boullemier, Wainwright, Lander, Rushton, Price, Capes, D. Simpson, Heames.

Venue: The Victoria Ground, Stoke-upon-Trent.
Attendance: 3,500.
Referee: Unknown.

THE SETTING
Stoke were eleventh in the First Division, having accumulated five points from their opening five matches, and had trounced Second Division Burton United 8-0 at home in the first round of the Staffordshire Cup a week before the local Derby. Vale occupied ninth position in the Second Division, likewise had gained five points from their first five games and also had progressed into the second round of the Staffordshire Cup, with a 5-2 win at the expense of Walsall a fortnight prior to the Derby. Stoke made three changes in their line-up for the local clash, selecting Baddeley, Whitehouse and Harris in place of Ashworth, Johnson and Hales, whilst Wainwright replaced Cook in Vale's team. The match was scheduled to kick off at 4 p.m. and the admission prices ranged from 6d. to 1s. 6d.

THE MATCH
The play was relatively even in the early stages, but Watkins and Higginson went close as Stoke's attacks gained impetus. However, the visitors retaliated and Heames became a constant threat to the Stoke defence. Vale went in front after twenty minutes when an error by the home keeper enabled a 'cluster' of opposing players to put the ball into the net. The visitors then threatened to extend their lead, but Capes struck the bar with a tremendous shot, whilst Rushton contrived to miss the target with an open goal ahead of him!

Stoke pressed strongly after the interval and Watkins quickly equalised, whilst Lockett fired them in front with a magnificent acute-angled shot just a minute later. As the flurry of activity continued, Price put Vale back on level terms shortly afterwards, although the rest of the match was mainly notable for action of a more violent nature as a series of 'unforeseen and regrettable incidents' occurred, the most extreme of which involved Rushton and Clark coming to blows!

THE AFTERMATH
The replay was scheduled for the following Monday and the only game that Stoke played prior to then was a 1-1 home draw in the league against Nottingham Forest on the Saturday beforehand, whilst Vale were hammered 4-0 at third from the bottom Barnsley on the same day.

46: MONDAY 7 OCTOBER 1901, BIRMINGHAM CUP, FIRST ROUND REPLAY

BURSLEM PORT VALE (2) 4 (2 rushes, Jones, Capes), STOKE (0) 0.

VALE: Cotton, Beech, Davies, Machin, Boullemier, Lander, Rushton, Price, Capes, D. Simpson, Jones.
STOKE: Boote, Meredith, Clark, Leech, Ashworth, Capewell, Johnson, Watkins, Higginson, Hales, Lockett.

Venue: The Athletic Ground, Cobridge.
Attendance: 1,500.
Referee: Unknown.

THE SETTING
Vale were twelfth in the Second Division and had lost 4-0 at lowly Barnsley on the Saturday before this cup replay. Stoke were one position better off, in the First Division, and had drawn 1-1 at home to Nottingham Forest on the same day. Vale made three changes in their line-up for the local clash, with Machin, Lander and Jones being drafted into the team, but Stoke were unchanged. The weather was extremely cold and the playing conditions were described as 'shocking', owing to a deluge of rain.

THE MATCH
After a fairly even opening, Vale adapted far better to the sticky pitch than did the visitors and attacked with speed and some fine passing which belied the nature of the conditions. The home side pressured their opponents almost throughout and the Stoke players persistently made fundamental mistakes as they attempted a short-passing game which didn't work. Although Vale were 'quite irresistible' in front of goal and had one effort disallowed as well as scoring four times, Boote, the visiting keeper, was far too slow to react to danger. Nevertheless, Stoke themselves had two goals disallowed and Cotton, the home custodian, was outstanding, but it was Vale's half-backs who were decisive in subduing the visiting forwards.

The home team opened the scoring in the twentieth minute when Boote allowed a cross by Jones to drift into the net and the Stoke keeper later made a hash of a clearance, which enabled the ball to be rushed over the line. The visitors then seemed to lose hope and Capes put Vale further in front with a long shot just after the interval, whilst the rout was completed a short time later when the ball was rushed through for a second time.

THE AFTERMATH
The local rivals were scheduled to meet once more, in a semi-final of the Staffordshire Cup a fortnight later, and prior to that Vale played two Second Division matches, one at home, which ended in victory, and the other away, which was lost. In between, they contested a semi-final of the Birmingham Cup at Stoke with First Division Wolverhampton Wanderers and gained an excellent 1-1 draw. Stoke also had two league fixtures to fulfil before they renewed Vale's acquaintance, but were only able to prise a single point from them.

47: MONDAY 21 OCTOBER 1901, STAFFORDSHIRE CUP, SEMI-FINAL

BURSLEM PORT VALE (1) 1 (unknown), STOKE (1) 2 (unknown, Johnson).

VALE: Cotton, Beech, Rushton and Capes played, but the team is otherwise unknown.
STOKE: Wilkes, Meredith, Clark, Capewell, Holford, Ashworth, Johnson, Whitehouse, Watkins, Harris, Lockett.

Venue: The Athletic Ground, Cobridge.
Attendance: 7,000 odd.
Referee: Unknown.

THE SETTING
Vale were twelfth in the Second Division, but had produced rather erratic form during the season thus far. Although they had drawn 1-1 with top flight Wolverhampton Wanderers in a semi-final of the Birmingham Cup a week before the local Derby, they had lost 2-0 at third-placed Preston North End in the league five days later. Stoke were sixth from the bottom of the First Division and were without a win in their previous six matches in all competitions. However, at least they had drawn 2-2 at home to struggling Blackburn Rovers on the Saturday prior to the Derby. Stoke selected a strong side for the local clash, but Vale's line-up has not been traced.

THE MATCH
Stoke produced 'exhilarating form' to overcome their opponents in an extremely hard-fought game. The visitors attacked with such precision in the opening quarter of an hour that it seemed that the Vale defence would be completely overrun. Not surprisingly, Stoke took the lead and Watkins was magnificent, spraying the ball out to both wings in fine style. The visitors were particularly threatening on their right flank, but Vale survived the onslaught, clawed their way back into the match and scored a 'clever' equaliser. Nevertheless, Stoke remained largely on top, although Capes proved difficult to control and Rushton was kept at bay only by Clark continually fouling him.

The second half was a ding-dong struggle, with Vale having more of the play, but the visitors looking exceptionally dangerous on the break. However, neither defence cracked until fifteen minutes from the end when Johnson netted a disputed winner with a tremendous shot. From then on, Vale brought tremendous pressure to bear on the visitors' defence, but the Stoke halves and backs proved themselves equal to the occasion.

THE AFTERMATH
Vale won just one of their next eleven league games and were eliminated from the Birmingham Cup by 2-0 at home to Wolves in the semi-final replay on 2 December. In contrast, Stoke gained three victories in their four First Division matches following the local Derby and progressed to the quarter-finals of the English Cup, although they were beaten 3-0 by Second Division West Bromwich Albion in the final of the Staffordshire Cup on 25 November.

48: MONDAY 21 APRIL 1902, FRIENDLY

BURSLEM PORT VALE (0) 0, STOKE (1) 1 (Whitehouse).

VALE: Cotton, Mullineux, Davies, Cook, Beech, Boullemier, Eardley, D. Simpson, Capes, Price, Heames.
STOKE: Wilkes, Burgess, Clark, Leech, Baddeley, Bradley, Whitehouse, Higginson, Watkins, Harris, Lockett.

Venue: The Athletic Ground, Cobridge.
Attendance: Not very large.
Referee: J. Ditchfield.

THE SETTING
This game was played as a benefit for Vale's long-serving forward, Danny Simpson. Vale were precariously perched at fourth from the bottom of the Second Division and still needed a point from their final match to be certain of avoiding a plea for re-election. A run of six league games without a win had seen them drop six places, from ninth, in just five weeks and they had only been able to draw 1-1 at home to struggling Newton Heath on the Saturday before the local Derby. Stoke were in an even more perilous position, fifth from the bottom in the First Division, having completed their programme, and were relying on the remaining results going in their favour in order to avoid relegation. However, their recent form had been good and they had gained a vital six points from their last four league games. Most critically of all, they had drawn 2-2 at Manchester City, the bottom side, two days prior to the Derby. Vale selected a strong line-up for the local clash, but Stoke fielded four reserves.

THE MATCH
The actual importance of the match was reflected in the somewhat slow pace of the proceedings. Nevertheless, it was an entertaining encounter, in which Stoke made most of the initial running. When Vale counterattacked, they found the visiting keeper to be in fine form and went behind after fifteen minutes. Harris shot at goal when well placed and the ball was cleared only as far as Whitehouse who slotted it home.

After the interval, Vale attacked almost incessantly, although they were unable to break down their opponents' rearguard. Both Heames and Price put in a number of fine efforts, but the Stoke defence proved equal to all that the home side could throw at them.

THE AFTERMATH
Vale's re-election worries were dispelled by their 1-0 victory at Glossop on the Saturday after the local Derby and they finished thirteenth out of eighteen teams. Stoke were also in the event relieved because they escaped relegation from the First Division by a single point and ended up third from the bottom. They even added to their celebrations by lifting the Walsall Cup as a result of beating Aston Villa 3-0 at home in the final, eight days after the Derby.

49: MONDAY 22 SEPTEMBER 1902, STAFFORD-SHIRE CUP, FIRST ROUND

BURSLEM PORT VALE (0) 1 (unknown), STOKE (0) 1 (Watkins).

VALE: Cotton, Mullineux, Hartshorne, Boullemier, Croxton, Perkins, Price, Loverseed, A. Capes, Jones, Heames.
STOKE: Wilkes (goalkeeper), A.J. Capes, Higginson, Watkins and Bridgett played, but the team is otherwise unknown.

Venue: The Athletic Ground, Cobridge.
Attendance: Some 4,000.
Referee: Mr. Lewis.

THE SETTING
Vale had failed to win any of their opening three Second Division matches in the 1902-1903 season, but had finally gained a victory, by 3-0 at home against Doncaster Rovers on the Saturday before the local Derby, which had lifted them to ninth place in the table. Although Stoke had begun their campaign in the First Division with a 5-0 hammering at Newcastle United, they had since recovered somewhat to attain eleventh position and had drawn 1-1 at Liverpool two days prior to the Derby. Vale made a single change to their team for the local clash, with Croxton replacing Cook, but Stoke's line-up has not been traced, although "The Staffordshire Sentinel" stated that they would be at full strength.

THE MATCH
The match was closely contested and Vale adopted a strong-running style of play which pressured the visitors, whilst Stoke countered by working the ball around more cleverly. Both sides had a number of good chances, but the visitors in particular finished poorly, although both Higginson and Arthur Capes were unlucky to hit the Vale bar with fine shots. Also, the home custodian made a series of excellent saves to keep Stoke at bay, but the Vale half-backs struggled to keep the opposing forwards under control. Nevertheless, Adrian Capes, Jones and Heames gave the Stoke defenders plenty to think about and the home team took the lead in the second half following a mistake by the visiting keeper, Wilkes. Although the game was hard fought, it was played in a good spirit and Watkins equalised for Stoke, after an error by Mullineux towards the end, when the home team began to fade. Thus justice was done because on balance there was little to choose between the two sides.

THE AFTERMATH
Vale were delighted to have taken £143 at the gate and it was the first time for quite some while that the £100 mark had been reached. The replay was scheduled for a fortnight hence and the two teams were also due to meet on the intervening Monday to contest a first round tie in the Birmingham Cup. Vale's preparations for this were hardly ideal as they were hammered 4-1 in the league at second-placed Lincoln City two days beforehand. However, Stoke were also defeated on the same day, by 1-0 at home to Sheffield United, in a First Division clash.

50: MONDAY 29 SEPTEMBER 1902, BIRMINGHAM CUP, FIRST ROUND

BURSLEM PORT VALE (0) 0, STOKE (0) 2 (Whitehouse, Clark).

VALE: Cotton, Mullineux, Hartshorne, Croxton, Cook, Perkins, Eardley, Loverseed, A. Capes, Price, Heames.
STOKE: Wilkes, Meredith, Clark, Ashworth, Holford, Baddeley, Johnson, Whitehouse, Watkins, A.J. Capes, Bridgett.

Venue: The Athletic Ground, Cobridge.
Attendance: 3,000.
Referee: J.T. Howcroft (Bolton).

THE SETTING
A 4-1 defeat at high-flying Lincoln City on the Saturday before the local Derby pushed Vale down to sixth from the bottom of the Second Division. Stoke also dropped in the league, to fourth from the bottom in the First Division, as a result of losing 1-0 at Sheffield United on the same day. Another tough game was anticipated following the 1-1 draw that the two local rivals had fought out in the Staffordshire Cup at Cobridge a week before and Vale made two changes in their line-up for the clash, with Cook and Eardley being selected. There were all of five alterations in Stoke's team with Wilkes, Clark, Ashworth, Whitehouse and Johnson replacing Roose, Burgess, Bradley, Forrest and Lockett.

THE MATCH
Vale attacked with the advantage of a stiff breeze and did their utmost to make it count, but Adrian Capes, Heames and especially Loverseed squandered golden opportunities to put them in front. However, Cook was extremely unlucky when he hit the Stoke bar with the visiting keeper well beaten. As Vale pressed aggressively, Eardley was outstanding on the right wing, but many of the fine moves he instigated were ruined by the 'shocking failure' of Loverseed, so that half-time arrived with no score.

After the interval, Stoke took command and bustled their way forward, shooting at every opportunity. Watkins really came into his own, spraying the ball out elegantly to his wingers, and caused the Vale defenders major problems with his pace. Although Cotton and Cook in particular worked overtime to stem the tide of the visiting forwards, Whitehouse eventually gave Stoke the lead following a wonderful solo run. Holford did much to disrupt Vale's increasingly rare attacks by committing a series of fouls and the visitors gradually wore their opponents down. Finally, Clark made the game safe by adding a second for Stoke who were then happy to keep possession of the ball and play out the remaining time.

THE AFTERMATH
Despite this being the second local Derby within a week, a pleasing £121 was taken at the gate. The two teams were due to meet again the following Monday to contest the Staffordshire Cup replay and Vale drew 2-2 at home to fourth-placed Small Heath in the league on the Saturday beforehand, whilst Stoke picked up the same result at third from the bottom Grimsby Town.

51: MONDAY 6 OCTOBER 1902, STAFFORDSHIRE CUP, FIRST ROUND REPLAY

STOKE (3) 5 (Watkins 3, Bridgett, A.J. Capes pen.), BURSLEM PORT VALE (0) 3 (Heames, A. Capes, Bourne).

STOKE: Wilkes, unknown, Clark, unknown, unknown, Bradley, Johnson, Whitehouse, Watkins, A.J. Capes, Bridgett.
VALE: Cotton, Boullemier, unknown, unknown, unknown, unknown, Bourne, unknown, A. Capes, D. Simpson, Heames.

Venue: The Victoria Ground, Stoke-upon-Trent.
Attendance: Under 1,500.
Referee: A. Wood (Shelton).

THE SETTING
Stoke remained fourth from the bottom of the First Division following a 2-2 draw at fellow strugglers, Grimsby Town, two days before the local Derby. On the same Saturday, Vale moved up one place to twelfth in the Second Division as a result of also obtaining a 2-2 draw, at home to promotion-chasing Small Heath. Neither side was selected at full strength for the local clash, although both teams included a fair proportion of first-choice players, and Vale had to move their centre-half, Boullemier, to right-back at the last minute when Mullineux turned up too late to be included in the third local Derby to be played within a fortnight.

THE MATCH
Stoke attacked from the outset and stamped their authority on the game, assisted by an early ankle injury to Boullemier which limited his effectiveness. In contrast, Watkins was superb for Stoke, scoring two goals and providing a constant stream of passes to both wingers. Bridgett also netted as the home side raced into a 3-0 lead, but the Vale attack itself was by no means inactive as they hit a post and had other goal-bound efforts cleared. Nevertheless, it looked as though the visitors were in for a real drubbing.

Soon after half-time, Watkins completed his hat trick and then had another goal disallowed for offside, but Vale surprisingly staged a major rally with Heames and Adrian Capes scoring to put them back in contention. As both sets of forwards continued to overwhelm the defenders in a remarkably open match, Simpson spurned a marvellous opportunity to reduce the arrears further, but Arthur Capes converted a disputed penalty to put Stoke safely back in control. Nevertheless, the visitors kept plugging away and Bourne scored a third goal for them near to the end.

THE AFTERMATH
The gate receipts did not total half the amount collected at the previous Derby a week earlier, although Stoke raised further funds by making it through to the final of the competition, which they lost. Also, they reached the semi-finals of the Birmingham Cup and the quarter-finals of the English Cup, whilst they finished sixth in the league. Although Vale had hardly any joy in their cup games, they ended up ninth in the Second Division.

52: MONDAY 14 SEPTEMBER 1903, STAFFORD-SHIRE CUP, FIRST ROUND

STOKE (4) 5 (A.J. Capes 2, Whitehouse, Holdcroft, Holford), BURSLEM PORT VALE (1) 2 (unknown).

STOKE: unknown, unknown, Hartshorne, unknown, Holdcroft, unknown, Whitehouse, Higginson, Holford, A.J. Capes, Pitt.
VALE: Cotton, unknown, Rowley, Holyhead, Simpson, Perkins, Eardley, Price, Loverseed, A. Capes, Heames.

Venue: The Victoria Ground, Stoke-upon-Trent.
Attendance: Unknown.
Referee: Unknown.

THE SETTING
Stoke were in tenth place in the First Division, but had lost two successive league matches after opening the season brightly with a 4-1 home win against Bury. Their most recent reverse had been a 1-0 defeat at Notts County on the Saturday before the local Derby. Vale were one position higher, in the Second Division, and had beaten Manchester United 1-0 at home on the same day. Although Stoke's full line-up was not given for the local clash, Pitt replaced the injured Davies, Holford (the usual centre-half) was moved to centre-forward and his position was occupied by Holdcroft. Vale were nearly at full strength, although their right-back, Mullineux, was unable to get to the match in time, whilst Croxton stood down in favour of Holyhead.

THE MATCH
Stoke opened strongly in a highly entertaining encounter and Whitehouse put them in front after just five minutes, but the visitors equalised about two minutes later. The game became evenly contested, although Arthur Capes gave Stoke the lead once more, from a fine pass by Holford, after about twenty minutes' play. Shortly afterwards, the same combination extended the home side's lead, but Vale's keeper pulled off a number of excellent saves to keep his team in contention. Nevertheless, Holdcroft put Stoke 4-1 up with a marvellous shot shortly before the interval.

Content with their lead, Stoke did not overexert themselves in the second half, even after the visitors had pulled a goal back. Simpson and Heames were particularly instrumental as Vale worked hard to try to reduce further the arrears, but shortly before the end Holford put the issue beyond doubt. Thus Stoke gained a relatively comfortable victory in a match notable for the players' individual skill.

THE AFTERMATH
Stoke lost their following two league games and slid towards the relegation zone, which was not ideal preparation for a second local Derby, to contest the first round of the Birmingham Cup, a fortnight later. Vale didn't fare too well either in the intervening period and picked up just one point from their two Second Division matches.

53: MONDAY 28 SEPTEMBER 1903, BIRMINGHAM CUP, FIRST ROUND

BURSLEM PORT VALE (0) 2 (A. Capes, Coxon), STOKE (2) 5 (Hartshorne 2 pens., Whitehouse, Holdcroft, Davies).

VALE: Cotton, Mullineux, Rowley, Croxton, Whittingham, Holyhead, Eardley, Price, Simpson, A. Capes, Coxon.
STOKE: Roose, Hartshorne, Benson, Baddeley, Holford, Bradley, Whitehouse, Holdcroft, Davies, A.J. Capes, Pitt.

Venue: The Athletic Ground, Cobridge.
Attendance: 2,000.
Referee: F. Heath (Small Heath).

THE SETTING

Vale were eleventh in the Second Division, but had won just one of their opening four league matches and had only drawn 1-1 at home against bottom of the table Glossop on the Saturday before the local Derby. Stoke were faring worse in the First Division and were third from the bottom, with four defeats in their initial five games, but at least they had beaten their Cobridge rivals 5-2 in the first round of the Staffordshire Cup a fortnight earlier. However, they had lost 1-0 at sixth-placed Newcastle United in the league two days prior to the Derby. Both clubs fielded strong sides for the local clash, although Vale drafted in two reserves, Holyhead and Coxon, whilst Bradley returned from injury for Stoke, who also selected two fringe players, Benson and Davies.

THE MATCH

Stoke proved themselves to be 'all-round superior' and exerted most of the pressure during the match. Nevertheless, Vale started well, but Rowley struck a penalty wide in the early stages. The significance of this quickly became apparent because Hartshorne put the visitors in front from a second spot kick in only the sixth minute and Whitehouse doubled their advantage following a fine move eighteen minutes later. Vale created and missed a number of chances to get back in contention, the easiest of which was spurned by Adrian Capes, although Pitt hit a post for Stoke shortly before half-time.

Stoke attacked vigorously after the interval and by the fifty-sixth minute had gained a four-goal lead thanks to Hartshorne converting a second penalty and Holdcroft applying the finishing touch to a cross by Pitt. Vale belatedly forced their opponents back and Adrian Capes reduced the arrears ten minutes from time, although Davies put the issue beyond doubt within a minute. Nevertheless, the home team made the score more respectable near to the end when an error by Roose enabled Coxon to strike the ball in.

THE AFTERMATH

Stoke got no further in the competition than the next round, the semi-finals, but shared the Staffordshire Cup with Wolverhampton Wanderers following two drawn games in the final. However, their league form generally remained poor and they finished third from the bottom. Vale eventually ended up sixth from the bottom of the Second Division, but at least successfully negotiated four rounds of the English Cup.

54: MONDAY 26 SEPTEMBER 1904, BIRMINGHAM CUP, FIRST ROUND

STOKE (0) 0, BURSLEM PORT VALE (0) 0.

STOKE: Whitley, Benson, Hartshorne, Baddeley, Holford, Bradley, Whitehouse, Rouse, Holdcroft, Godley, Coxon.
VALE: Box, Mullineux, Whittingham, Croxton, Allman, Bradbury, Eardley, Capes, Loverseed, Price, Bowen.

Venue: The Victoria Ground, Stoke-upon-Trent.
Attendance: 800.
Referee: Unknown.

THE SETTING
Stoke had begun the 1904-1905 season badly, with four defeats in their opening five league matches, which left them second from the bottom of the First Division. The only bright note was that they remained in the Staffordshire Cup, having secured a 2-2 draw at Second Division Burton United in the first round a week before the local Derby. Vale were not doing especially well either and, after drawing their initial four Second Division games, had suffered their first defeat on the Saturday prior to the Derby, by 2-1 at struggling Bradford City, which put them in twelfth place. Also, they had already been eliminated from the Staffordshire Cup by Wolverhampton Wanderers. Stoke were virtually at full strength for the local clash and Vale also fielded a strong line-up, though they were without three regular members of their defence.

THE MATCH
Vale showed great determination right from the outset and dominated the play in the first half. Their forwards combined extremely well and the home keeper performed wonders to keep out a series of shots that were rained in on his goal, especially by the outstanding Loverseed. The Stoke defence worked tirelessly to keep the visiting forwards at bay and Bradley was particularly noteworthy for his excellent tackles, blatant fouls and 'smart footwork'.

After the interval, Stoke came more into the game and the visiting custodian pulled off a few good saves during occasional moments of danger, whilst Whitehouse hit the bar. Nevertheless, Croxton, Whittingham and Mullineux were instrumental in minimising the danger and Capes kept the forwards flowing, so that Vale still looked the likelier side to break the deadlock. Indeed, "The Staffordshire Sentinel's" reporter, "The Potter", stated that he'd never seen Vale 'play so well and so accurately against Stoke' and that they were 'decidedly unlucky' not to win.

THE AFTERMATH
The replay was scheduled for the following Monday and, two days beforehand, Stoke gained their first away victory of the campaign, by 1-0 at Nottingham Forest in the league. However, on the same Saturday, Vale played poorly in losing 1-0 at home to Lincoln City in a Second Division clash.

55: MONDAY 3 OCTOBER 1904, BIRMINGHAM CUP, FIRST ROUND REPLAY

BURSLEM PORT VALE (1) 3 (Simpson 2, Williams), STOKE (1) 1 (Haworth).

VALE: Cotton, Mullineux, Whittingham, Croxton, Holyhead, Bradbury, Price, Allman, Simpson, Williams, Mountford.
STOKE: Benton, Meredith, Benson, Sturgess, Beswick, Huffadine, Hesham, Haines, Haworth, Holdcroft, Leonard.

Venue: The Athletic Ground, Cobridge.
Attendance: 4,000.
Referee: Unknown.

THE SETTING
Although Vale were twelfth in the Second Division, they had still to win a league match and had lost 1-0 at home to Lincoln City in their most recent outing two days before the local Derby. Stoke had two league victories to their credit and had won 1-0 at Nottingham Forest on the Saturday prior to the Derby, but were third from the bottom of the First Division. Vale fielded a strong line-up for the local clash, although they were without Capes, their regular inside-right, and both their first-choice wingers, Bowen and Eardley, who were ill. However, Stoke decided to rest most of their first team players and only Benson and Holdcroft were selected from the side which had beaten Nottingham Forest.

THE MATCH
The Vale supporters were extremely angry when they realised that Stoke had effectively sent a reserve team for the occasion, even though the home side progressed quite comfortably into the next round of the competition. Nevertheless, the first half was evenly contested and Simpson had a brilliant shot saved by the Stoke keeper before Haworth gave the visitors the lead in the fortieth minute when he niftily converted a cross by Hesham. However, Simpson scored a fine equaliser two minutes before the interval.

Vale dominated the second period, with Croxton in excellent form and the forwards exhibiting some crisp inter-passing. Price increasingly wreaked havoc on the right wing through clever dribbling and the provision of a series of accurate crosses which carved out innumerable scoring opportunities for the home team. One of these was adeptly taken by Williams in the fifty-seventh minute, whilst Simpson put Vale further in front with a wonderful solo goal and then struck a post and the bar. The visitors fell apart and Holdcroft failed dismally with a spot kick after Whittingham had been penalised for hand ball.

THE AFTERMATH
Vale protested to the Birmingham Football Association that Stoke had broken the rules by not sending their strongest side, but they were told that nothing could be done because other clubs had been allowed to get away with exactly the same thing! Vale exited from the competition in the next round (the semi-finals) and had to apply for re-election to the Second Division after finishing third from the bottom, although Stoke had more joy in the league and ended up twelfth.

56: MONDAY 18 SEPTEMBER 1905, BIRMINGHAM CUP, FIRST ROUND

BURSLEM PORT VALE (1) 3 (Croxton, P. Smith, Carter), STOKE (0) 0.

VALE: Box, Jones, Cope, P. Smith, Croxton, Bradbury, Carter, Price, Mountford, Capes, Crombie.

STOKE: Whitley, Cartlich, Dawson, Turner, Shaw, Huffadine, Griffiths, Cartlidge, Gallimore, A. Smith, Usherwood.

Venue: The Athletic Ground, Cobridge.
Attendance: About 2,500.
Referee: J. Wilson (West Bromwich).

THE SETTING

Vale were thirteenth in the Second Division and although they'd scored eight goals in their opening four league matches, they had conceded ten. They had drawn 2-2 at home to Grimsby Town in their most recent outing on the Saturday before the local Derby. In contrast, Stoke stood proudly at the top of the First Division, with four straight victories from the start of the campaign, and had netted ten times. Their most recent success had been by 2-1 at fourth from the bottom Bolton Wanderers two days prior to the Derby. Vale were effectively at full strength for the local clash, except for their regular centre-half, Whittingham, being absent with an injury, but Stoke selected a team of reserves so as not to risk jeopardising their league prospects.

THE MATCH

Unexpectedly, Stoke opened brightly and had most of the play initially, but after fifteen minutes a solo run by Mountford led to a loose ball reaching Croxton, who powered Vale in front through a ruck of players. This reverse spurred the visitors into greater efforts, but gradually the passing ability of the Vale players began to make its mark and only a series of marvellous saves by Whitley prevented the home side from extending their lead. Also, Carter shot wildly over the bar when presented with a good opportunity by Croxton shortly before half-time.

After the interval, Vale applied intense pressure to the visitors' goal and Whitley pulled off a remarkable save almost immediately to deny Mountford. Soon after, the visiting keeper thwarted another fine effort, by Carter, but, as Vale monopolised the action, Philip Smith extended their lead, with the help of a deflection off Cartlich. Croxton continually surged forward, whilst Carter caused havoc on the Vale right, especially once the visiting left-back, Dawson, had injured his leg. Although Whitley continued to perform heroics between the posts, particularly in saving a penalty by Croxton, he was unable to prevent Carter from adding a third goal for Vale, which they thoroughly deserved.

THE AFTERMATH

The two clubs were due to meet again the following Monday, this time in the first round of the Staffordshire Cup. On the Saturday beforehand, Vale were hammered 4-0 in the league at fourth from the bottom Barnsley, but Stoke beat Woolwich Arsenal 2-1 at home in the First Division on the same day.

57: MONDAY 25 SEPTEMBER 1905, STAFFORD-SHIRE CUP, FIRST ROUND

STOKE (0) 0, BURSLEM PORT VALE (2) 5 (Price 2, Crombie, P. Smith, Carter).

STOKE: Benton, Cartlich, Dawson, Turner, Ward, Huffadine, Griffiths, Haines, A. Smith, Cartlidge, Usherwood.
VALE: Box, Hamilton, Cope, Croxton, Whittingham, Horrocks, Carter, Price, P. Smith, Mountford, Crombie.

Venue: The Victoria Ground, Stoke-upon-Trent.
Attendance: A few hundred.
Referee: T. Armitt (Leek).

THE SETTING
Stoke had beaten Woolwich Arsenal 2-1 at home on the Saturday before the local Derby and had thereby retained their position at the top of the First Division, with maximum points from their opening five matches. However, Vale were struggling at third from the bottom of the Second Division and had lost 4-0 at lowly Barnsley two days prior to the Derby. As they had done in the previous local clash a week earlier, Stoke preferred to choose a side made up entirely of reserves, although Vale fielded a very strong line-up. Nevertheless, Stoke's decision and bad weather severely limited the size of the crowd.

THE MATCH
Stoke lost the toss and attacked against the wind a man down because Alf Smith was ten minutes late in joining the fray! Not surprisingly, Vale had the better of the initial play and Price shot against the bar, but the home side held firm, especially through the herculean efforts of their custodian, Benton. Generally, Vale's shooting was poor, although Crombie opened the scoring after half an hour when Carter provided an excellent cross following a solo run. This inspired the visitors to produce some fine inter-passing and, five minutes before the break, a shot from Price extended their lead.

The second half opened in a rather tame manner, but Stoke were unable to make any headway and Box became virtually a spectator. Then, fifteen minutes into the period, a precise pass by Carter enabled Price to put Vale 3-0 up. Ten minutes later, Ward made a hash of clearing a Price centre and Philip Smith pounced to strike the ball into the net to extend the visitors' lead still further. By now, Vale were comfortably in command, but Box was forced to make his first save of the match fifteen minutes from the end. There still remained time for Carter to add a fifth goal to complete Vale's all-time record local Derby victory, whilst Whittingham was forced to retire with an injury soon afterwards.

THE AFTERMATH
Stoke suffered their first league defeat on the following Saturday, then drifted off the pace and finished tenth. Their interest in the English Cup lasted only as far as the second hurdle and this performance was equalled by Vale in all three major cup competitions. However, Vale gained three successive wins in the Second Division after the local Derby, but still ended up fourth from the bottom.

58: MONDAY 29 APRIL 1907, FRIENDLY

STOKE (1) 1 (Brown), BURSLEM PORT VALE (0) 1 (Mountford).

STOKE: Roose, Burgess, Mullineux, G. Baddeley, Bentley, Sturgess, Williamson, Brown, Holford, Arrowsmith, Griffiths.
VALE: Box, Cope, Hamilton, Bradbury, Brough, Gleave, Carter, Dodds, Beats, Mountford, Coxon.

Venue: The Victoria Ground, Stoke-upon-Trent.
Attendance: Small.
Referee: Unknown.

THE SETTING
This was a benefit game for Ted Holdcroft, a former player of both clubs, who had retired because of an ankle injury and who had suffered a serious illness which prevented him from working. Stoke had been relegated from the First Division in their penultimate match nine days before the local Derby and had finished at the bottom of the table, with only eight victories to their credit all season. This had therefore set up the prospect of their first ever league meeting with Vale during the following campaign and at least Stoke had ended their top flight connection with dignity by drawing 2-2 at Preston North End two days prior to the Derby. Vale had not fared particularly well either during the 1906-1907 season and had saved themselves from a re-election plea only by a 3-0 home win against Blackpool in their final Second Division game on the Saturday before the Derby. Both clubs fielded very strong teams for the local clash and Vale included Gleave, their latest recruit, from Stockport, but the attendance was adversely affected by the counterattraction of the Sentinel Cup final between Goldenhill Villa and Halmerend Gymnastics!

THE MATCH
Stoke pressed strongly in the first half and their defence restricted the visitors to only temporary raids. Although the home forwards didn't greatly trouble the Vale keeper, Brown gave Stoke the lead with a fierce shot. Griffiths' speed caused Vale considerable problems, but at the other end Roose had just one noteworthy shot to stop.

The second period saw no more attempts at goal than the opening half had witnessed and Burgess could only strike the Vale bar from a penalty after Arrowsmith had been fouled. Nevertheless, Stoke had most of the play, although Holford missed a string of chances, created especially by fine crosses from Williamson. Finally, the home team were left to rue their spurned opportunities because Mountford equalised with a clever shot five minutes from the end.

THE AFTERMATH
Not only was this contest the last match of the season for both teams, but it was also the final game ever played by Burslem Port Vale because a decision was taken in June to wind up the club as a consequence of an insoluble financial crisis. Stoke were major beneficiaries of Vale's demise in that they picked up several freed players to strengthen their squad for the forthcoming season: Arthur Box, William Cope, Joe Brough, Tom Coxon and centre-half, Sam Baddeley.

59: SATURDAY 26 DECEMBER 1908, MAY BANK CUP, SECOND ROUND

STOKE RESERVES (1) 2 (F. Eardley, Fielding), PORT VALE (1) 1 (B. Eardley).

STOKE RESERVES: Garry, J. Williams, James, T. Millward, Harding, Hawe, Myatt, F. Eardley, Hargreaves, Fielding, Howshall.
VALE: Osborne, Benson, Meigh, Moss, Coleman, Croxton, Fieldhouse, Turner, Mayland, Beech, B. Eardley.

Venue: The Victoria Ground, Stoke-upon-Trent.
Attendance: Good.
Referee: Mr. Bailey (Hanley).

THE SETTING
Stoke Reserves were in second place in the North Staffordshire Federation League and had won 3-2 at Vale Reserves in the competition on the day before this May Bank Cup match. They had also reached the semi-finals of the Staffordshire Junior Cup before being eliminated. The original Burslem Port Vale had folded in 1907 and the current outfit was the direct descendant of the Cobridge Church club. They were at the foot of the North Staffordshire And District League, with nine defeats in their opening twelve league games, and had lost 3-1 at Hanley Swifts, the league leaders, on Christmas Day. Both clubs had had a bye through the first round of the May Bank Cup and fielded their strongest available sides for the local clash, but Vale included their recently-signed former stalwarts, Harry Croxton and Bert Eardley.

THE MATCH
Much of the initial play was concentrated in midfield, but after ten minutes Bert Eardley put Vale ahead with an effort which Garry should have stopped. Afterwards, the contest swung from end to end and the home keeper made amends for his earlier error by making a wonderful save from a fierce shot by Beech. Howshall then headed just over for Stoke Reserves before Frank Eardley put them level upon receiving the ball from Hargreaves.

After the interval, Stoke Reserves attacked strongly and Myatt struck a shot against the bar. The rebound fell nicely for Fielding, who rushed in and crashed the ball into the net with Osborne well beaten. The home side continued to press, but eventually Vale broke away and Beech was upended in the penalty area. The resulting kick was taken by Coleman, but Garry pulled off a marvellous save to keep his team ahead. Vale attacked vigorously in search of the equaliser, although the closest that either side came to adding to the score was when Fielding scraped the bar with a shot for Stoke Reserves.

THE AFTERMATH
Stoke Reserves went on to win the cup, thrashing Leek United 5-0 in the final at Vale's Athletic Ground on 9 April, and completed a fine season by finishing as runners-up in the North Staffordshire Federation League. Vale turned the corner at the end of January and remarkably won nine consecutive league matches to end up eighth out of fourteen teams!

60: SATURDAY 11 SEPTEMBER 1909, NORTH STAFFORDSHIRE AND DISTRICT LEAGUE

PORT VALE (2) 3 (Peplow 3), STOKE RESERVES (0) 1 (Greaves).

VALE: Cliffe, Meigh, Benson, Croxton, Coleman, Cook, B. Eardley, Beech, Peplow, Capes, Fieldhouse.
STOKE RESERVES: Rathbone, James, Turner, Hawe, Harding, Williams, Dyke, F. Eardley, Greaves, Bourne, A. Baddeley.

Venue: The Athletic Ground, Cobridge.
Attendance: Quite 3,500.
Referee: J. Lowndes (Cheadle).

THE SETTING
Vale had opened their season in the North Staffordshire And District League with a 2-0 win at Goldenhill Wanderers a week before the local Derby and two days later had trounced Kidsgrove Wellington 7-0 at home in the first round of the Burslem Park Cup. Stoke Reserves had commenced their league programme even more convincingly with a 6-1 triumph at home to Goldenhill United, but could only draw 2-2 at Hanley Swifts in the Burslem Park Cup on the Monday prior to the Derby. For the local clash, both teams were at full strength.

THE MATCH
Vale quickly got into their stride and Beech struck a post with a long shot before much time had elapsed. Rathbone worked overtime to keep the home side at bay and on one occasion was bundled into the net with the ball by Beech, but the referee disallowed the goal. However, a couple of minutes later, Vale did succeed in taking the lead when Peplow blasted the ball in direct from a free kick. The home team continued to dominate the play and Bert Eardley hit the Stoke Reserves bar and then had a goal disallowed for offside. In addition, Fieldhouse squandered several good opportunities, although Peplow supplied the finishing touch to a fine move involving Bert Eardley and Capes just before half-time to put Vale further in front.

Shortly after the break, Peplow completed his hat trick with another strong shot and effectively made the game safe for the home side. Until then, it was all that Stoke Reserves could do to 'obtain temporary relief' from Vale's 'almost unremitting attack', but they increasingly gained more of the play as the home team tired. The pressure mounted from the visitors until it was Vale who were hanging on, but their defences were only finally breached a couple of minutes before the end when Greaves scored a consolation goal.

THE AFTERMATH
Vale quickly rose to head the league table and collected a remarkable twenty-seven points from their first fourteen matches! They also made spectacular progress in four cup competitions and won the locally prestigious Staffordshire Junior Cup the following March. Stoke Reserves also performed well in the league and, although they had their work cut out to stay in touch with Vale, their championship challenge remained intact into the spring. In addition, they fought their way to the final of the Hanley Cup to take on Vale once more.

61: MONDAY 28 MARCH 1910, HANLEY CUP, FINAL

STOKE RESERVES (2) 2 (Horrocks 2), PORT VALE (0) 0.

STOKE RESERVES: Rathbone, James, Hutsby, Hawe, Harding, Steel, Dyke, Eardley, Greaves, Horrocks, Bourne.
VALE: Everill, Meigh, Benson, Croxton, Coleman, Cook, Smith, Brough, Cavenor, Capes, Peplow.

Venue: The Victoria Ground, Stoke-upon-Trent.
Attendance: 8,000.
Referee: T. Armitt (Leek).

THE SETTING

Stoke Reserves were in third position in the North Staffordshire And District League, but were only three points behind Vale, the leaders, and had confirmed their challenge by beating fourth from the bottom Dresden Queen's Park 2-0 at home on the Saturday before the local Derby. Vale had annihilated Congleton Town 8-1 at home on the same day and also had won the locally coveted Staffordshire Junior Cup earlier in the month. Both clubs fielded their strongest available line-ups in this second Derby of the season, which attracted a record crowd for the competition.

THE MATCH

At first the contest was end to end, but gradually Stoke Reserves got on top and Bourne went close with a shot when a cross would almost certainly have led to a goal. Nevertheless, Horrocks put the home side in front from a pass by Greaves after twenty-three minutes and brilliant play then forced the Vale keeper to pull off two fine saves in quick succession. However, the visitors retaliated and Peplow slashed well wide from a clear opportunity, whilst Rathbone produced a marvellous save to deny Brough. Cavenor then missed another golden chance for Vale, but Capes twice had to leave the pitch with a serious knee injury and, while he was absent, Horrocks extended the home team's lead with a header from a precisely-flighted free kick by Steel.

Shortly after the interval, Brough netted for Vale, but the whistle had already been blown for a foul, whilst Eardley had a goal disallowed for their opponents through offside a little later. Then Capes was forced to retire for a third and final time, although Vale pressed strongly nevertheless. However, the Stoke Reserves defence remained rock-solid and near to the end Rathbone saved magnificently to foil Cavenor. At the final whistle, the home custodian was carried off shoulder high.

THE AFTERMATH

Stoke Reserves not only won the cup as a result of their efforts, but also collected competition record gate receipts of £114 19s. 4d. and afterwards continued their challenge to Vale for the league championship. Vale permanently lost the services of the influential Adrian Capes, who was forced to retire through his injury, and they were surprisingly beaten 4-1 by Fegg Hayes in the second replay of a Burslem Park Cup semi-final the following month.

62: SATURDAY 23 APRIL 1910, NORTH STAFFORD-SHIRE AND DISTRICT LEAGUE

STOKE RESERVES (0) 0, **PORT VALE** (1) 2 (Grundy 2) (match abandoned).

STOKE RESERVES: Rathbone, James, Hutsby, Hawe, Harding, Williams, Dyke, F. Eardley, Greaves, Horrocks, Bourne.
VALE: Roose, Meigh, Benson, B. Eardley, Chapman, Croxton, Smith, Brough, Grundy, Cavenor, Heaton.

Venue: The Victoria Ground, Stoke-upon-Trent.
Attendance: Quite 7,000.
Referee: S. Davies (Longton).

THE SETTING
The championship of the North Staffordshire And District League hinged entirely on the result of the local Derby, the final match of the season for both teams. Vale were top, a point in front of their rivals who needed to win the game to take the trophy. The visitors had led the table for virtually all the season, but a 4-1 defeat at Congleton Town in their penultimate fixture a week before the Derby had opened the door for Stoke Reserves to pip them at the post. To help prevent this from happening, the Vale committee enlisted the services of four 'brilliant amateurs': Dickie Roose (a Welsh international formerly with Stoke), Frederick Chapman (an English amateur international), William Grundy (from Huddersfield Town) and Herbert Heaton (late of Preston North End), although Stoke fielded their regular reserve side.

THE MATCH
As Vale kicked off, it was apparent that the home supporters resented the presence of 'the strangers' and especially Roose in the visiting team. Nevertheless, Stoke Reserves pressed vigorously, but Grundy put Vale into the lead from a cross by Smith in the tenth minute. This only served to spur the home side into even greater efforts and Horrocks shot against an upright, whilst Roose pulled off a string of wonderful saves, for which he was loudly booed at half-time!

Stoke Reserves redoubled their endeavours after the interval and soon claimed a penalty, which was denied by the referee, and shortly afterwards Grundy extended the visitors' lead from a breakaway. Then, when Roose charged down Horrocks' shot after a marvellous solo run, a large section of the Stoke crowd could endure no more and invaded the pitch. They surrounded Roose and carried him towards the River Trent, whilst Horrocks was knocked unconscious in attempting to intervene! As utter chaos prevailed, the referee abandoned the match.

THE AFTERMATH
Although Roose was eventually rescued, further play was impossible. The league therefore ordered the game to be replayed, but Vale refused and appealed to the Staffordshire F.A. for the points. This claim was dismissed, although Stoke's ground was ordered to be closed for the first two weeks of the following season and the league championship was declared void because the competition hadn't been completed!

63: SATURDAY 8 OCTOBER 1910, NORTH STAFFORDSHIRE AND DISTRICT LEAGUE

PORT VALE (0) 0, STOKE RESERVES (2) 3 (Horrocks, Brown pen., Greaves).

VALE: Heeks, Meigh, Benson, Croxton, Coleman, Cook, Smith, Eardley, Mitchell, Tunnicliffe, Lamonby.
STOKE RESERVES: Baxter, James, Williams, Dixon, Latham, Owen, Dyke, Hawe, Greaves, Horrocks, Brown.

Venue: The Athletic Ground, Cobridge.
Attendance: 9,000.
Referee: F. Leigh (Hanley).

THE SETTING
Vale were at the top of the North Staffordshire And District League and had suffered their only defeat in five matches by 2-1 at second-placed Hanley Swifts on the Saturday before the local Derby. Stoke Reserves were in fourth position and had moved to within a point of the leaders by annihilating fifth from the bottom Goldenhill Wanderers 9-0 at home on the same day. Both clubs fielded their strongest available line-ups for the Derby, with Vale making three changes from their last game and Stoke two.

THE MATCH
Although Stoke's first team were also playing at home, an extremely large crowd gathered to see Horrocks run through and score with a fine shot to give the visitors the lead just one minute after the kickoff. Vale retaliated and Eardley forced Baxter to make a marvellous save, whilst Latham cleared another effort off the line. However, Stoke Reserves went further in front when Brown stroked a penalty into a corner of the net after Greaves had been fouled in the area. The visitors almost extended their lead shortly before half-time when Brown broke away, but his goal-bound shot was touched in by Greaves who was standing offside.

After the interval, Stoke Reserves continued to look dangerous and exhibited superior passing. Brown went close with a tremendous shot, but Lamonby and Tunnicliffe were too slow to take advantage for Vale when they were presented with excellent openings. Although the home side dominated the play, Horrocks scraped the bar in a Stoke Reserves breakaway and then Mitchell failed to reduce the arrears when he remarkably headed over the woodwork whilst standing on the goal line! However, the visitors made the game safe twelve minutes from time when Greaves tapped the ball in from a cross by Hawe.

THE AFTERMATH
Record league receipts of £120 were collected from a crowd which was a mere thousand fewer than had watched Stoke's first team that same day! As a result of their defeat, Vale dropped to fourth place and they won only two of their next seven league matches. Stoke Reserves moved up into second position and mounted a serious championship challenge, although both sides lost on the following Saturday, two days before they were due to meet again, this time in cup action.

64: MONDAY 17 OCTOBER 1910, NORTH STAFFORD-SHIRE NURSING SOCIETY'S CUP, SEMI-FINAL

STOKE RESERVES (0) 2 (Horrocks, Dixon), **PORT VALE** (0) 1 (Billings).

STOKE RESERVES: Rathbone, Burns, Williams, Hawe, Dixon, Owen, Dyke, Bourne, Greaves, Horrocks, Swarbrick.
VALE: Heeks, Benson, Brockley, Moss, Hood, Croxton, Morgan, Tunnicliffe, Billings, Cork, Lamonby.

Venue: The Victoria Ground, Stoke-upon-Trent.
Attendance: A good one.
Referee: B. Davies (Tunstall).

THE SETTING
Stoke Reserves dropped to fourth in the North Staffordshire And District League after suffering a 3-2 defeat at fifth-placed Hanley Swifts on the Saturday before the local Derby. Vale occupied only fifth position despite having commenced the 1910-1911 season with four straight league victories because three consecutive defeats had followed, the most recent by 5-2 at the table-toppers, Kidsgrove Wellington, two days prior to the Derby. Stoke Reserves preferred to make four changes from their previous game, whilst Vale brought in only two new men despite the need to arrest their slide.

THE MATCH
Much of the early play was end to end, but, after Morgan had proved too slow to take advantage of a clear-cut opportunity for Vale, the home side piled on the pressure. Burns hit the Vale bar with a long shot and Horrocks spoiled an excellent chance to open the scoring by hesitating, probably thinking he was offside. The visitors' goal came under siege and a superb back-pass by Horrocks led to Swarbrick shooting just wide, whilst Bourne inexplicably failed to touch in a fine cross from the left winger just before the interval.

In the second half, Stoke Reserves resumed where they'd left off and only a desperate goal line clearance by Benson prevented them from taking the lead. Although Greaves then had a goal disallowed for an infringement and heavy rain began to make the pitch very slippery, the home team finally broke the deadlock when Horrocks netted with an angled drive. Vale's keeper performed heroics to keep them in contention and twelve minutes from time, Billings swept the ball home for an equaliser from a pass by Tunnicliffe. Both sides then searched for a winner and it came to Stoke Reserves right on time when Dixon powerfully headed in from a corner.

THE AFTERMATH
Stoke Reserves went on to win the cup, beating Hanley Swifts 3-1 in the final, and remained in the North Staffordshire And District League championship race throughout the rest of the autumn. Vale were also eliminated from the Staffordshire Junior Cup before the turn of the year, although they annihilated Goldenhill Catholics 9-0 at home on 10 December to progress into the third round of the Hanley Cup. However, their league form continued to be inconsistent.

65: MONDAY 26 DECEMBER 1910, NORTH STAFFORDSHIRE AND DISTRICT LEAGUE

STOKE RESERVES (1) 3 (Dixon, Boulton, Bourne), PORT VALE (0) 1 (Beech).

STOKE RESERVES: Baxter, Taylor, Hay, Hawe, Dixon, James, Dyke, Bourne, Boulton, Horrocks, Swarbrick.
VALE: Champion, Meigh, Brockley, Croxton, Hood, Davies, Smith, Beech, Billings, Tunnicliffe, Lamonby.

Venue: The Victoria Ground, Stoke-upon-Trent.
Attendance: About 9,000.
Referee: F. Leigh (Hanley).

THE SETTING

Stoke Reserves were in fifth place in the North Staffordshire And District League, three points behind the leaders, and had won their last match 3-1 at second from the bottom Chesterton White Star nine days before the local Derby. Vale were in seventh position, but had not won in the league since 5 November and had lost 1-0 at home to Goldenhill Wanderers on the Saturday prior to the Derby. Stoke Reserves showed two team changes from their previous game, but Vale made four alterations as they attempted to halt their decline.

THE MATCH

Stoke Reserves kicked off towards the Town goal and the play quickly became end to end, although neither side came close to scoring for a long time, mainly because of the alertness of both goalkeepers. Nevertheless, towards the end of the first half, Stoke Reserves took the lead when Dixon thumped the ball just under the angle of the bar and post. Vale hit back almost immediately and Billings struck an upright with a smart shot, but then Boulton had a goal disallowed for the home team because the ball had already gone out of play.

After the interval, Vale attacked strongly, although a precise flick-on by Horrocks from a corner allowed Boulton to head Stoke Reserves further in front. As the pressure mounted, the visiting custodian made two fine saves, but when he could only parry a hard shot by Boulton, Bourne responded quickly to slot in the rebound and put the home side well in command. Nevertheless, the play continued to be very open and both keepers remained heavily involved, but eventually Beech squeezed a shot inside a post to reduce the arrears for Vale, although they proved unable to make any further impact.

THE AFTERMATH

A second holiday period victory moved Stoke up into second place and put them just a single point behind the league leaders, whilst Vale remained seventh. The two sides were scheduled to meet again on 14 January in the third round of the Hanley Cup and in the meantime, Stoke Reserves intensified their championship challenge by winning 1-0 at Goldenhill Wanderers on New Year's Eve. Vale's only activity in the intervening period was in the Burslem Park Cup, from which they were knocked out by 3-1 at home to Hanley Swifts in a second round replay on 31 December.

83

66: SATURDAY 14 JANUARY 1911, HANLEY CUP, THIRD ROUND

PORT VALE (1) 2 (Cork, Baxter o.g.), STOKE RESERVES (2) 4 (Horrocks, Boulton, Greaves, Dixon pen.).

VALE: Heeks, Coleman, Brockley, Croxton, Hood, Davies, Smith, Beech, Cork, Tunnicliffe, Lamonby.
STOKE RESERVES: Baxter, James, Williams, Hawe, Burton, Dixon, Bourne, Greaves, Boulton, Horrocks, Swarbrick.

Venue: The Athletic Ground, Cobridge.
Attendance: Unknown.
Referee: W.H. Gibson (Wolstanton).

THE SETTING
Vale had not played any matches in the North Staffordshire And District League since 26 December and had dropped to sixth from the bottom of the table, whilst Stoke Reserves were second in the same league, just a point behind the leaders. In the previous round of the Hanley Cup, Vale had trounced Goldenhill Catholics 9-0 at home, whilst Stoke Reserves had hammered Stockton Brook 5-0 at the Victoria Ground. Both sides were at their fullest available strength for the local clash, which was the fourth of the season.

THE MATCH
The game got off to a sensational start with two goals within the first five minutes. After Beech had shot just wide for Vale, Greaves broke away for the visitors and put Horrocks through to open the scoring. Vale then attacked straight from the restart and when Baxter parried a shot by Beech, Cork was on hand to slot in the rebound. Not long afterwards, Boulton put Stoke Reserves back in front by tapping home after the ball had hit a post and Tunnicliffe then squandered a marvellous chance to equalise once more, by firing wide as the play swept from one end to the other. Towards half-time, Vale took complete command, although they were unable to effect a further breakthrough.

After the interval, Vale continued to attack, but a precise cross by Swarbrick in a breakaway by the visitors enabled Greaves to walk the ball around Heeks and place it in an empty net. This setback stung Vale into even greater efforts and they reduced the arrears when the visiting keeper was bundled over the line during a scrimmage. End to end play created much further excitement and Stoke Reserves made the game safe near to the death when Dixon converted a penalty after Boulton had been upended by Brockley. Thus the visitors triumphed over Vale for the fourth successive time that season.

THE AFTERMATH
Vale remained in contention for honours in only the May Bank Cup, from which they were eventually eliminated in the third round, although they finished fourth in the league. Stoke Reserves went on to win the Hanley Cup and ended up one position below Vale in the league. Although it was not known at the time, this was the last ever local Derby to be played at Cobridge because when the clubs next met, in 1914, it was at Vale's new ground in Hanley.

67: SATURDAY 4 APRIL 1914, BIRMINGHAM CUP, FINAL

PORT VALE (0) 0, STOKE (0) 0.

VALE: Bateup, Cameron, Jones, Shelton, Suart, A. Smith, J. Smith, Brough, Young, Weir, Yule.
STOKE: Herron, Smart, James, Baddeley, Parker, Bradley, Hargreaves, A.R. Smith, Watkin, Ellis, Tempest.

Venue: The Old Recreation Ground, Hanley.
Attendance: 16,929.
Referee: E.H. Spiers (Redditch).

THE SETTING

Vale were top of the Central League, a point clear of their nearest rivals, and had played a remarkable nine games in the English Cup, but had got no further than the first round proper. However, they had annihilated Wednesbury Old Athletic 12-1 and Darlaston 9-1 on their way to the Birmingham Cup final as they attempted to retain the trophy, whilst Stoke had yet to concede a goal in the competition. Also, Stoke were in fourth place in the Second Division of the Southern League, but were nine points behind the leaders. Although Vale selected their strongest available line-up for the local contest, Stoke included five reserves. Eighty-two policemen and three horses were on duty to keep order amongst the then record Derby crowd, which included many people blowing trumpets in eager anticipation of the first local clash to be played at Hanley.

THE MATCH

The game started at a furious pace in spite of drizzle, but chances were few and far between as both defences proved to be firmly on their mettle. Nevertheless, Weir shot just wide for Vale and Young forced Herron to his knees to save a free kick before Baddeley dragged Yule down with his hands in the penalty area. However, to the great disappointment of the home crowd, Young fired the resulting kick straight at the Stoke keeper. Despite this failure, Vale pressed their opponents hard, although the visitors came close to breaking the deadlock when Tempest spurned a fine opportunity and shot over the bar.

Vale started the second period on the offensive and several times threatened to take the lead before Yule and Weir both left the simple task of putting the ball into an empty net to each other until it was too late! The home side applied relentless pressure and Young struck the underside of the Stoke bar, but the visitors weathered the storm and the play became more even in the latter stages. Nevertheless, both defences proved to be impregnable.

THE AFTERMATH

The match receipts were a highly welcome £608 11s. and the directors and players of both clubs celebrated by dining together that evening at the Saracen's Head Hotel in Hanley. The replay was fixed for 20 April and in the meantime Vale's Central League championship challenge faded as they took only four points from their intervening four games. Stoke fared even worse and lost three of their four league matches during the same period.

68: MONDAY 20 APRIL 1914, BIRMINGHAM CUP, FINAL REPLAY

STOKE (2) 2 (Watkin, Ellis), PORT VALE (0) 1 (Young).

STOKE: Herron, James, Milne, Baddeley, Parker, Bradley, Hargreaves, A.R. Smith, Watkin, Ellis, Tempest.
VALE: Bateup, Cameron, Leese, Shelton, Hood, Suart, Walker, Weir, Young, A. Smith, Yule.

Venue: The Victoria Ground, Stoke-upon-Trent.
Attendance: 21,324.
Referee: Unknown.

THE SETTING
With one match to play, Stoke were fourth in the Second Division of the Southern League, but could not finish any higher. A 4-1 defeat at Pontypridd on the Saturday before the local Derby had finally scotched their hopes of securing third position, but Vale led the Central League and were a point clear of their nearest rivals. However, their chances of securing the championship had diminished considerably a week prior to the Derby when they had been beaten 2-0 at fourth-placed Blackburn Rovers Reserves. Stoke made only one change in their line-up for the local clash from the team fielded in the initial final, owing to an injury to Smart, whilst Vale were forced to include two reserves, Hood and Walker. A new record local Derby crowd gathered in anticipation of a battle royal.

THE MATCH
Straight from the outset, Stoke went on the offensive and looked altogether more lively than their opponents who seemed jaded, perhaps as a result of having played fifty-three matches during the season. A mistake by Cameron allowed Watkin to put Stoke in front in the eighth minute and Ellis extended their lead just five minutes later. The home side were generally quicker to the ball, which moved rapidly on the hard ground, and their youthful attackers gave Vale's defence little respite, but failed to make the most of their frequent opportunities.

After Weir had reverted to his normal position of inside-left in the second half, Vale improved, although Tempest should have made the game safe for the home team, but struck a spot kick yards wide of a post! Vale then forced their opponents back and Stoke desperately, but successfully, resisted constant pressure in the final seven minutes after Young had reduced the arrears with a fine header from a corner.

THE AFTERMATH
The gate receipts of £633 surpassed even those of the initial tie and the officials and players of the two clubs took the opportunity to dine together afterwards once more, this time at the North Stafford Hotel. However, Stoke lost their final Southern League game at home and thereby finished in fifth place, whilst Vale were hammered 4-1 at Blackpool Reserves in their last league fixture and ended up a disappointing fourth.

69: MONDAY 14 DECEMBER 1914, BIRMINGHAM CUP, THIRD ROUND

PORT VALE (0) 1 (Brough), STOKE (2) 5 (Watkin 4, Tempest).

VALE: Bateup, Holford, Leese, Shelton, Suart, Vincent, Davies, Brough, Young, Nelson, Yule.
STOKE: Herron, Turner, Milne, Bradley, Parker, Jones, Hargreaves, A.R. Smith, Watkin, A. Smith, Tempest.

Venue: The Old Recreation Ground, Hanley.
Attendance: 5,691.
Referee: W.J. Heath (Burslem).

THE SETTING
Vale were making a firm bid for the championship of the Central League and were third, two points behind the leaders, but with a match in hand. Although they had lost 2-1 at third from the bottom Stalybridge Celtic on the Saturday before the local Derby, Vale had slaughtered Burton Rangers 14-1 and Brierley Hill Alliance 10-1 in previous rounds of the Birmingham Cup. The form of the cup holders, Stoke, was even more outstanding as they had already trounced Willenhall 7-0 and Darlaston 7-1 in the competition and annihilated Stourbridge 11-0 in the English Cup, whilst they stood proudly at the top of the Second Division of the Southern League, six points clear of the field. Although both clubs selected their strongest available line-ups for the Derby, Vale made three team changes as a result of the Stalybridge defeat.

THE MATCH
Both sides made light of the pitch that had in places been turned into a quagmire by heavy rain and the play initially moved swiftly from one end to the other. Vale then gained command and Herron was kept busy by a string of shots, but in the eighteenth minute the visitors took the lead as Watkin prodded the ball home after an effort by Tempest had been parried. Watkin then shot over when excellently placed and Brough committed an absolute howler by treading on the ball on the goal line when he should have equalised! This proved costly because immediately before the interval, Watkin extended Stoke's lead with a tap-in after the home keeper had misdirected his clearance.

Five minutes into the second period, Watkin ran through to complete his hat trick and Tempest put Stoke further ahead by firing the ball through a crowd of players. Watkin increased Vale's discomfort by heading a fifth goal from a corner fifteen minutes from time, although shortly afterwards Brough reduced the arrears by finishing off a fine passing move. There still remained time for Tempest to hit the bar for Stoke and for Young to shoot wide from a penalty for the home team.

THE AFTERMATH
The two sides were scheduled to meet again in a semi-final of the North Staffordshire Infirmary Cup on 25 January and in the meantime Vale took thirteen out of a possible sixteen league points, whilst Stoke were unbeaten in five Southern League games.

70: MONDAY 25 JANUARY 1915, NORTH STAFFORDSHIRE INFIRMARY CUP, SEMI-FINAL

PORT VALE (1) 3 (Young, A. Pearson, Munro), STOKE (0) 0.

VALE: Bateup, Bentley, Holford, Shelton, Bennett, Suart, Brough, A. Pearson, Young, Nelson, Munro.
STOKE: Herron, Turner, Milne, Jones, Parker, Bailey, Hargreaves, A.R. Smith, Watkin, A. Smith, Ellis.

Venue: The Old Recreation Ground, Hanley.
Attendance: Over 3,000.
Referee: I. Baker (Crewe).

THE SETTING
This match was played in a new competition designed to raise funds for the hospital and both clubs responded to the need by selecting strong line-ups. Vale were second in the Central League and in an excellent position, having two games in hand on the leaders and being only a single point behind. They had annihilated the bottom team, Blackpool Reserves, 9-2 at home on 2 January, but had been knocked out of all the major cup competitions. Stoke were in a tremendous position to secure the championship of the Second Division of the Southern League, being ten points clear of their nearest rivals, although they had managed only a 0-0 draw at Barry two days before the local Derby and had already been eliminated from the English Cup.

THE MATCH
Although both teams pressed strongly to try to open the scoring, Vale generally had the better of the early play and most of the opportunities. Nevertheless, neither side went particularly close to breaking the deadlock, with the exception of a Young shot which flashed just wide for Vale. However, Nelson missed a golden opportunity to put the home team in front in the latter stages of the first half when he ballooned the ball high over the bar from a penalty! Despite this, a hard drive by Young did indeed give Vale the lead, six minutes from the interval.

Vale started the second period largely on the offensive and Pearson put them two up by slotting in the rebound after Nelson had hit a post fourteen minutes into the half. The Stoke keeper then made two wonderful saves to deny Brough and Young, but Munro duly extended the home side's lead with a nicely-placed shot just inside a post. Although Holford limped through the remainder of the game, Vale gave as good as they got and ran out well-deserved winners, with the satisfaction of becoming the first team that season to score three times against their opponents in the same match.

THE AFTERMATH
Vale continued to challenge for the Central League title and were victorious in five of their next seven matches. In addition, they won the North Staffordshire Infirmary Cup by beating Macclesfield 3-0 in the final after a replay on 25 March. Stoke carried on relentlessly towards claiming the Southern League, Second Division title and took six points from their following four games.

71: MONDAY 29 MARCH 1915, FRIENDLY

STOKE (1) 2 (Ellis 2), PORT VALE (0) 1 (Munro).

STOKE: Gadsden, Smart, Turner, Baddeley, Jones, Bradley, Tompkinson, Herbert, Morris, Ellis, Tempest.
VALE: Bateup, Bentley, Cooper, Shelton, Bennett, Suart, Munro, Lockett, Young, A. Pearson, Bourne.

Venue: The Victoria Ground, Stoke-upon-Trent.
Attendance: A negligible quantity.
Referee: W.J. Heath (Burslem).

THE SETTING

Stoke were top of the Second Division of the Southern League, eight points clear of their nearest rivals, and needed a maximum of only three points from their remaining three matches to clinch the championship. However, a 2-0 defeat at home by Birmingham in the final of the Birmingham Cup on the Saturday before the local Derby had not given them the best psychological preparation for the contest. Vale were also bidding for glory, in the Central League, and were in third position with games in hand on the teams above them, having secured three victories in succession. They had also been bolstered by winning the North Staffordshire Infirmary Cup four days prior to the Derby and fielded a strong side for the local clash, although Stoke experimented and included only four players from their previous match.

THE MATCH

Although no detailed report has been found, the game was played in a 'decidedly friendly' manner in front of an extremely disappointing crowd. Although neither team seemed to make much effort, Ellis put Stoke in front in the first half and Munro equalised just after the interval. Vale exerted most of the pressure and appeared to be the more determined to win, although Ellis completed the scoring and thus secured the victory for the home side.

THE AFTERMATH

Because the essential objective of the match had been to raise funds, the tiny number of spectators in attendance entirely discouraged the two clubs from playing the planned return, which was consequently cancelled. Although Stoke lost two of their final three games, they annihilated bottom of the table Ebbw Vale 10-0 in their penultimate fixture, which was sufficient to secure the Southern League, Second Division championship with a point to spare and thereby to gain them promotion. In the event, they did not compete in the Southern League's top flight because on 19 July they were elected to the Football League, but were fined £500 by the former competition for resigning beyond the official deadline! Unfortunately, Vale went off the boil in April and lost four of their last eight Central League matches, although they still ended up in third place.

72: SATURDAY 30 SEPTEMBER 1916, FOOTBALL LEAGUE, LANCASHIRE REGIONAL SECTION

STOKE (0) 0, PORT VALE (0) 0.

STOKE: Herron, G. Turner, Twemlow, Jones, Parker, Dobson, Harrison, McCarthy, A.R. Smith, Bridgett, Brooks.
VALE: Powell, Bentley, Cameron, J. Shelton, Bennett, Holford, J. Smith, G. Shelton, Brough, Needham, Dyke.

Venue: The Victoria Ground, Stoke-upon-Trent.
Attendance: Near 16,000.
Referee: W. Chadwick (Blackburn).

THE SETTING
This, the first ever league encounter between the senior sides of the two rival clubs, was played in one of the Football League's wartime regional competitions. Stoke were in eighth place, out of sixteen teams, but had been annihilated 9-2 at third from the bottom Bolton Wanderers on the Saturday before the local Derby! Vale were fifth from the bottom, still had to register a victory in the 1916-1917 season and had only drawn 2-2 at home to struggling Bury a week prior to the Derby. Because both clubs had lost players to the services and war occupations, and as the league rules had been relaxed in recognition of the circumstances, the two sides included guest players in addition to their regulars for the local clash.

THE MATCH
Stoke won the toss and chose to play towards the Boothen goal, but the visitors quickly threatened. However, Brough headed wide with only the keeper to beat and Dyke shot well off target after both players had been set up by Jack Smith. Nevertheless, Vale continued to press, with Needham producing some delightful touches, and Brough had a goal disallowed for offside. Stoke then came back into the match, but Dick Smith and Brooks ruined a marvellous opportunity by colliding as they both attempted to score, whilst McCarthy twice fired over the bar when excellently placed.

Shortly after the interval, the referee awarded a goal to Stoke when a close-range shot from Brooks went over the line, but, following a strong protest from the visiting players, the official decided that the ball had passed through a hole in the side of the net! Nevertheless, Stoke dominated for long spells in the second period and on one occasion Dick Smith seemed certain to score, but was fouled on the edge of the penalty area. Then, in the final minute, Powell kept the score level by grabbing a loose ball almost on the line.

THE AFTERMATH
Despite their failure to beat their local rivals, Stoke generally fared well over the next several months and lost only four of their following fourteen matches. In contrast, Vale were defeated in their next four games, extended their dismal sequence to eleven matches without a win and sank to second from the bottom of the table. Then, remarkably, they trounced Blackpool 11-1 at home on 18 November to record their all-time biggest victory in a league competition!

73: SATURDAY 13 JANUARY 1917, FOOTBALL LEAGUE, LANCASHIRE REGIONAL SECTION

PORT VALE (0) 1 (Griffiths), STOKE (1) 2 (Whittingham, Harrison).

VALE: Bateup, Bentley, Lyons, J. Shelton, Groves, Needham, Smith, G. Shelton, Griffiths, Colclough, Wootton.

STOKE: Herron, Allman, G. Turner, Limer, Jones, Dobson, Harrison, Herbert, Howell, Whittingham, Bridgett.

Venue: The Old Recreation Ground, Hanley.
Attendance: 10,000.
Referee: W. Chadwick (Blackburn).

THE SETTING

Vale were second from the bottom of the wartime regional league, but their three victories had included an 11-1 annihilation of Blackpool, whilst a week before the local Derby they had finally secured their first away win, by 3-1 at struggling Bury. Stoke were faring much better in sixth place and had trounced lowly Bolton Wanderers 7-0 at home on the same day. Both clubs made one team change for their first ever league clash at Vale, with Limer replacing Parker for Stoke and Broadhurst standing down in favour of Smith for the home side. In addition, Vale's left-back, Collins, missed his train so that Bentley had to step into the breach at the last minute. A large crowd assembled to watch the contest, despite lying snow (which was cleared off the pitch) and a hard overnight frost.

THE MATCH

Stoke won the toss and chose to defend the Far Green goal. They took the lead after only seven minutes when Whittingham pounced as the Vale defence failed to clear its lines and the visitors continued to have the better of the exchanges thereafter. Nevertheless, there was little goalmouth action of note, although Colclough forced Herron to make a fine save at the foot of a post as Vale searched for the equaliser.

Shortly after the interval, Stoke went further in front when Harrison retrieved the ball from a scrimmage and netted with a marvellous fifteen-yard cross-shot. Vale's efforts then became rather disjointed, but Griffiths put them back in contention with a tremendous strike after dribbling inside from the left wing. Although Bentley was injured shortly afterwards and became a passenger, Vale attacked strongly with new heart and only two fine saves from the visiting keeper prevented Griffiths from levelling the score.

THE AFTERMATH

Although Vale's form improved considerably and they took ten points from their remaining eleven matches, it was not sufficient to prevent them from finishing second to the bottom of the league. However, Stoke won seven of their final ten games, scoring thirty-two goals in the process, and ended up in third position.

74: SATURDAY 7 APRIL 1917, FOOTBALL LEAGUE, LANCASHIRE REGIONAL SECTION, SUBSIDIARY TOURNAMENT

PORT VALE (1) 3 (Needham, Brough, Holford), STOKE (0) 2 (Whittingham 2).

VALE: Powell, Cameron, Collins, Price, Groves, J. Shelton, Broadhurst, G. Shelton, Brough, Needham, Holford.
STOKE: Herron, G. Turner, Milne, Jones, Parker, Limer, Harrison, Whittingham, Howell, Herbert, Bridgett.

Venue: The Old Recreation Ground, Hanley.
Attendance: Quite 12,000.
Referee: H. Oxley (Stockport).

THE SETTING
Vale had completed their main regional section league programme the day before the local Derby with a 3-0 home win against Manchester United, but had still finished second from the bottom of the table. In contrast, Stoke had secured third place, largely through four straight victories at the death, in which they had scored seventeen goals! Vale had begun the Subsidiary Tournament with a defeat, whilst Stoke had won their first match in the competition, but had then lost 1-0 at Manchester City on the day prior to the Derby. Vale made two changes from their victorious Good Friday team, with Price and Needham returning to the fray, whilst Stoke preferred to make four alterations in their side and recalled Parker, Limer, Harrison and Bridgett.

THE MATCH
Although the pitch was rather heavy, both teams started at a cracking pace, but Vale were the first to threaten seriously when Needham attempted to shoot too precisely when presented with a clear opportunity by Broadhurst. Nevertheless, the home side went in front in the twenty-third minute as Needham stroked the ball into an empty net following superb play by Brough. This had the effect of further increasing the tempo, although the outcome was a great deal of foul play.

Vale extended their lead two minutes into the second period when Brough, who was seemingly offside, received a pass from Needham and scored with a low drive. Stoke then exerted tremendous pressure as they attempted to get back into the game and Powell made brilliant saves from Whittingham and Jones before the former reduced the arrears with a wonderful swerving overhead kick eleven minutes into the half. However, fourteen minutes later, Holford increased Vale's lead by converting a Broadhurst centre, although Whittingham stabbed in a rebound for Stoke just two minutes afterwards. Exciting end to end play followed, but neither team was able to add any further goals.

THE AFTERMATH
Although Vale gained a much-needed boost from beating their local rivals, they did not win either of their intervening matches in the competition before they faced Stoke again in the return. Stoke performed rather better and thrashed Manchester City 5-0 in their next game, but then suffered another defeat.

75: SATURDAY 21 APRIL 1917, FOOTBALL LEAGUE, LANCASHIRE REGIONAL SECTION, SUBSIDIARY TOURNAMENT

STOKE (1) 2 (Howell, Herbert), PORT VALE (0) 0.

STOKE: Herron, Allman, G. Turner, Jones, Parker, Limer, Harrison, Whittingham, Howell, Herbert, Bridgett.
VALE: Powell, Cameron, Collins, Price, Groves, J. Shelton, Broadhurst, G. Shelton, Brough, Needham, Holford.

Venue: The Victoria Ground, Stoke-upon-Trent.
Attendance: Unknown.
Referee: H. Oxley (Stockport).

THE SETTING
Stoke were not faring particularly well in the league's Subsidiary Tournament and had lost three of their five previous matches, although they had had the satisfaction of thumping Manchester City 5-0 at home twelve days before the local Derby. Vale were doing even worse, with their only victory thus far in the competition being by 3-2 at the expense of their local rivals two weeks earlier. Both clubs made a single change to their line-ups from their previous games, with Allman replacing Milne for Stoke, whilst Vale reintroduced Price at right-half to field the same team that had accounted for their rivals fourteen days earlier.

THE MATCH
"The Staffordshire Sentinel" gave no report of the match, but "Onward" of "The Athletic News" described in detail the 'unpleasant incidents', which 'quite destroyed the pleasure' of watching the contest. Players not only carried on a feud amongst themselves, but also argued with a section of the crowd in the enclosure in front of the main stand, whilst the referee himself was threatened. Nevertheless, Stoke quickly gained control of the game and maintained their superiority throughout. Their forwards combined impressively and it was only the stubborn resistance of the Vale defence that restricted them to a single goal lead at the interval. This resulted from a brilliant pass by Whittingham which presented Howell with a simple opportunity to score. However, just before half-time, Holford (an ex-Stoke player) left the pitch to engage in a dispute with some spectators who had been barracking him!

Stoke continued their fine form in the second period and Herbert shot them further in front after being set up by Bridgett. Only a series of wonderful saves by the Vale keeper prevented the home team from running riot, whilst Cameron and Collins also worked overtime to keep the score respectable.

THE AFTERMATH
The directors of both clubs met after the match and subsequently decided to arrange another local Derby for the benefit of the North Staffordshire Prisoners of War Fund. As a result of their victory, Stoke finished sixth in the Subsidiary Tournament, whilst Vale ended up fifth from the bottom following a 5-2 home win against Manchester United in their final game.

93

76: SATURDAY 5 MAY 1917, FRIENDLY

STOKE (1) 2 (Herbert 2), PORT VALE (0) 1 (Needham).

STOKE: Gebhard, Allman, G. Turner, Jones, Parker, Limer, A.R. Smith, Whittingham, Johnson, Herbert, Bridgett.
VALE: Powell, Twemlow, Collins, J. Shelton, Groves, Arrowsmith, Broadhurst, Davies, Brough, Needham, Cunliffe.

Venue: The Victoria Ground, Stoke-upon-Trent.
Attendance: Disappointing.
Referee: W.J. Heath (Burslem).

THE SETTING
This was the fifth local Derby of the season and had been arranged for the benefit of the North Staffordshire Regiment Prisoners of War Fund, but the anticipated large crowd did not materialise to support it. Both teams had concluded their league campaigns, with Stoke finishing third in the Lancashire Regional Section competition and sixth in the subsequent Subsidiary Tournament. In contrast, Vale had ended up second from the bottom and fifth from the bottom respectively in the same tournaments. Stoke's first-choice forwards, Harrison and Howell, were unable to play in the Derby because of work commitments, whilst Vale's George Shelton was in the same boat and the Liverpool left winger, Tommy Cunliffe, replaced Holford, who had been conscripted into the forces. In addition, Stoke's full-back, Twemlow, made a guest appearance for Vale.

THE MATCH
Stoke won the toss and chose to attack with the advantage of a strong wind, which soon helped to put them in the ascendancy. Although the home side pressed strongly, the Vale keeper was not unduly troubled until the twenty-fifth minute when Herbert squeezed the ball in from a tight angle to put Stoke in front. The visitors then worked hard to try to get back on level terms, but it was Stoke who came the closer to scoring, with both Herbert and Bridgett firing over the bar when well placed.

The second period started without a break, but before Vale could take advantage of the wind, the home side extended their lead. Only four minutes had elapsed when Herbert slotted in a rebound from a shot by Bridgett, although Needham put Vale back in contention with a hard drive almost straight from the restart. Nevertheless, it was Stoke who had the better of the remaining exchanges and Johnson and Herbert both went close, but they were eventually indebted to Gebhard, who made a superb save from a Needham rocket, to clinch their victory.

THE AFTERMATH
The Derby was the final match of the campaign for both clubs, which were relatively inactive in the close season regarding the recruitment of new players owing to the suspension of the normal transfer system during the war period. Indeed, it was all they could do to retain their existing players in the face of conscription and both lost several to the war effort. Nevertheless, relieved of the burden of paying players' wages, Stoke announced a tidy profit of £810 on the season and Vale £692 9s. 2½d.!

77: SATURDAY 29 SEPTEMBER 1917, FOOTBALL LEAGUE, LANCASHIRE REGIONAL SECTION

PORT VALE (0) 0, STOKE (1) 2 (Herbert, Whittingham).

VALE: Bateup, Lyons, Cameron, J. Shelton, H. Pearson, Arrowsmith, Spooner, Bowcock, Holford, A. Pearson, Edgeley.
STOKE: Peers, Allman, G. Turner, J. Jones, Parker, Smith, Harrison, Whittingham, H. Howell, Herbert, Bridgett.

Venue: The Old Recreation Ground, Hanley.
Attendance: 10,000.
Referee: I. Baker (Crewe).

THE SETTING

Stoke were third in the wartime regional league and had won their opening four matches, scoring eighteen goals in the process! In their previous game, a week before the local Derby, they had hammered Preston North End 4-0 at home and on that same day Vale had recorded their first victory of the season, by 4-2 at Southport Central. This left them in tenth position out of sixteen teams. Three players who had enlisted in the armed forces made welcome appearances in the Derby: Tom Holford and Jack Shelton for Vale and George Turner for Stoke, but neither club made any further changes to their sides of the previous week. Warm weather attracted a large crowd and a collection was held for the ·'comforts fund' of the North Staffordshire Regiment!

THE MATCH

The play quickly became end to end, but little of note occurred in the early stages, other than Herbert firing just wide from a good position for Stoke. However, in the twenty-first minute, Whittingham was upended in the penalty area by three Vale players when running through on goal and put the rebound wide after Bateup had brilliantly parried the spot kick. Shortly afterwards, Herbert netted for Stoke, but was ruled offside, although a fine move led to the same player opening the scoring with a volley from an acute angle after half an hour. Vale almost equalised in the latter stages of the half, but Smith kicked the ball off the line with Bowcock about to apply the finishing touch.

The play remained open after the interval and, although Holford hit a terrific shot only a foot wide of an upright, Vale found it difficult to exert any sustained pressure because their passing was not particularly accurate. Nevertheless, their opponents were increasingly forced on the defensive, but Howell missed an open goal from a Stoke breakaway before Whittingham extended their lead by lashing the ball into the net from a scrimmage twelve minutes from time. Thereafter, the visitors went on the rampage, but were unable to add to their score.

THE AFTERMATH

As a result of their victory, Stoke went up to the top of the table, whilst Vale remained tenth. It was already clear that Stoke were making a strong challenge for the championship and that they possessed a formidable attacking triumvirate in Whittingham, Howell and Herbert, who had scored sixteen goals between them in just five games! For Vale, the picture was ominously otherwise.

78: SATURDAY 6 OCTOBER 1917, FOOTBALL LEAGUE, LANCASHIRE REGIONAL SECTION

STOKE (0) 4 (Whittingham 2, Howell, Herbert), PORT VALE (0) 1 (Hill).

STOKE: Peers, Maddock, Twemlow, J. Jones, Parker, Smith, Harrison, Whittingham, H. Howell, Herbert, Bridgett.
VALE: Bateup, Lyons, Holmes, Phillips, H. Pearson, Arrowsmith, Spooner, Brough, A. Pearson, Edgeley, Hill.

Venue: The Victoria Ground, Stoke-upon-Trent.
Attendance: Excellent.
Referee: I. Baker (Crewe).

THE SETTING
Undefeated Stoke had become the leaders of the wartime regional league by winning 2-0 at Vale a week before the return Derby and had scored twenty goals in their opening five matches. Their local rivals, however, were tenth, with just a single victory to their credit. Stoke's line-up for the clash showed a new full-back pairing, but was otherwise identical to that of the previous meeting, whilst Vale made four changes, partly as a result of the demands of the armed services. Fine weather prompted a large turnout to watch the contest.

THE MATCH
The game commenced at a fast pace and there was considerable action, but scoring opportunities were few and far between. Those that did materialise fell mainly to Stoke and Howell twice headed over the bar, whilst Jones forced Bateup to bring off an excellent save and then headed the ball against a post. Although Brough replied with a hard volley, which the home keeper collected, Stoke exerted further pressure before the interval.

Stoke finally went in front a minute and a half into the second period when Whittingham received a pass from Jones and lofted the ball over the head of the visiting custodian and into the net. Vale then rose to the challenge and kept Peers busy, but the home side broke away and Harrison centred for Whittingham to head them further in front twenty-two minutes into the half. Vale's problems were compounded when Albert Pearson was injured and became a passenger and Harrison furthered their misery after seventy-five minutes by providing a pinpoint cross for Howell to steer the ball in. Nevertheless, Vale battled on gamely and reduced the arrears when Hill converted a Harry Pearson centre five minutes from time, but Herbert added a fourth goal for Stoke straight from the restart.

THE AFTERMATH
As a result of their convincing victory, Stoke remained as the league leaders and they continued their sequence of consecutive victories from the start of the season until 3 November when they first tasted defeat. Nevertheless, they still accused Vale of paying their players more than the legally permitted wartime expenses! Vale sank to fifth from the bottom as a consequence of their second local Derby defeat, but then began a five-match unbeaten run.

79: TUESDAY 25 DECEMBER 1917, FRIENDLY

PORT VALE (1) 1 (Brough), STOKE (2) 2 (P. Jones 2).

VALE: Hammond, Holmes, Cameron, Holford, J. Bennett, Lawton, Spooner, Brough, Bowcock, A. Pearson, Hill.
STOKE: Herron, Milne, Twemlow, J. Jones, Parker, E. Turner, Smith, A. Howell, P. Jones, Herbert, Bridgett.

Venue: The Old Recreation Ground, Hanley.
Attendance: More than 3,000.
Referee: W.J. Heath (Burslem).

THE SETTING

Vale had recovered from a poor start to the 1917-1918 season to rise to eighth place, out of sixteen sides, in the Lancashire Regional Section league as a result of sustaining just a single defeat in their last eleven games before the local Derby. Their 2-0 win at fifth from the bottom Bolton Wanderers on the Saturday prior to the Derby marked their third victory in four league matches. Stoke were second, two points behind the leaders but with a game in hand, and had annihilated Blackburn Rovers 16-0 and 8-1 the previous month! However, their most recent success, three days before the local clash, had been a modest 1-0 win against struggling Bury. Both Vale and Stoke made four changes in their line-ups for the Derby, but were fairly strongly represented nevertheless.

THE MATCH

Play started fifteen minutes late and Vale quickly went on the offensive, with Herron excelling to save a swerving shot from Brough. However, after ten minutes, Stoke took the lead when Percy Jones scrambled the ball in from a magnificent Bridgett centre. Thereafter, Vale pressed even more strongly, but Pearson contrived to tread on the ball when it just needed to be prodded over the line, Spooner shot wide from a clear opportunity and Brough hit the bar with the visiting keeper beaten! Nevertheless, Brough equalised for Vale from a scrimmage in the thirty-eighth minute, although Percy Jones restored Stoke's advantage almost immediately.

Stoke dominated the contest in the second period, but the play was scrappy and the defences were firmly in command. As the match proceeded, both sets of forwards became less effective, especially as their passing deteriorated and the goalkeepers were rarely seriously troubled. The only major incident of note occurred when Herron appeared to fall over the line in making a save, but this Vale equaliser was disallowed.

THE AFTERMATH

"The Wanderer", the match reporter for "The Staffordshire Sentinel", complained bitterly that the spectators had been cheated because they had paid to see two halves of only forty minutes' duration each! Nevertheless, the supporters were not to be deprived of local Derby action for long because a return game had been arranged at the Victoria Ground for the following day.

80: WEDNESDAY 26 DECEMBER 1917, FRIENDLY

STOKE (2) 2 (Bridgett, P. Jones), PORT VALE (0) 0.

STOKE: Herron, Maddock, Milne, Limer, J. Jones, E. Turner, Whittingham, A. Howell, P. Jones, Herbert, Bridgett.
VALE: Hammond, Holmes, Cameron, J. Bennett, H. Pearson, Lawton, Spooner, Foster, Bowcock, A. Pearson, Holford.

Venue: The Victoria Ground, Stoke-upon-Trent.
Attendance: Good.
Referee: F. Leigh (Hanley).

THE SETTING
The local Derby was the return match of two friendlies played over the festive season. Stoke had been boosted by their 2-1 victory against their rivals the previous day and by their lofty position (second) in the Lancashire Regional Section wartime league. Although Vale had been defeated on Christmas Day, the contest had been very closely fought and they were also cheered by their excellent recent form which had taken them up to eighth place in the same league. Although the Derby was played only the day after the last one, Stoke made three team changes and Vale two, which perfectly illustrated how line-ups fluctuated with circumstances during the war period.

THE MATCH
Vale kicked off, but the home side quickly took control. Whittingham missed the target by inches with a powerful rising shot and then Howell dallied far too long when presented with a golden opportunity to score. Nevertheless, Stoke went in front when Bridgett netted with a cross-shot and the visiting keeper was brought into almost constant action afterwards. Shortly before the interval, Stoke extended their lead when Percy Jones tapped the ball in after Hammond had dropped a centre from Bridgett.

Early in the second half, Stoke were desperately unlucky not to add to their score because a tremendous shot by Whittingham struck Cameron on the line and bounced clear. The home side continued to dominate the play and only a remarkable save by the visiting custodian prevented Whittingham from netting from a free kick. Although Vale came back into the game near the end, the home team almost struck again, but Bridgett had an effort ruled out because of offside.

THE AFTERMATH
Stoke continued their chase for the league championship with a vengeance and gained twenty-one points from their following thirteen matches, which included a 7-0 thrashing of Oldham Athletic and a 9-0 annihilation of struggling Burnley, both at home. However, Vale's league form fell away badly so that eight of their remaining thirteen games were lost and they disappointingly finished sixth from the bottom.

81: FRIDAY 29 MARCH 1918, FOOTBALL LEAGUE, LANCASHIRE REGIONAL SECTION, SUBSIDIARY TOURNAMENT

PORT VALE (0) 0, STOKE (1) 2 (Herbert, P. Jones).

VALE: Hammond, J. Bennett, Cameron, Arrowsmith, H. Pearson, Hawley, Spooner, Brennan, Rogers, Foster, A. Pearson.
STOKE: Morris, Wootton, Twemlow, J. Jones, Parker, E. Turner, Smith, Martin, P. Jones, Herbert, Bassett.

Venue: The Old Recreation Ground, Hanley.
Attendance: Unknown.
Referee: I. Baker (Crewe).

THE SETTING

This was the opening game for both clubs in the Lancashire Regional Section's Subsidiary Tournament. Vale had completed their main league programme with a 2-0 home defeat by struggling Blackburn Rovers on the Saturday before the local Derby and had finished sixth from the bottom. In contrast, as a result of a 2-0 victory at Burnley six days prior to the Derby, Stoke only had to avoid a defeat by three clear goals at home to sixth-placed Rochdale in their final game in order to win the championship of the same competition. Vale made four team changes for the local clash, one of which was enforced by their regular right-back, Lyons, arriving too late, whilst Stoke's side showed five alterations from their previous match and the inclusion of several reserves.

THE MATCH

Stoke won the toss, decided to defend the Town goal and quickly exerted their authority. Fine interplay between Percy Jones and Herbert led to the latter firing just wide, but then Rogers forced the visiting keeper to make a tremendous save to prevent Vale from taking the lead. Many good Stoke moves were ruined by Bassett's slowness, but he redeemed himself after twenty minutes by providing a pinpoint centre for Herbert to open the scoring with a low drive. With their inside-left an inspiration, Stoke dominated the rest of the first period, but were unable to add to their tally.

At the very start of the second half, Rogers let a splendid opportunity to equalise pass by dithering with the ball at his feet and Brennan proceeded to do likewise shortly afterwards. Relieved by their good fortune, Stoke then pressed strongly and Percy Jones had a goal disallowed for an infringement, whilst Herbert struck the crossbar. Their efforts were finally rewarded when Percy Jones took advantage of a misclearance to extend their lead, although Albert Pearson almost reduced the arrears when he shot just outside a post.

THE AFTERMATH

Vale continued their poor run of form by losing 4-1 at home to Manchester City in the same tournament the following day, which did not help their preparation for the return local Derby on the Easter Monday. Stoke were also beaten in the meanwhile, for the first time since 9 February, but at least this was only by 2-1 at Manchester United.

82: MONDAY 1 APRIL 1918, FOOTBALL LEAGUE, LANCASHIRE REGIONAL SECTION, SUBSIDIARY TOURNAMENT

STOKE (3) 6 (Herbert 2, E. Turner, Martin, Lockett, Smith pen.), PORT VALE (0) 0.

STOKE: Morris, Maddock, Twemlow, J. Jones, Parker, E. Turner, Smith, Martin, Lockett, Herbert, Bassett.
VALE: Hammond, Lyons, Cameron, Holmes, Arrowsmith, Jolly, Malkin, Brennan, Rogers, Foster, A. Pearson.

Venue: The Victoria Ground, Stoke-upon-Trent.
Attendance: Unknown.
Referee: Unknown.

THE SETTING
Although Stoke were top of the Lancashire Regional Section league, with maximum home points and the championship within their grasp, their vital last match was not due to be played until 27 April. They had opened their Subsidiary Tournament account with a 2-0 win at Vale three days before this return local Derby, but had then lost 2-1 at Manchester United twenty-four hours later. Vale had already ended up sixth from the bottom of the Lancashire Regional Section main competition and had started the Subsidiary Tournament with two home defeats, which included a 4-1 reverse to Manchester City two days prior to the return Derby. Stoke made two alterations in their line-up from their previous match, with Martin and Bassett replacing Cooper and Percy Jones, whilst Jim Bennett stood down in favour of Jolly for Vale.

THE MATCH
Only scant references to the game have been traced, but, according to "The Staffordshire Sentinel", Vale were 'distinctly overplayed'. "The Athletic News" added that 'the home eleven from the start showed a complete mastery of the situation'. Eli Turner opened the scoring for Stoke and Herbert added a brace of goals before half-time. Martin and Lockett further extended the home side's lead after the interval, whilst Smith converted a penalty close to the final whistle as Stoke ran out convincing winners. Thus Stoke were victorious for the sixth time in six matches that season against their old rivals.

THE AFTERMATH
Stoke picked up only two points from their remaining three Subsidiary Tournament games and finished a disappointing ninth. However, they won the Lancashire Regional Section main championship in spite of losing their final match 2-1 at home to sixth-placed Rochdale on 27 April. This triumph set up a two-leg League Championship Cup tie against the Midland Section winners, Leeds City, which Stoke unfortunately lost 2-1 on aggregate, although the National Footballers' War Fund benefited to the tune of approximately £918 from the donation of the total gate receipts to the cause. Vale were defeated in their following two Subsidiary Tournament games, but won their final fixture to end up third from the bottom.

83: SATURDAY 5 OCTOBER 1918, FOOTBALL LEAGUE, LANCASHIRE REGIONAL SECTION

STOKE (0) 3 (Bowser, Turner, McGregor), PORT VALE (2) 2 (Foster 2).

STOKE: Peers, Garratly, Twemlow, A. R. Smith, J. Jones, McGregor, Harrison, Bowser, Lockett, Herbert, Turner.
VALE: Hammond, Lyons, Holmes, Arrowsmith, H. Pearson, A. Smith, Daley, McCarthy, Brown, Foster, A. Pearson.

Venue: The Victoria Ground, Stoke-upon-Trent.
Attendance: Unknown.
Referee: Unknown.

THE SETTING

Stoke, the reigning champions, had started their Lancashire Regional Section league programme impressively, with three straight victories, before losing 3-1 at Oldham Athletic a week before the local Derby. This left them fourth in the table and undefeated Vale were just one place below their old rivals, but with only a single win under their belts. Their latest draw had been 1-1 at home to struggling Blackpool seven days before the Derby, for which they made three team changes, with Hammond, Brown and Foster replacing Dennis (who had a broken leg), Davies and Marsden. Stoke's line-up also showed three alterations, with Morris, Emery and Flaherty standing down in favour of Peers, Dick Smith and McGregor. However, the occasion was tarnished by the recent news that Stoke's stalwart goalkeeper, Dickie Herron, and Vale's long-serving right-half, Jack Shelton, had been killed in action in the First World War.

THE MATCH

Although the match was contested in a very sportsman-like manner, it still proved a really thrilling encounter. Vale took a two-goal lead in the first half, thanks to some incisive passing, especially by Brown, who twice set up Foster to score. Although Stoke attacked vigorously throughout most of the first period, they were unable to hit the target, mainly because of a lack of teamwork, and at the interval they looked a beaten side.

Early in the second half, Brown had a marvellous opportunity to extend Vale's lead, but dallied too long in possession, which was especially unfortunate because Stoke then concentrated on working the ball to Harrison, who inspired them with a 'wonderful' display and set up Bowser to reduce the arrears. Turner equalised and McGregor completed their rally by scoring with a 'masterpiece' a few minutes from the end, as Stoke's superior stamina made their offensive 'irresistible'. Nevertheless, Brown should have levelled the score just before the final whistle, but contrived to miss whilst standing virtually on the line!

THE AFTERMATH

"The Staffordshire Sentinel" carried a sizable article in its edition that evening about the deaths of and injuries sustained by several Stoke and Vale players and it was against this background that the two clubs made their preparations for the return Derby the following Saturday.

84: SATURDAY 12 OCTOBER 1918, FOOTBALL LEAGUE, LANCASHIRE REGIONAL SECTION

PORT VALE (0) 1 (Davies), STOKE (3) 8 (Whittingham 4, Lockett 2, Bowser pen., Herbert).

VALE: Hammond, Marsden, Holmes, Arrowsmith, H. Pearson, A. Smith, Daley, Davies, Rogers, Foster, A. Pearson.
STOKE: Peers, Garratly, Twemlow, H. Wootton, Bowser, A. R. Smith, Harrison, Whittingham, Lockett, Herbert, Tempest.

Venue: The Old Recreation Ground, Hanley.
Attendance: Unknown.
Referee: Unknown.

THE SETTING

Vale's 3-2 defeat at Stoke a week previously was their first of the 1918-1919 season in the Lancashire Regional Section league, in their fifth match, whilst the same result marked Stoke's fourth victory in their opening five league games. Vale were weakened for the return local Derby by the unavailability of their full-back, Lyons; their inside-right, McCarthy, and their guest centre-forward, David Brown, whose places were taken by Marsden, Davies and Rogers. However, Stoke were strengthened by the return of Whittingham, whilst Joey Jones and Turner were unable to play and were replaced by Harold Wootton and Tempest.

THE MATCH

Although it was generally expected that Stoke would win the match, the high score came as a great surprise. This was the third-biggest league home defeat in Vale's entire history and created the all-time record score for a Potteries Derby. The disparity between the relative strengths of the two sides became obvious right from the outset and Stoke dominated the play almost entirely. The visitors produced a marvellous footballing display and the Vale defence was 'almost powerless' to keep Stoke's 'irresistible' forwards at bay. Harrison, in particular, wreaked havoc and, along with Tempest, supplied an almost endless number of pinpoint centres, but Whittingham spurned a series of 'gift openings'. Nevertheless, he found the target four times after Bowser had put the visitors in front from a penalty and Lockett, with two goals, and Herbert completed the rout. Vale rarely threatened, although a rearrangement of their forwards in the second half brought some improvement and Albert Pearson set up Davies to score a consolation goal.

THE AFTERMATH

Vale's disastrous defeat marked the start of a sequence of poor results which lasted until Christmas. During this period, they lost seven of their eleven league games, conceded thirty-five goals in the process and plummeted to fifth from the bottom of the table. Stoke followed up their local Derby triumph by trouncing Blackburn Rovers 7-0 and 6-0 and continued their championship challenge by winning eleven of their sixteen fixtures to the beginning of February. However, in comparison with the death in the war of Vale's long-serving half-back, Bob Suart, which was announced six days after the Derby, it mattered little.

85: WEDNESDAY 25 DECEMBER 1918, FRIENDLY

PORT VALE (0) 0, STOKE (1) 5 (Whittingham 2, Turner, Bowyer, Nicklin).

VALE: Hammond, Holmes, Cameron, Davies, H. Pearson, J. Smith, Nash, Burgess, Brennan, Fitchford, Millward.
STOKE: Peers, French, Twemlow, J. Jones, C. Parker, H. Wootton, Harrison, Whittingham, Nicklin, Bowyer, Turner.

Venue: The Old Recreation Ground, Hanley.
Attendance: Large.
Referee: F. Leigh (Hanley).

THE SETTING

Vale were fifth from the bottom of the Lancashire Regional Section league, but had won three of their last six matches to stage something of a recovery after a dire start. However, they had crashed 5-1 at lowly Manchester United on the Saturday before the local Derby. Stoke were in third place in the same competition, were undefeated in their previous five league games and had trounced fourth-placed Bolton Wanderers 7-1 at home four days prior to the Derby. Although both clubs fielded their strongest available teams for the local clash, Vale were obliged to make no fewer than seven changes from their previous match, whilst Stoke's side showed four alterations and included the West Stanley player, French, and Nicklin of Col. Blizzard's XI.

THE MATCH

The ball was set in motion at around 10.45 a.m. and Whittingham opened the scoring for Stoke in the fifteenth minute with a tremendous twenty-yard drive. Although this proved to be the only goal of the first period, both Brennan and Davies struck the Stoke bar, the latter from a free kick. Also, both teams had further opportunities, but these were wasted either by slow anticipation or inaccurate shooting.

Vale's centre-half, Pearson, did not appear for the second half, having picked up an injury, and Stoke quickly took advantage as Whittingham centred for Turner to head them into a two-goal lead. A few minutes later, Whittingham prodded the visitors further in front after Hammond had parried a shot by Turner, who had appeared to be yards offside before cutting in. Then Bowyer dribbled half the length of the pitch and teed up Whittingham to net once more, but the latter had strayed offside. In a belated Vale rally, Millward shot well wide with only the keeper to beat and Stoke sealed their eleventh successive local Derby victory through fine efforts by Bowyer and Nicklin, as the home side finished with nine men because Smith also retired injured.

THE AFTERMATH

The following day, a joint Vale and Stoke team (which included only two Vale players!) took on Col. Blizzard's XI at the Victoria Ground in another friendly game and lost 7-5! Nevertheless, Vale won their next four league matches, although they then fell apart and finished fifth from the bottom. In contrast, Stoke gained six consecutive league victories and ended the season in second place.

86: MONDAY 21 APRIL 1919, FOOTBALL LEAGUE, LANCASHIRE REGIONAL SECTION, SUBSIDIARY TOURNAMENT

STOKE (1) 2 (J. Wootton, Phillips), PORT VALE (2) 2 (Briscoe, Brennan).

STOKE: Kay, Smart, Twemlow, Clarke, J. Jones, Smith, J. Wootton, Phillips, Whipp, Martin, Tempest.
VALE: Hammond, Lyons, Leese, A. McGarry, H. Pearson, Newton, Broadhurst, Brennan, Briscoe, Fitchford, Hill.

Venue: The Victoria Ground, Stoke-upon-Trent.
Attendance: Big.
Referee: H. Holland (Stockport).

THE SETTING
Stoke had finished as the runners-up in the Lancashire Regional Section league, but had started the Subsidiary Tournament with only one victory in their first three matches, by 1-0 at Manchester United on the Saturday before the local Derby. Vale had ended up fifth from the bottom of the same league, having lost eight of their final ten games, and had begun the Subsidiary Tournament badly with three straight defeats, the last of which had been by 1-0 at home to Manchester City two days prior to the Derby. Both clubs selected their strongest available teams for the local clash and Stoke included Tom Kay, their new goalkeeper, signed from Rochdale, although Charlie Parker was unavailable because he was playing in a Y.M.C.A. charity match!

THE MATCH
The game was keenly contested, but there was little initial excitement as neither set of forwards could do more than probe the opposing defence. However, Stoke went close from a scrimmage before Briscoe pounced on a bouncing ball in the thirty-second minute and placed it just inside a post to give Vale the lead. Only six minutes later, Brennan sprinted clear from forty yards out to put the visitors further in front, but shortly before the interval, Wootton reduced the arrears with a well-placed shot while Vale vainly appealed for offside.

Stoke pressed hard upon the resumption of play, but the visitors ought to have extended their lead when Brennan broke away but shot harmlessly behind. Although Tempest had a shot kicked off the line, Vale came into the ascendancy and Kay produced an excellent save to deny Brennan. Nevertheless, Stoke equalised when Phillips stroked the ball into an open goal, although Brennan missed a golden opportunity to secure both points for the visitors near to the death. Despite this, Vale had finally broken their dismal sequence of eleven consecutive Derby defeats.

THE AFTERMATH
The two teams were due to meet again in their final Subsidiary Tournament match a week later and Stoke beat Manchester United 4-2 at home in their penultimate fixture on the Saturday beforehand, whilst Vale were hammered 4-1 at Manchester City on the same day.

1. TOMMY CLARE, who made 26 appearances in the Potteries Derbies (22 for Stoke, 4 for Vale) between 1884 and 1898.

2. BILLY ROWLEY, who made 14 appearances in the Potteries Derbies (13 for Stoke, 1 for Vale) between 1886 and 1892.

3. WILLIE DICKSON, who scored 7 goals for Stoke in the Potteries Derbies between 1894 and 1896.

4. JIM BEECH, who made 15 appearances for Vale in the Potteries Derbies between 1894 and 1902.

5. TOM HOLFORD, who made an all-time record 28 appearances in the Potteries Derbies (19 for Vale, 9 for Stoke) between 1899 and 1922.

6. ARTHUR BRIDGETT, who made 12 appearances for Stoke in the Potteries Derbies between 1902 and 1917.

7. JOE BROUGH, who made 19 appearances for Vale in the Potteries Derbies between 1910 and 1922.

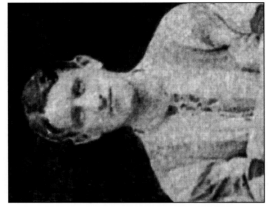

9. BOB WHITTINGHAM, who scored an all-time record 13 goals for Stoke in the Potteries Derbies between 1917 and 1920.

8. BILLY TEMPEST, who made 24 appearances in the Potteries Derbies (20 for Stoke, 4 for Vale) between 1914 and 1925.

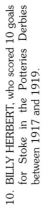

10. BILLY HERBERT, who scored 10 goals for Stoke in the Potteries Derbies between 1917 and 1919.

11. JACK MADDOCK, who made 17 appearances in the Potteries Derbies (11 for Vale, 6 for Stoke) between 1917 and 1929.

12. BILLY BRISCOE, who made 22 appearances for Vale in the Potteries Derbies between 1919 and 1930.

RULE 14.—Each Club must send the results of League Matches, together with the names of the Players competing therein and Officials, to the League Secretary, within 4 days of each match.   In case of default, a fine of 10/- to be imposed.

THE FOOTBALL LEAGUE.

SEASON 1918-19.

Date of Match _28th April_ 191 9

Home Club _Port Vale_   Visiting Club _Stoke_

Result :—Home Club _4_ Goals, Visiting Club _1_ Goals.

Total No. of Matches Played _6_

Signed _Mitchell_   Secretary of _Port Vale_ Club

TEAM.

Note.—The Surname, with Full initials, must be given.

Goal	_A Hammond_
Backs (Right)	_Jq Lyons_
„ (Left)	_b Fletcher_
Half-Backs (Right)	_a McGarry_
„ (Centre)	_H Pearson_
„ (Left)	_QT Holford_
Forwards (Outside Right)	_Donaldson_
„ (Inside Right)	_R Whittingham_
„ (Centre)	_H Arrell_
„ (Inside Left)	_J Smith_
„ (Outside Left)	_WH Fitchford_

Advertised Time of Kick-off _____

Referee _H Holland_

Linesman _JJ McAter_
F Reid

Any comments for assistance of the Management Committee.

-2- MAY 1919

13. THE VALE REPORT OF THE 28 APRIL 1919 POTTERIES DERBY, as submitted to the Football League.

14. THE STOKE REPORT OF THE 28 APRIL 1919 POTTERIES DERBY, as submitted to the Football League.

15. POTTERIES DERBY ACTION AT THE VICTORIA GROUND, thought to be during the first ever full Football League clash between the two clubs at Stoke, on 13 March 1920.

17. BOB McGRORY, who made 22 appearances for Stoke in the Potteries Derbies between 1921 and 1935.

16. TOM PAGE, who made 17 appearances for Vale in the Potteries Derbies between 1920 and 1928.

18. TOM FERN, who kept a clean sheet for Vale in four consecutive Potteries Derbies played between 20 September 1924 and 7 September 1925.

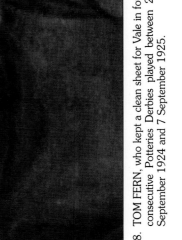

19. WILF KIRKHAM, who scored 8 goals in the Potteries Derbies (7 for Vale, 1 for Stoke) between 1925 and 1930.

21. TOMMY SALE, who scored 10 goals for Stoke in the Potteries Derbies between 1931 and 1945.

20. WATTIE BUSSEY, who scored 5 goals for Stoke in the Potteries Derbies between 1928 and 1931.

23. FREDDIE STEELE, who scored 6 goals for Stoke in the Potteries Derbies between 1936 and 1945.

22. STANLEY MATTHEWS, who scored 5 goals for Stoke in the Potteries Derbies between 1932 and 1936 and tormented Vale's defenders during several matches.

24. THE STOKE TEAM WHICH BEAT VALE 2-0 IN THE FOOTBALL LEAGUE NORTH ON 18 NOVEMBER 1944:
Back Row: Neil Franklin, Frank Mountford, Manny Foster, John McCue, John Jackson, Cyril Watkin.
Front Row: Stanley Matthews, Frank Bowyer, Freddie Steele, Tommy Sale, John Mannion.

25. JOHN McCUE, who made 17 appearances for Stoke in the Potteries Derbies between 1944 and 1959.

26. A caricature of FRANK BOWYER, who made 13 appearances for Stoke in the Potteries Derbies between 1944 and 1959.

27. GEORGE MOUNTFORD, who scored 9 goals for Stoke in two Potteries Derbies within the space of eleven weeks in 1945.

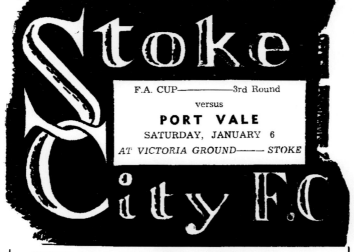

28. THE PROGRAMME OF THE F.A. CUP CLASH BETWEEN STOKE AND VALE ON 6 JANUARY 1951, which attracted the all-time record Potteries Derby crowd of 49,500.

29. HARRY OSCROFT, who made 14 appearances in the Potteries Derbies (11 for Stoke, 3 for Vale) between 1951 and 1961.

30. TOM CHEADLE, the pivot of Vale's famous "Iron Curtain" defence, who appeared in seven consecutive Potteries Derbies between 1951 and 1955.

31. A caricature of ROY SPROSON, who made 15 appearances for Vale in the Potteries Derbies between 1951 and 1970.

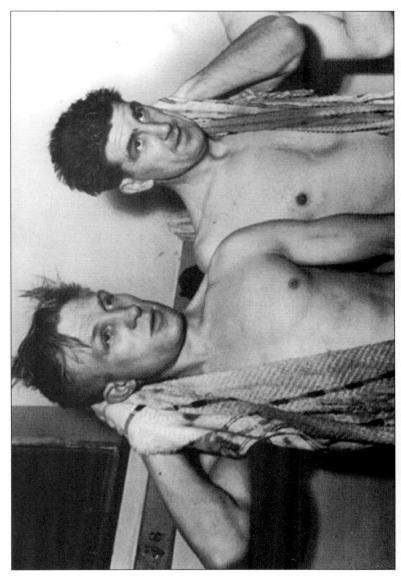

32. STAN TURNER AND REG POTTS, the regular full-backs in Vale's "Iron Curtain" defence, who helped the visitors to gain a 0-0 draw at Stoke on 4 September 1954 in the first full Football League local Derby for over 21 years.

33. KEN GRIFFITHS, whose goal for Vale in a 1-1 draw at Stoke on 31 March 1956 kept them in the Second Division promotion race.

34. TIM COLEMAN (second from the right) shoots past Vale's goalkeeper, RAY KING, during Stoke's 3-1 home win on 10 October 1956. This was the first league game played under Stoke's newly-installed £15,000 floodlights.

36. JIMMY O'NEILL, the Stoke keeper, whose own goal clinched the Supporters' Clubs' Trophy for Vale at the Victoria Ground on 24 April 1961.

35. AN ADMISSION TICKET TO THE BOXING DAY 1956 POTTERIES DERBY, which was postponed because of up to five inches of lying snow on the pitch at Vale Park. The match was in the event played on 29 April 1957.

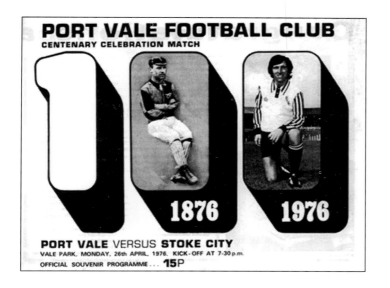

38. THE PROGRAMME OF THE FRIENDLY MATCH ON 26 APRIL 1976 TO CELEBRATE VALE'S CENTENARY.

37. BOBBY GOUGH, who scored the winning goal in Vale's surprise 3-2 victory at Stoke in a friendly match on 1 May 1970.

40. LEE CHAPMAN, who scored a hat trick for Stoke in a 3-2 home win against Vale in a Wedgwood Trophy match on 21 April 1982.

39. JEFF COOK, who scored a hat trick for Stoke in a 6-1 win at Vale in a friendly match on 14 August 1981.

41. MARK HARRISON AND MARK CHAMBERLAIN, who were transferred from Vale to Stoke for a combined fee of £181,000 after impressing in a pre-season Potteries Derby on 13 August 1982.

42. DAVID RILEY AND TONY HENRY in action in a friendly match at Vale Park on 16 August 1988, which resulted in Vale's first Potteries Derby victory for over eighteen years.

43. ROBBIE EARLE AND CHRIS KAMARA shake hands on 23 September 1989 before the start of the first Football League Potteries Derby for over thirty-two years.

44. SIMON MILLS, who was inspirational in midfield for Vale in their 1-1 draw at Stoke in the league on 23 September 1989.

45. NEIL ASPIN, who made 13 appearances for Vale in the Potteries Derbies between 1989 and 1997.

46. DEAN GLOVER, who made 12 full appearances and 1 as a substitute for Vale in the Potteries Derbies between 1989 and 1998.

47. RAY WALKER AND PAUL WARE in action during Stoke's 2-1 home win against Vale in the league on 24 October 1992.

48. JOHN RUDGE, the manager who masterminded Vale to five victories against Stoke in competitive matches between 1992 and 1996.

49. ROBIN VAN DER LAAN, who scored Vale's goal in a 1-0 victory at Stoke in a Southern Area semi-final of the Autoglass Trophy on 3 March 1993. Vale went on to win the trophy.

50. MARK STEIN (centre) wheels away after scoring Stoke's first goal in their vital 2-0 league victory at Vale on 31 March 1993. Stoke went on to win the Second Division championship that season.

51. MARTIN FOYLE (by the right-hand goalpost) celebrates after scoring Vale's goal in a 1-0 victory at Stoke on 22 April 1995, which was their first league win at the Victoria Ground since 1927.

52. ANDY PORTER (who made 12 full appearances in the Potteries Derbies between 1988 and 1998) leads Vale out to play Stoke at home in a league match on 12 March 1996.

53. IAN BOGIE scores for Vale after just twelve seconds to notch the only goal of their match at home to Stoke on 12 March 1996, which completed their first league double over their local rivals since 1925.

54. A MELEE during the last ever Potteries Derby played at the Victoria Ground, on 20 April 1997.

55. MIKE SHERON (far right) celebrates after scoring the last ever Potteries Derby goal at the Victoria Ground, during Stoke's 2-0 league win on 20 April 1997.

56. RICHARD FORSYTH (right) receives the congratulations of KEVIN KEEN (left) after scoring the first ever Potteries Derby goal at the Britannia Stadium, during Stoke's 2-1 league win on 12 October 1997.

57. ANDY HILL AND PETER THORNE in action during Stoke's 2-1 home win in the league on 12 October 1997.

87: MONDAY 28 APRIL 1919, FOOTBALL LEAGUE, LANCASHIRE REGIONAL SECTION, SUBSIDIARY TOURNAMENT

PORT VALE (1) 4 (Howell 2, Smart o.g., Joe Smith), STOKE (0) 1 (Herbert).

VALE: Hammond, Lyons, Fletcher, A. McGarry, H. Pearson, Holford, Donaldson, Whittingham, Howell, Joe Smith, Fitchford.
STOKE: Morris, Smart, Twemlow, J. Jones, C. Parker (Turner), H. Wootton, Harrison, Phillips, Boxley, Herbert, Tempest.

Venue: The Old Recreation Ground, Hanley.
Attendance: 16,000.
Referee: H. Holland (Stockport).

THE SETTING

Vale were faring badly in the Subsidiary Tournament, having gained just one point from their first five matches, and had lost 4-1 at Manchester City on the Saturday before the local Derby, whilst Stoke had beaten Manchester United 4-2 at home on the same day to accumulate six points from their first five games. Vale made five team changes and included five guest players in their line-up for the Derby, two of whom (Bob Whittingham and Harry Howell) had previously rendered sterling service for their local rivals. Stoke themselves were somewhat under full strength because of injuries.

THE MATCH

Although Stoke had the better of the early play, especially through the forceful runs and accurate centres of Harrison, their inside-forwards failed to make much of the opportunities he created. This proved costly because Parker was carried off with an ankle injury and Vale then naturally gained the upper hand against their ten opponents. They took the lead after twenty-six minutes when Howell deftly headed in a cross from Fitchford, but they sportingly then allowed Stoke to send on a substitute, Turner.

After the interval, Stoke pressed strongly, but the home team went further ahead when Smart deflected a free kick from Whittingham into his own net, although Smith then squandered a penalty by kicking the ball straight at the Stoke keeper. However, Smith made amends by converting a Donaldson centre and Howell added a fourth goal for Vale, but Herbert reduced the arrears near the end with a low drive.

THE AFTERMATH

The collection of £300 in gate receipts helped to soften the blow to Vale of ending up bottom (out of four teams) of Section C of the Subsidiary Tournament, whilst Stoke finished second. Far more important to both clubs were the summer preparations for the resumption of league football proper the following season. Vale signed three players 'of proven ability' (Peter Pursell, for £2,500 from Rangers, Willie Aitken and Robert Waine) to boost their chances in the Central League, whilst Stoke acquired George Jarvis from Celtic and Jock Stirling from Bradford City to assist them upon their return to the Football League.

88: MONDAY 6 OCTOBER 1919, FRIENDLY

PORT VALE (2) 5 (Lockett 3, Briscoe, Hill), STOKE (0) 0.

VALE: Bourne, Ellis, Pursell, McGarry, Pearson, Holford, Aitken, Lockett, Briscoe, Dyke, Hill.
STOKE: Morris, Taylor, Twemlow, Wootton, Goodwin, Smith, Wainwright, Phillips, Martin, Herbert, Bassett.

Venue: The Old Recreation Ground, Hanley.
Attendance: About 4,000.
Referee: F. Leigh (Hanley).

THE SETTING
This game was played as a benefit for Vale's long serving centre-half, Harry Pearson. Vale were third in the Central League, a point behind the leaders but with a match in hand. However, they had lost their unbeaten record with a 3-2 defeat at Manchester United Reserves nine days before the local Derby. Stoke were also performing well and were in fifth position in the Second Division, a single point adrift of a promotion place. They had gained a creditable 1-1 draw at West Ham United two days before the Derby, for which they fielded seven reserves. Vale, however, selected a strong side for the occasion in recognition of Harry Pearson's important contribution to the club.

THE MATCH
The match was played in a good spirit and Vale passed the ball around impressively, whilst Aitken and Hill produced exciting wing play throughout the entire game. In the tenth minute, Lockett hit a post with a tremendous shot for Vale and nine minutes later put them in front after Hill had created the opening. The home side continued to press strongly and Briscoe doubled their lead with a beautiful angled volley in the twenty-eighth minute, although Smith forced the Vale keeper into an excellent save to show that Stoke still posed a threat.

After the interval, Stoke attacked vigorously and both Phillips and Herbert went close, but Pursell made a series of 'masterly' interceptions to relieve the home defence. In due course, Vale stepped up their efforts and in the sixty-fifth minute Aitken put the ball on a plate for Lockett to add a third goal. Hill then twice squandered opportunities to extend Vale's lead, although Lockett completed his hat trick by heading in from a corner ten minutes from time. The scoring was completed right at the death when Lockett rolled the ball back for Hill to drive home and secure for Vale their equal largest ever local Derby victory.

THE AFTERMATH
There was a remarkable development just a week after the local Derby when Leeds City were expelled from the Football League amidst allegations of illegal payments and Vale were elected to take their place in the Second Division. Vale's consequent elation was barely dampened by the 2-0 defeat they suffered at fifth from the bottom South Shields in their first match on 18 October. After the Derby, Stoke gained two points from two league games against Stockport County, which provided good preparation for a Staffordshire Cup tie against Vale scheduled for 20 October.

106

89: MONDAY 20 OCTOBER 1919, STAFFORDSHIRE CUP, FIRST ROUND

PORT VALE (1) 1 (Hill), STOKE (0) 0.

VALE: Hammond, Ellis, Pursell, McGarry, Perry, Newton, Aitken, Lockett, Briscoe, Holford, Hill.
STOKE: Kay, Smart, Twemlow, Clarke, Jones, Smith, Stirling, Phillips, Boxley, Martin, Page.

Venue: The Old Recreation Ground, Hanley.
Attendance: More than 8,000.
Referee: H. Pollitt (Manchester).

THE SETTING

Vale had sensationally been elected to the Second Division just a week before the local Derby and were required to fulfil the fixtures of Leeds City, who had been expelled from the Football League for failing to answer allegations of illegal payments. However, Vale had lost their opening match by 2-0 at fifth from the bottom South Shields on the Saturday prior to the Derby. Stoke were in seventh position in the division, but had been defeated 3-1 at Stockport County on the same day. Both clubs fielded strong sides for the local clash, although Vale were without their usual right-back, Lyons, whilst Stoke were weakened by the absence of Milne, a regular defender, and Herbert, their normal inside-left.

THE MATCH

Vale attacked from the outset and went in front after only four minutes when Hill shot the ball in from a scrimmage. Shortly afterwards, McGarry hit the bar and the Stoke defenders resorted to 'some wild kicking' to relieve the relentless pressure. Although the visitors began to fight back, Vale were awarded a penalty when Briscoe was tripped in the area by Smith, but Ellis could only strike the bar from the spot kick. Play then became more even, but just before the interval, Holford squandered a good opportunity to extend Vale's lead by firing wide with only the keeper to beat.

After half-time, Vale continued to dominate, but the visitors almost equalised when Clarke hit a tremendous shot just wide. Nevertheless, it was Vale who looked the more likely to score and strong wing runs by Hill created continual danger, whilst Stoke's custodian smothered a goal-bound effort from Briscoe. Kay was kept active by the Vale forwards, but the closest they came to increasing their lead was near the end when Lockett blasted the ball into the side netting.

THE AFTERMATH

Although Vale went on to win the cup, they found the Second Division a struggle and won only three of their first fifteen matches in spite of their purchase in November of the hard-shooting centre-forward, Bob Blood, for £50 from Leek Alexandra. Stoke were reinforced by the capture of two fine forwards, Bob Whittingham and David Brown, shortly after the Derby and five consecutive league victories temporarily pushed them up into second place before they fell away badly.

90: SATURDAY 6 MARCH 1920, FOOTBALL LEAGUE, SECOND DIVISION

PORT VALE (0) 0, STOKE (2) 3 (Whittingham, Watkin, Brown).

VALE: Bourne, Lyons, Pursell, McGarry, Perry, Holford, Aitken, Brough, Blood, Fitchford, Hill.

STOKE: Kay, Maddock, Twemlow, Jarvis, Jones, Clarke, Crossthwaite, Whittingham, Brown, Watkin, Tempest.

Venue: The Old Recreation Ground, Hanley.
Attendance: 22,697.
Referee: E.H. Spiers (Redditch).

THE SETTING

This was the first ever full Football League Potteries Derby and it attracted the all-time record crowd at the Old Recreation Ground and a then record attendance for a local Derby. Vale were eleventh in the Second Division and had won five of their previous seven matches to make up for a sluggish start after they'd been elected into the league in October 1919. A week before the Derby, they had beaten sixth from the bottom Rotherham County 4-2 at home, with centre-forward Blood scoring all their goals. Stoke were in sixth position, but were seven points off the promotion pace and had played more games than their key rivals. They had lost their last match 1-0 at Bury the previous Saturday, but had since signed a new right winger, Harry Crossthwaite, from Stockport County for a then club record fee. Vale were strengthened for the local clash by the return of Holford, Brough and Hill to their team, whilst Crossthwaite made his debut for Stoke and Watkin regained his place after recovering from a long-term injury. The turnstiles were closed an hour before the scheduled starting time and thousands of people were turned away.

THE MATCH

The game began a quarter of an hour early to reduce the impact of the rain on the spectators, a large group of whom were gathered on top of the Supporters' Stand, whilst clusters of others peered from the roofs of houses outside the ground! Vale had the better of the early play and Aitken shot just wide before Whittingham thundered a twenty-yard drive into the net to put the visitors in front after seventeen minutes. Vale then swarmed around the Stoke goal, but the visitors extended their lead in the thirty-third minute when Crossthwaite centred for Watkin to turn the ball in. The home side continued to push forward, although they found the Stoke rearguard to be impenetrable.

Vale plugged away after the interval, but were still unable to effect a breakthrough and, in a rare Stoke attack, Brown kicked the ball out of Bourne's hands and over the line to add to their tally. Vale pressed none the less strongly thereafter, although a decisive finish remained elusive.

THE AFTERMATH

Vale sank to thirteenth place in the league as a result of their defeat, whilst Stoke's success pushed them up to fifth and after the match the two clubs began their preparations for the return the following Saturday.

91: SATURDAY 13 MARCH 1920, FOOTBALL LEAGUE, SECOND DIVISION

STOKE (0) 0, PORT VALE (0) 0.

STOKE: Kay, Maddock, Twemlow, Jarvis, Jones, Smith, Crossthwaite, Whittingham, Brown, Watkin, Tempest.
VALE: Bourne, Lyons, Pursell, McGarry, Perry, Holford, Aitken, Brough, Briscoe, Fitchford, Wootton.

Venue: The Victoria Ground, Stoke-upon-Trent.
Attendance: Approximately 27,000.
Referee: E.H. Spiers (Redditch).

THE SETTING

This match was the first ever full Football League Potteries Derby to be played at Stoke. As a result of their 3-0 victory at Vale a week previously, Stoke had climbed to fifth position in the Second Division, albeit six points adrift of a promotion place and having played more games than their key rivals. Vale had dropped two places to thirteenth, but were well clear of the danger zone. Stoke fielded an unchanged side for the return Derby, with the exception that their left-half, Clarke, was absent because of a bereavement. Vale were without the services of their regular centre-forward, Blood, who had been injured towards the end of the last match, and Wootton was selected instead of Hill on the left wing. A new record local Derby crowd gathered to witness the clash and created a tremendous din with their bells.

THE MATCH

Stoke won the toss and chose to kick with the advantage of a strong wind. They quickly got into their stride and Brown hit a post from a corner, although Aitken ballooned the ball over the bar when presented with a good opportunity for the visitors. However, Stoke dominated the play and after Watkin, Whittingham and Brown had all gone close, McGarry handled a Crossthwaite centre to give them a penalty. Although Twemlow struck the kick like a rocket, the visiting keeper caught the ball brilliantly, which greatly spurred Vale on and four minutes before half-time Brough had a goal disallowed.

With the wind at their backs, Vale attacked strongly after the interval, but were unable to 'hit the mark for toffee'! Brough skied the ball over the bar to ruin two marvellous opportunities, whilst Kay pulled off two wonderful saves to deny Fitchford. Although Vale continued to press for the winner, they proved unable to make the breakthrough.

THE AFTERMATH

The magnificent crowd yielded gate receipts of over £1,600, which went a long way to make up for Stoke's failure to close the gap on the leading teams. However, their promotion challenge faded altogether as they won only two of their remaining ten games and finished in tenth position. Vale's point from the local Derby did not prevent them from dropping a place in the table, but four victories in their final ten matches were sufficient to enable them to end up a highly satisfactory thirteenth in their first season back in the league.

92: MONDAY 3 MAY 1920, NORTH STAFFORDSHIRE INFIRMARY CUP

STOKE (0) 0, PORT VALE (0) 0.

STOKE: Kay, Maddock, Milne, Clarke, Parker, Smith, Crossthwaite, Brown, Jarvis, Watkin, Tempest.
VALE: Bourne, Lyons, Pursell, McGarry, Perry, Holford, Aitken, Brough, Blood, Briscoe, Wootton.

Venue: The Victoria Ground, Stoke-upon-Trent.
Attendance: Between 4,000 and 5,000.
Referee: I. Baker (Crewe).

THE SETTING

This resurrected cup competition had been trimmed down in size so that it was thenceforth contested only by Stoke and Vale. Stoke had fallen away in the last month of the season to finish a disappointing tenth in the Second Division, although they had won their final match 3-0 at home to fourth from the bottom Wolverhampton Wanderers on the Saturday before the local Derby. Vale had completed their league programme on the same day with a 4-0 hammering at sixth-placed Fulham, which had left them a respectable thirteenth in the table. Both clubs fielded their strongest available teams for the Derby, with Stoke's secretary-manager, Arthur Shallcross, replacing Boxley with Jarvis at centre-forward, whilst Vale were entirely unchanged from their previous game.

THE MATCH

The match was closely contested and played in a good spirit, with some interesting football exhibited. Stoke had the better of the early exchanges, although the visitors were the first to pose a serious threat when Brough broke through, but he shot wide from a very favourable position. Watkin then spurned a golden opportunity to head Stoke in front from a Crossthwaite centre, whilst Parker came within an ace of scoring two minutes before the interval.

Soon after the resumption of play, the Vale keeper saved a snap-shot by Watkin at the second attempt, but the visitors then pressed strongly and both Aitken and Wootton struck hard drives wide of the mark. Stoke retaliated with Crossthwaite and Tempest supplying a stream of crosses, but these were all cleared by the visiting defenders. In the closing stages, Vale dominated the proceedings, although they were no more successful in breaking through their opponents' defence.

THE AFTERMATH

As a result of the draw, the trophy was shared by the two clubs and the hospital gained £309 in funds raised at the gate. Nevertheless, a week after the local Derby, Stoke were disappointed to lose 3-0 at Birmingham (who had finished third in the Second Division) in the final of the Birmingham Cup in their last game of the season. However, Vale secured the Staffordshire Cup on 15 May by beating Birmingham Reserves 1-0 in the final of the competition at the Victoria Ground.

93: SATURDAY 25 SEPTEMBER 1920, FOOTBALL LEAGUE, SECOND DIVISION

PORT VALE (2) 2 (Page, Briscoe), STOKE (1) 1 (McColl).

VALE: Bourne, Lyons, R. Pursell, Brough, P. Pursell, Holford, Price, Page, Blood, Briscoe, Fitchford.
STOKE: Kay, Brittleton, Milne, Clarke, Parker, Smith, Crossthwaite, Brown, McColl, Watkin, Tempest.

Venue: The Old Recreation Ground, Hanley.
Attendance: 20,000.
Referee: E. Shutt (Burnley).

THE SETTING
Although Vale were eleventh in the Second Division, they had not won since their opening match. Nevertheless, they had gained a 1-1 draw at Rotherham County a week before the local Derby. In contrast, Stoke had begun the 1920-1921 season in fine style, undefeated in their first five games, and were second in the table. However, their unbeaten run had ended with a 1-0 home defeat by fourth from the bottom Sheffield Wednesday on the Saturday prior to the Derby. Peter Pursell was selected for the local clash by Joe Schofield, the Vale secretary-manager, and Fitchford replaced Wootton, who was unwell, but Stoke were unchanged from their previous match. The bright sunshine attracted a large and boisterous crowd, who were well armed with rattles, although it was believed that many people had stayed away to avoid being crushed in Vale's small ground.

THE MATCH
Both sides opened tentatively and the initial play was scrappy, but McColl soon struck a post for Stoke. The visitors continued to press and Tempest also had bad luck when he cut in from the left wing and thumped a shot against the bar after twenty minutes. However, Tempest was instrumental in Stoke taking the lead just five minutes later when he centred the ball perfectly to enable McColl to walk it over the line. This spurred Vale into action and only two more minutes passed before a flowing move gave Page the chance to lash the ball into the roof of the net for the equaliser. Then, shortly before the interval, they went in front through Briscoe, who squeezed a shot in from an acute angle.

Vale began the second half on top, although the visitors eventually gained the ascendancy and Brown seemed certain to level the score, but Lyons flung his body in the way of the shot. Vale then retained possession for long periods and took the sting out of the game, although the Stoke players clamoured for a penalty at the death when the ball appeared to strike Lyons' hand.

THE AFTERMATH
Vale moved up one position in the division as a result of their success, whilst Stoke tumbled six places, to eighth. The return Derby was scheduled for the following Saturday and the Stoke players prepared for it with a visit to Nantwich brine baths for massage treatment.

94: SATURDAY 2 OCTOBER 1920, FOOTBALL LEAGUE, SECOND DIVISION

STOKE (0) 0, PORT VALE (0) 1 (Blood).

STOKE: Kay, Brittleton, Milne, Clarke, Parkes, Smith, L. Page, Brown, Watkin, McColl, Tempest.
VALE: Bourne, Lyons, R. Pursell, Brough, P. Pursell, Holford, Price, T. Page, Blood, Briscoe, Fitchford.

Venue: The Victoria Ground, Stoke-upon-Trent.
Attendance: 27,455.
Referee: E. Shutt (Burnley).

THE SETTING

Stoke had dropped from second position to eighth in the Second Division as a result of their 2-1 defeat at Vale the Saturday before the return local Derby. Vale had moved up only one place, to tenth, as a result of their victory, but were below their old rivals only on goal average. Stoke were without their regular centre-half, Parker, who had sustained a leg injury in the first meeting, whilst Louis Page was tried at outside-right instead of Crossthwaite. Not surprisingly, in view of their success a week earlier, Vale were unchanged. The local railways were hard-pressed to transport the hordes of spectators to the match and a crowd of 15,000 had already assembled an hour before the kickoff, whilst the final number constituted a new local Derby record.

THE MATCH

Vale showed a tremendous spirit and work rate throughout the match and defended stoutly when under pressure, with Bob and Peter Pursell and Lyons inspirational. In contrast, the Stoke half-backs tended to kick the ball too far ahead of their forwards, whilst at times some of their players 'wandered badly'. Nevertheless, the game was played in a sporting manner on an excellent pitch and Stoke gave the visiting keeper plenty to think about in the first period. McColl drove the ball over the bar for the home team when presented with a fine opportunity, whilst the Vale forwards persisted in straying offside and Brough shot weakly when well placed just before half-time.

Almost immediately after the interval, Brittleton injured his head and retired for ten minutes for attention, as a result of which Vale took command. Kay came to the rescue for Stoke to prevent Milne from scoring an own goal and to deny Price, but in the sixty-third minute Blood headed the visitors into the lead. It then began to pour down with rain and although Stoke tried hard to equalise, it was Vale who proved the more dangerous with Price hitting a post just before the whistle.

THE AFTERMATH

As a result of their third consecutive defeat, Stoke fell to twelfth position in the table, whilst Vale climbed to fifth. However, both sides fared badly during most of the rest of the season. Both exited from the English Cup at the first hurdle and Stoke finished third from the bottom of the league, whilst Vale ended up just three places and one point better off.

95: MONDAY 9 MAY 1921, NORTH STAFFORDSHIRE INFIRMARY CUP

PORT VALE (1) 3 (Briscoe 2, Hayes), STOKE (2) 5 (Tempest 2 [1 pen.], Watkin, Spencer, Dickie).

VALE: Bourne, Holford, Birks, Brough, Collinge, Perry, Crook, Page, Evans, Hayes, Briscoe.
STOKE: Steventon, McGrory, Milne, Brittleton, Clarke, Dickie, Spencer, Smith, Whitehurst, Watkin, Tempest.

Venue: The Old Recreation Ground, Hanley.
Attendance: Not more than 3,000 or 4,000.
Referee: I. Baker (Crewe).

THE SETTING
Vale had completed their Second Division programme on the Saturday before the local Derby with a 2-0 home defeat against the already promoted league leaders, Birmingham. This had left the Valiants in seventeenth place and just a single point clear of the penultimate team. Stoke had fared even worse and only goal average had prevented them from finishing second from the bottom of the same division. In addition, they had lost 1-0 at struggling Barnsley two days prior to the Derby to end their campaign on a depressing note. Vale were forced to make no fewer than six alterations in their line-up from their last match because of injuries and travelling problems, but Stoke were unchanged.

THE MATCH
The initial ten minutes' play was rather uneventful, although Tempest shot well wide for Stoke when presented with an excellent opportunity. As the contest livened up, Smith handled the ball when he only had to chest it into the net, but after twelve minutes Stoke went in front through Tempest, who squeezed a firm drive inside a post. Two minutes later, Watkin seized upon a weak back-pass by Holford and doubled the visitors' advantage. After half an hour, the unmarked Evans and Hayes dithered too long with only the Stoke keeper to beat, but Vale reduced the arrears five minutes before the break with a shot by Briscoe. Then the latter was upended in the penalty area, but Page fired the spot kick wide.

Vale equalised five minutes into the second period through an acute-angled rocket shot by Hayes and took the lead after fifty-five minutes when Briscoe placed the ball beyond the visiting keeper's reach. However, Tempest put Stoke level with a penalty fifteen minutes from the end, whilst Spencer slipped the ball inside a post in the eighty-fifth minute and Dickie completed a remarkable comeback by the visitors by prodding home from a scrimmage with two minutes remaining.

THE AFTERMATH
In spite of their problems on the playing front, Vale made a profit of £1,187 3s. 11d. on the season and £1,000 of this was spent on acquiring the services of Jack Hampson, a half-back from Aston Villa. Stoke also strengthened their team in the close season, especially with the purchase of the forwards Tommy and Jimmy Broad at a total cost of £3,000.

96: SATURDAY 24 SEPTEMBER 1921, FOOTBALL LEAGUE, SECOND DIVISION

STOKE (0) 0, PORT VALE (0) 0.

STOKE: Lee, McGrory, Milne, Clarke, Beswick, A.R. Smith, T. Broad, Shore, J. Broad, Watkin, Tempest.
VALE: W. Smith, Twemlow, P. Pursell, Collinge, Connelly, Hampson, Firth, Page, Agnew, Pearson, Briscoe.

Venue: The Victoria Ground, Stoke-upon-Trent.
Attendance: Nearly 30,000.
Referee: H. Rylance (Earlestown).

THE SETTING
Stoke were in twelfth position in the Second Division, but had lost their last league match 1-0 at Clapton Orient a week before the local Derby. Vale were struggling, sixth from the bottom, having suffered defeat in four of their opening five matches, although they had won their most recent game 2-1 at home to West Ham United on the Saturday prior to the Derby. To 'foster the friendly spirit already existing between the two clubs', the directors of both had had dinner together at the North Stafford Hotel the night before the match! Stoke were unchanged from their previous game, apart from introducing their new goalkeeper, John Lee, whilst Vale also made just one alteration, at right-back, and appeared in new white shirts, on which the letters "P.V.F.C." were displayed in red silk.

THE MATCH
A new record local Derby crowd assembled to see Stoke initially kick with the advantage of the wind and have more of the early play, but the exchanges were generally scrappy. As the teams settled down, the football became more flowing and Jimmy Broad shot just wide for Stoke. In due course, Vale came more into contention and Page was presented with a scoring opportunity, but hastily shot wide. The home keeper twice made good saves to keep the match goalless, whilst both Briscoe and Page fired over the bar when well placed.

The second half began at a cracking pace and Firth wildly shot wide for Vale before Watkin came within an ace of putting the home side ahead with a tremendous strike which hit the base of a post. This served only to increase the tempo further, but the best efforts of both teams were spoiled by erratic shooting. Nevertheless, Stoke strove hard to snatch the winner and Jimmy Broad thumped a terrific drive just wide, whilst Beswick saw a powerful effort glance a post. However, at the final whistle, the deadlock remained unbroken.

THE AFTERMATH
The hard-earned point proved to be of benefit to both clubs because it pushed Stoke up one place to eleventh in the table and Vale likewise to sixteenth. There was also the prospect of at least one of the Potteries sides making further progress the following Saturday, on which the return local Derby was due to be played.

97: SATURDAY 1 OCTOBER 1921, FOOTBALL LEAGUE, SECOND DIVISION

PORT VALE (0) 0, STOKE (1) 1 (J. Broad).

VALE: W. Smith, Twemlow, P. Pursell, Collinge, Connelly, Hampson, Firth, Page, Agnew, Lauder, Briscoe.
STOKE: Lee, McGrory, Milne, Clarke, Beswick, A.R. Smith, T. Broad, Shore, J. Broad, Watkin, Tempest.

Venue: The Old Recreation Ground, Hanley.
Attendance: Well over 20,000.
Referee: H. Rylance (Earlestown).

THE SETTING
Vale had risen one place in the league, to sixteenth, as a result of the point they had gained in a goalless draw at Stoke the previous Saturday. The draw had also enabled Stoke to climb one position, to eleventh. The two teams were unchanged from their last clash, except that Vale's secretary-manager, Joe Schofield, replaced Pearson with Alex Lauder, a trialist from Partick Thistle, at inside-left. Fine weather conditions helped to attract a crowd estimated at over 20,000 at the kickoff, with many of the Stoke supporters carrying red and white celluloid dolls. Spectators hung from telegraph poles overlooking the pitch and a tremendous roar greeted the arrival of the two sides on the field.

THE MATCH
Vale dominated the initial play, but the first real opportunity fell to the visitors when Tommy Broad shot weakly wide with only the keeper to beat. His brother, Jimmy, then went close with a tremendous effort, although Vale began to exert their authority and Page became a constant danger, forcing the visiting custodian to make several smart saves, shooting inches wide and then striking an upright with a header. However, this merely proved the prelude to Stoke taking the lead midway through the half with their very next attack when Jimmy Broad thumped a direct free kick straight into the net. Vale were stung into even greater efforts and Lee made a superb save from an Agnew hook shot, whilst Page skimmed the bar.

Vale pressed hard after the interval in search of an equaliser, but their shooting was erratic and the visitors almost went further in front when Jimmy Broad forced the home keeper to push the ball round a post. The play became more even in the latter stages, but Vale were unable to level the score, although Firth spurned an excellent chance.

THE AFTERMATH
The marvellous crowd produced gate receipts of £1,200, which helped to soften the blow of Vale's defeat and their drop in the table to third from the bottom. Although Alex Lauder impressed sufficiently to be signed permanently for £300 the following month, Vale continued to struggle and won only three of their next seventeen league matches, which left them adrift at the bottom. However, Stoke's local Derby victory lifted them into ninth place, whilst their steady, if unspectacular, form took them into a promotion-challenging seventh position by the end of the year.

98: SATURDAY 7 JANUARY 1922, ENGLISH CUP, FIRST ROUND

PORT VALE (1) 2 (Page, Brough), STOKE (2) 4 (Watkin 3, Tempest).

VALE: Peers, Twemlow, R. Pursell, Collinge, P. Pursell, Holford, Firth, Brough, Connelly, Page, Pearson.
STOKE: Lee, McGrory, Milne, Clarke, Beswick, Brittleton, T. Broad, Groves, J. Broad, Watkin, Tempest.

Venue: The Old Recreation Ground, Hanley.
Attendance: 14,471.
Referee: S. Rothwell (St. Annes).

THE SETTING

Vale were in penultimate position in the Second Division and had been hammered 4-1 at fourth from the bottom Coventry City a week before the local Derby. Stoke, however, were seventh, and had drawn 1-1 at home to Sheffield Wednesday on the same day. Vale made four changes in their line-up from their last game and included a new goalkeeper, Teddy Peers, a Welsh international signed from Wolverhampton Wanderers to replace the injured regular custodian, Smith. Stoke's secretary-manager, Arthur Shallcross, preferred to make just one alteration and welcomed back his usual centre-half, Beswick, who had recovered from an injury. The crowd appeared surprisingly subdued until the band encouraged the Vale supporters to take up their song, "The Port Vale War-Cry".

THE MATCH

The match began at a furious pace and Stoke did most of the early attacking. Although the visitors threatened to open the scoring several times, the game remained goalless until the thirty-fourth minute when Watkin finished a marvellous solo run with a fine low drive to put Stoke ahead. They extended their lead just four minutes later, with Tempest firing in an acute-angled shot during a melee in the home goalmouth, although Page reduced the arrears from a header only two minutes afterwards.

Stoke opened the second period brightly, but the home side were unlucky not to equalise when Page hit a post. However, in the fifty-third minute, Watkin converted a centre by Tommy Broad to put Stoke further in front and shortly afterwards Tempest raced in to strike a post with a terrific shot. Vale began to flag and Watkin converted a rebound in the seventy-fourth minute to complete his hat trick. Nevertheless, Vale salvaged some pride when Brough headed in from a corner ten minutes from time.

THE AFTERMATH

Although the size of the crowd had been rather disappointing, a useful £1,138 15s. was taken at the gate. Better things still were ahead for Stoke, who reached the third round of the cup and drew a then club record home attendance of 43,689 against Aston Villa before being eliminated after a replay by their First Division opponents. Even more importantly, they finished their league campaign as runners-up and thereby gained promotion to the top flight, whilst Vale at least staged a major recovery to end up eighteenth and avoid the drop.

99: TUESDAY 9 MAY 1922, NORTH STAFFORDSHIRE INFIRMARY CUP

STOKE (0) 0, PORT VALE (0) 0.

STOKE: Lee, McGrory, Milne, Clarke, Massey, Smith, Twemlow, Groves, Whitehurst, Watkin, Tempest.
VALE: Peers, Birks, P. Pursell, E. Collinge, Hampson, Briscoe, Firth, Page, Cartledge, Fitchford, Holford.

Venue: The Victoria Ground, Stoke-upon-Trent.
Attendance: About 3,000.
Referee: D.H. Asson (West Bromwich).

THE SETTING

Stoke had beaten second from the bottom Bristol City 3-0 at home in their final match, on the Saturday before the local Derby, to secure the runners-up spot in the Second Division and thereby gain promotion. Whilst Stoke were thus basking in glory, Vale had lost 2-0 on the same day at the bottom club, Bradford Park Avenue, and had finished eighteenth. Stoke's secretary-manager, Arthur Shallcross, selected eight of his promotion-winning side plus three reserves for the Derby, whilst Vale also fielded a strong line-up.

THE MATCH

Neither team played flat out, but some 'interesting football' was exhibited and the contest 'ended amicably' in a goalless draw, largely because both sets of forwards failed to take advantage of the many scoring opportunities that were created. The first of these occurred in only the third minute when Peers made an almost miraculous save from a swerving shot by Groves. The Vale keeper later denied Whitehurst, who tried to glance the ball in, whilst the visitors also had their moments in the first half, especially when a Cartledge drive skimmed the Stoke bar and a Fitchford header was brilliantly saved by Lee.

The second period witnessed a number of glaring misses, in particular when Whitehurst and Watkin got in each other's way with only the Vale keeper to beat. Then Cartledge missed a simple chance for the visitors and fired the ball way off target. Nevertheless, both defences were on top form and it was their excellence as much as the forwards' failures that prevented the deadlock from being broken.

THE AFTERMATH

Neither side wished to play extra time nor to decide the outcome in a replay and so it was agreed that the trophy should be shared. The attendance and the gate receipts were considered a little disappointing, but at least the hospital received a financial return. John Lee and Charlie Twemlow were amongst the Stoke players released at the end of the season and only three newcomers were signed from Football League clubs in readiness for the big First Division test, although a number of ground improvements were carried out. Robert Firth and Frank Cartledge were freed by Vale and their four main summer signings were all forwards, although none was particularly eminent.

100: MONDAY 7 MAY 1923, NORTH STAFFORD-SHIRE INFIRMARY CUP

STOKE (1) 3 (J. Broad 2, Davies), PORT VALE (1) 1 (Thompson).

STOKE: Dixon, McGrory, Lennon, Brough, Kasher, Rouse, Rutherford, Davies, J. Broad, J. Smith, Nicholas.
VALE: Peers, Twemlow, Pursell, Gordon, Connelly, Collinge, Harrison, Thompson, Reid, Butler, Prince.

Venue: The Victoria Ground, Stoke-upon-Trent.
Attendance: Unknown.
Referee: D.H. Asson (West Bromwich).

THE SETTING
Stoke had finished second from the bottom of the First Division and had been relegated. The result of their final match, a 1-0 defeat at Liverpool (who were already the champions) two days before the local Derby, had made no difference to their fate, which was already sealed. Vale had fared only marginally better in ending up sixth from the bottom in the Second Division and escaping the drop by just two points. At least they had finished their campaign with a 2-2 home draw against seventh-placed Sheffield Wednesday on the Saturday prior to the Derby. Although both sides fielded strong teams with a smattering of reserves for the local clash, Stoke's new secretary-manager, Jock Rutherford, selected himself and Joe Smith, the captain of the English Cup winners, Bolton Wanderers, was also included in their line-up.

THE MATCH
A larger crowd than had been attracted by the previous year's fixture assembled to see a contest more notable for its 'delightful touches' than the players' fighting spirit. Nevertheless, the match started sensationally with Broad converting a left-wing centre for Stoke in their very first attack. However, Vale equalised when Thompson ran clean through the opposing defence and coolly drilled the ball past the home keeper.

Stoke regained the lead in the second period as a result of Broad firing home an accurate long drive and they then made the game safe through a left-foot hook shot by Davies during a spell of intense pressure on the Vale goal.

THE AFTERMATH
The cup was presented to the winning team in the Directors' Pavilion and the Stoke players each received a Copeland plaque, whilst those of Vale were given a Wedgwood jasper flowerpot. The gross gate receipts of £250 enabled a more substantial sum to be donated to the infirmary than had been the previous year and it was one which Stoke could have well done with themselves because the following month they announced a then club record loss of £2,223 10s. 9d. on the past season. Not surprisingly, they had little money available with which to strengthen their team in the summer. Vale's position was even worse because the campaign's accounts had ended up £2,400 in the red despite stringent economies, although they still managed to attract several new players with not inconsiderable pedigrees.

101: SATURDAY 6 OCTOBER 1923, FOOTBALL LEAGUE, SECOND DIVISION

STOKE (0) 1 (Clarke), PORT VALE (0) 0.

STOKE: Campbell, Brittleton, Howe, Clarke, Beswick, Brough, T. Broad, Kelly, J. Broad, Eyres, Tempest.
VALE: Lonsdale, Maddock, Birks, Dark, Connelly, Hampson, Lowe, Page, Howard, Butler, Bookman.

Venue: The Victoria Ground, Stoke-upon-Trent.
Attendance: 21,685.
Referee: G.D. Nunnerley (Ellesmere).

THE SETTING
Stoke had adjusted reasonably well to life in the Second Division following their relegation from the top flight at the end of the previous season. They were currently in twelfth place, but had lost 2-0 at second from the bottom Nelson the week before the local Derby. Vale were two positions and two points behind their rivals, but had a match in hand. The previous Saturday, they had beaten third-placed Leicester City 2-1 at home to move clear of the relegation zone. Stoke's player-coach, Tom Brittleton, who was in temporary control of team affairs, made three alterations in their side from their last game and recalled Beswick, Brough and Kelly. Vale were unchanged and played in black and white to avoid a clash of strips.

THE MATCH
Early Stoke pressure forced Hampson to head out an Eyres effort from almost under the bar and Birks then produced a virtually carbon copy clearance to deny Clarke. However, Vale managed to stem the tide, despite Hampson being forced on to the left wing because of an injury, and they increasingly began to control the game. Despite this, they were unable to take full advantage of their possession, especially as a result of Howard spurning two excellent opportunities.

After the interval, the play became end to end, but in the fifty-fifth minute Clarke headed into the roof of the net from a corner to put Stoke ahead. Hampson then returned to the Vale defence, which remained under pressure, and Tommy Broad skimmed the corner of the bar and post with an acute-angled shot. His brother, Jimmy, fired over shortly afterwards with only the Vale keeper to beat, whilst Kelly twice went close and then the visitors' goal underwent a remarkable escape as successive shots from Jimmy Broad, Eyres and Tempest thundered in. Lonsdale dislocated a finger during this bombardment and Dark took over as the custodian, but was not seriously tested during the remaining time.

THE AFTERMATH
Stoke's first ever Football League home victory against Vale pushed them up to ninth position, whilst their old rivals dropped to sixteenth. The two teams were set to clash again in the return Derby the following Saturday and Stoke received a great boost the day before when the experienced Tom Mather was appointed as their new secretary-manager.

102: SATURDAY 13 OCTOBER 1923, FOOTBALL LEAGUE, SECOND DIVISION

PORT VALE (2) 2 (Page, Butler), STOKE (2) 4 (J. Broad 2, Eyres 2).

VALE: Radford, Maddock, Birks, Dark, Connelly, Hampson, Lowe, Page, Reid, Butler, Bookman.
STOKE: Campbell, Brittleton, Howe, Clarke, Kasher, Brough, T. Broad, Kelly, J. Broad, Eyres, Tempest.

Venue: The Old Recreation Ground, Hanley.
Attendance: 16,800.
Referee: G.D. Nunnerley (Ellesmere).

THE SETTING
As a result of their 1-0 defeat at Stoke the previous Saturday, Vale had sunk to sixteenth position in the Second Division, whilst Stoke had climbed to ninth and were just a single point adrift of second place. Vale were without their regular goalkeeper, Lonsdale, for the return Derby because he had dislocated a finger in the first clash and they preferred Reid to Howard at centre-forward. Stoke had appointed a new secretary-manager, Tom Mather, the day before the match and selected an unchanged team except for the return of Kasher to centre-half.

THE MATCH
The match began at a cracking pace and after only eight minutes Stoke went in front from a twenty-five-yard shot by Jimmy Broad which sailed into the roof of the net. Vale were level just four minutes later when Page ran through and squeezed the ball past the visiting keeper. Then, in the nineteenth minute, the home side took the lead through a thumping shot by Butler, but the excitement was far from over and Jimmy Broad equalised for Stoke six minutes afterwards by tapping the ball in from a superb low centre delivered by his brother, Tommy. The thrills continued with Butler hitting the bar for Vale and Radford making several fine saves to deny the visitors.

Stoke attacked vigorously after half-time and the home custodian resumed his heroics, but, as Vale gradually disputed more of the play, Bookman fired harmlessly behind from a wonderful opening. However, it was Stoke who regained the lead ten minutes from time when Eyres ended a marvellous solo run by slipping the ball past Radford and into the net. Eyres made the game safe just a minute later by converting a left-wing centre, although Vale continued to fight hard right to the end.

THE AFTERMATH
As a result of their defeat, Vale dropped to sixth from the bottom of the table, just a point clear of the relegation zone, whilst Stoke moved up to fifth place and were adrift of the promotion positions merely on goal average. Vale continued to struggle throughout most of the rest of the season and finally preserved their Second Division status only in their penultimate match. Stoke led the table for nearly two months in the new year, but fell away in the spring and finished sixth.

103: MONDAY 28 APRIL 1924, NORTH STAFFORD-SHIRE INFIRMARY CUP

PORT VALE (0) 0, STOKE (0) 1 (Sam Brown).

VALE: Sidney Brown, Maddock, Birks, Hampson, Connelly, Pursell, Lowe, Page, Kirkham, Briscoe, Prince.
STOKE: Knott, Milne, Howe, Walker, Stentiford, Maddison, Ralphs, Nicholas, Sam Brown, Sellars, Tempest.

Venue: The Old Recreation Ground, Hanley.
Attendance: Unknown.
Referee: F.J.Proctor (Trentham).

THE SETTING

Vale were fifth from the bottom of the Second Division with one game remaining, but were safe from relegation and had drawn 2-2 at home to Hull City two days before the local Derby. Stoke had completed their league programme that same Saturday with a 2-1 defeat at fifth from the bottom Bradford City and occupied sixth place. Vale's secretary-manager, Joe Schofield, selected a full-strength and unchanged side for the Derby, but Stoke fielded only two players who had appeared at Bradford City and turned out a team largely composed of reserves. This was most unfortunate as the annual competition was billed as 'the great local championship match'!

THE MATCH

The game proved an immense disappointment as a spectacle of good football and it seemed that the effects of a long season had taken their toll on the players, especially those of Vale, who on paper were the favourites to win. Both sides missed a series of scoring opportunities and Stoke were reduced to ten men for the whole of the second period after their left-half, Maddison, was forced to retire with a knee injury. Nevertheless, Sam Brown struck the deciding goal for them ten minutes after the interval to ensure a surprise victory.

THE AFTERMATH

A disappointing crowd yielded gate receipts of only around £100, whilst a competition for the match ball raised another £1 6s. 8d. towards the infirmary funds. Each of the winning players received a decorated salad bowl and those from the losing team were presented with four-piece smokers' sets adorned with Greek figures! Vale completed their league programme the following Saturday with a 2-1 victory at Hull City and climbed two places in the table to end up sixteenth, whilst Stoke finished in sixth position. Jack Hampson and Peter Pursell were both freed by Vale during the close season and Arthur Prince was transferred to Sheffield Wednesday for £750. The club decided to adopt a policy of developing local players and consequently there were only two new signings of note: Tom Fern, a veteran goalkeeper from Everton, and Billy Tempest, Stoke's outside-left, who cost £1,000. Stoke released nine professionals and asked a number of others to take a cut in wages, but some of the players affected deliberately caused damage to the ground in response! There were no newcomers of note.

104: SATURDAY 20 SEPTEMBER 1924, FOOTBALL LEAGUE, SECOND DIVISION

STOKE (0) 0, PORT VALE (1) 1 (Connelly).

STOKE: Dixon, McGrory, Brittleton, Brough, Dawson, Rouse, Ralphs, Davies, Armitage, Sellars, Nicholas.
VALE: Fern, Maddock, Birks, Collinge, Connelly, Blunt, Lowe, Page, Kirkham, Briscoe, Tempest.

Venue: The Victoria Ground, Stoke-upon-Trent.
Attendance: 22,747.
Referee: A.F. Kirby (Preston).

THE SETTING
Stoke were thirteenth in the Second Division, with five points from their opening five matches, and had won 1-0 at Leicester City the week before the local Derby. Vale were one point and two places below their rivals, having lost 2-0 at home to unbeaten Portsmouth on the Monday prior to the contest. Both sides were unchanged from their previous games and bright sunshine helped to attract a sizable crowd.

THE MATCH
After only five minutes' play, Vale were unlucky not to take the lead when Connelly hit the bar following a melee in the home goalmouth. The visitors continued to press strongly and Connelly had a tremendous long drive well saved, whilst Tempest continually caused problems for the Stoke defence. However, the home side were awarded a penalty in their first serious attack after about half an hour when Sellars was upended by Maddock, but Armitage ballooned the spot kick over the bar. This miss proved vital because Vale scored the only goal of the game ten minutes later as Connelly stroked the ball into the net from a partially-cleared corner.

Although the second half began slowly, the play soon became end to end, but Vale made the best two openings from which Kirkham headed and then shot wide. Nevertheless, with the wind in their favour, Stoke gradually got on top, although their efforts were not sufficiently constructive to pose much danger. However, Armitage missed a fine chance to equalise as the match neared its end when he shot over from a pinpoint centre by Ralphs.

THE AFTERMATH
Stoke dropped to fifth from the bottom of the division as a result of their defeat, although they then gained two successive victories and stabilised themselves in the middle of the table for the rest of the year. However, their line-up almost constantly changed as injuries took their toll, which disrupted their pattern of play, and they exited from the English Cup at the first hurdle. Vale moved up to tenth place after their local Derby triumph, but then went five games without a win and transferred their left-back, Len Birks, to Sheffield United the following month for 'a substantial sum'. Nevertheless, they made spectacular progress in the English Cup, scoring fourteen goals in two qualifying rounds!

122

105: SATURDAY 24 JANUARY 1925, FOOTBALL LEAGUE, SECOND DIVISION

PORT VALE (0) 2 (Kirkham, Tempest), STOKE (0) 0.

VALE: Fern, Cooper, Briscoe, Collinge, Connelly, Blunt, Lowe, Strange, Kirkham, Jones, Tempest.
STOKE: Dixon, McGrory, Milne, Brough, McClure, Rouse, Ralphs, Kelly, Blackie, Eyres, Watkin.

Venue: The Old Recreation Ground, Hanley.
Attendance: 17,936.
Referee: A.F. Kirby (Preston).

THE SETTING

Vale were fifteenth in the Second Division, but had matches in hand on most of the other teams. On the Saturday before the local Derby, they had won 1-0 at sixth from the bottom Middlesbrough, whilst a fortnight previously they had been thrashed 7-2 at Aston Villa in the first round of the English Cup! Stoke were two league places and one point better off than their rivals, but had played two games more. They had gained a 1-1 home draw with fourth-placed Leicester City a week prior to the Derby after being eliminated from the English Cup by the same club seven days earlier. Vale made just one change for the local clash, with Tempest replacing Page, who had become a flu victim. However, Stoke were without Davies, their inside-right, who was injured, and Tom Mather, the club's secretary-manager, recalled McClure, Kelly and Eyres to the side.

THE MATCH

The contest began at a furious pace, but little skill was exhibited and nothing of note occurred until Watkin forced the Vale keeper to make a full-length save. In response, Strange lofted a good opportunity skywards, whilst Fern injured his left eye in diving at Watkin's feet and had to retire for treatment after forty minutes. Briscoe took over in goal and almost immediately was forced to rush out to kick clear from Eyres.

The Vale custodian returned to the fray a few minutes after the interval and saved well from a rising shot by Kelly, but this proved the prelude to the home team taking the lead in their very next attack in the fifty-fourth minute when Tempest centred for Kirkham to lash the ball in. As Stoke strove for an equaliser, Fern stopped a pile-driver from Kelly, but Lowe regularly tormented the left side of their defence and from one of his crosses, after sixty-five minutes, Kirkham hooked in a dropping volley. The Stoke keeper was only able to touch this against a post and Tempest was on hand to drill in the rebound. The visitors then exerted some belated pressure, but their efforts came to nought, partly as a result of Blackie being carried off with a knee injury ten minutes from time.

THE AFTERMATH

A handy £1,103 2s. 6d. was taken at the gate, whilst Vale climbed two positions in the division as a result of their victory and eventually finished eighth. Stoke, however, lost seven of their next eight games and slumped to the foot of the table before they rallied to avoid relegation by a single point and a single place.

123

106: MONDAY 31 AUGUST 1925, FOOTBALL LEAGUE, SECOND DIVISION

PORT VALE (1) 3 (Kirkham 2 [1 pen.], Strange), STOKE CITY (0) 0.

VALE: Fern, Maddock, Oakes, Collinge, Connelly, Briscoe, Lowe, Page, Kirkham, Strange, Tempest.
STOKE: Campbell, McGrory, Howe, Brough, Dawson, S. Johnson, Ralphs, Davies, R. Johnson, Clennell, Archibald.

Venue: The Old Recreation Ground, Hanley.
Attendance: 19,997.
Referee: H. Clayton (Derby).

THE SETTING

This was the first local Derby in which Stoke played using the addition of "City" to their name, in reflection of the new status of Stoke-on-Trent. Vale had opened their 1925-1926 Second Division campaign with a 2-1 win at Clapton Orient on the Saturday before the local Derby, whilst Stoke had also begun brightly, defeating Stockport County 3-0 at home on the same day. Vale's secretary-manager, Joe Schofield, made one team change for the local clash, replacing the injured Cooper with Maddock at right-back, whilst Stoke not surprisingly fielded the same line-up which had triumphed in their last match. The interest was so great that the ground was densely packed with spectators and thousands of people were turned away, especially because of the reduction in the stadium's capacity by the replacement of banking by terracing.

THE MATCH

The match was notable for Vale's direct tactics based on speed, which became apparent almost immediately as Lowe surged down the wing and centred for Strange to force the visiting keeper into a fine save. Although Dawson shot just wide for Stoke, Tempest hit the bar at the other end and in the thirteenth minute the home side went in front when Kirkham headed in from a chip by Strange. Stoke then pressed strongly for the equaliser, but Briscoe made several timely interceptions and only a marvellous save by Campbell prevented Kirkham from extending Vale's lead shortly before the interval.

Vale attacked forcefully at the outset of the second half, but Strange missed a golden opportunity when Lowe centred perfectly, although the former made amends in the sixty-second minute by tapping in another pinpoint cross from Lowe. Stoke then exerted relentless pressure, but Archibald squandered three excellent chances, which proved costly because Kirkham made the game safe near the end from a penalty after McGrory had handled in the area.

THE AFTERMATH

Although Vale found the result and the gate receipts of £1,229 highly satisfactory, their mood was changed abruptly the following Saturday when they were trounced 6-0 at home by Chelsea, who brilliantly exploited the opportunities offered by the new offside rule. Stoke, however, bounced back from their local Derby defeat to win 4-2 at Fulham on the same day.

107: MONDAY 7 SEPTEMBER 1925, FOOTBALL LEAGUE, SECOND DIVISION

STOKE CITY (0) 0, PORT VALE (2) 3 (Kirkham 3).

STOKE: Campbell, McGrory, Howe, Brough, Dawson, S. Johnson, Ralphs, Davies, Armitage, Hallam, Archibald.
VALE: Fern, Maddock, Oakes, Maddison, Blunt, Briscoe, Lowe, Page, Kirkham, Strange, Tempest.

Venue: The Victoria Ground, Stoke-upon-Trent.
Attendance: 21,869.
Referee: H. Clayton (Derby).

THE SETTING
Stoke were fifth in the Second Division, having lost only one of their opening three matches, against Vale, who were two places below them in the league table but had accumulated the same number of points. On the Saturday before the local Derby, Stoke had won 4-2 at Fulham, but Vale had been hammered 6-0 at home by high-scoring Chelsea! Stoke's secretary-manager, Tom Mather, named an unchanged side for the local clash, whilst Vale were forced to call up Maddock and Maddison to replace the injured Cooper and Connelly.

THE MATCH
The match proved to be a scrappy affair with some ill feeling which followed Maddock's unnecessarily aggressive tackle on Ralphs in the first minute. This fractured the latter's collarbone, although he played throughout the rest of the game after receiving attention! While he was absent, Kirkham seized upon a Briscoe centre and placed the ball out of the home keeper's reach to put Vale in front after only two minutes. The visitors then attacked vigorously and Stoke's problems were compounded in the tenth minute when Hallam received a serious head wound in a collision with Armitage, which sidelined him for a quarter of an hour for bandaging. This enabled Briscoe to undertake a roving role and after twenty-four minutes Kirkham extended Vale's lead by tapping the ball in from a misplaced clearance.

There was even less flowing football in the second period, which was littered with fouls, and although Stoke dominated the play, their handicapped forwards could make little impact. Indeed, Hallam retired on the hour, whilst Armitage hit a post to spurn a golden opportunity provided by Archibald and Kirkham wrapped up the points for Vale five minutes from time when he converted a Tempest cross to complete his hat trick.

THE AFTERMATH
As a result of their defeat, Stoke dropped to eighth place, but far worse was to come as they slid further down the table to be relegated after finishing second to the bottom. Vale climbed to fifth position in achieving the double over their old rivals and early the following April got to within four points of a promotion place, but then fell away to end up eighth. In addition, neither team impressed in the English Cup, with Vale being eliminated at the first hurdle, whilst Stoke were hammered 6-3 at Second Division Swansea Town in the next round.

108: THURSDAY 5 MAY 1927, NORTH STAFFORD-SHIRE ROYAL INFIRMARY CUP

STOKE CITY (1) 5 (Davies 3, Cull, Armitage pen.), PORT VALE (0) 0.

STOKE: Dixon McGrory, Beachill, Armitage, Williamson, Eastwood, Cull, Davies, Johnson, Eyres, Archibald.
VALE: Matthews, Maddock, Oakes, Whitcombe, Connelly, Rouse, Lowe, Anstiss, Kirkham, Page, Briscoe.

Venue: The Victoria Ground, Stoke-upon-Trent.
Attendance: 5,950.
Referee: E.R. Westwood (Bloxwich).

THE SETTING
The two Potteries clubs renewed their rivalry in this fundraising competition, which had been in abeyance since 1924. Stoke had won the championship of the Third Division (North) and therefore promotion with two matches left to play and had celebrated by winning 3-1 at Lincoln City on the Saturday before the local Derby. Vale had risen to eighth place in the Second Division as a result of drawing 1-1 at home to Swansea Town on the same day, but no longer had any chance of going up. Stoke's line-up showed three changes from their previous game, although Tom Mather, their secretary-manager, fielded his strongest available team, whilst Vale were unchanged.

THE MATCH
The match was keenly contested, but at the outset the Vale players appeared to be overconfident. Nevertheless, they dominated the early exchanges, although Page lofted the ball way over the bar when he was clean through and Briscoe and Kirkham also squandered good opportunities. However, in Stoke's first real attack, Eyres hit a post, which seemed to unsettle the visiting defence and marked a turning point in the game. Thereafter, the home side's accurate passing proved decisive and shortly before the interval, Davies put them in front from a pinpoint corner by Archibald.

Stoke extended their lead five minutes after the restart when Cull fired in a delightful cross-shot. The home team then further increased the pressure and in the sixty-eighth minute Davies ran on to a short pass from Johnson and struck the ball past the Vale keeper. Davies completed his hat trick just three minutes later when he converted a Johnson flick-on and the scoring ended with Armitage firing in a penalty kick after Eyres had been brought down by Maddock. Nevertheless, Stoke's relentless attacks continued and only the alertness of the visiting keeper prevented Eyres and Johnson from adding to their tally.

THE AFTERMATH
A competition record £365 1s. 8d. was taken at the gate and the players of the winning team were presented with Cauldon plaques, whilst the losers received Cauldon boxes. Stoke rounded off their fine season on the Saturday after the Derby by thrashing fourth-placed Halifax Town 5-1 at home, whilst Vale triumphed 3-0 at Nottingham Forest, who were four positions above them, in their final match on the same day to end up eighth in their division.

109: SATURDAY 5 NOVEMBER 1927, FOOTBALL LEAGUE, SECOND DIVISION

STOKE CITY (0) 0, PORT VALE (1) 2 (Anstiss, Kirkham).

STOKE: Dixon, McGrory, Spencer, Armitage, Williamson, Sellars, J. Williams, Davies, Wilson, Johnson, Archibald.
VALE: Bennett, Maddock, Oakes, Briscoe, Connelly, Rouse, Anstiss, Page, Kirkham, Gillespie, Trotter.

Venue: The Victoria Ground, Stoke-upon-Trent.
Attendance: 31,493.
Referee: T. Crew (Leicester).

THE SETTING
Stoke had fared extremely well in the early stages of the 1927-1928 Second Division campaign and were third in the table, with only two defeats in their opening twelve matches. Indeed, on the Saturday before the local Derby, they had won 2-1 at Wolverhampton Wanderers. Vale had tasted victory five times in their last seven games, following a poor start to the season, and had hammered fifth from the bottom Southampton 4-0 at home a week prior to the Derby, which had moved them up to thirteenth position. Both teams were unchanged for the resumption of their league rivalry and the morning's continuous rain failed to deter a new record crowd for the fixture from assembling and letting off fireworks in excited anticipation.

THE MATCH
Stoke came close to taking the lead straight from the kickoff when a header from Williams landed on top of the visitors' net. Although the exchanges became vigorous, good football was plentiful and the home team dominated, but Williams missed three fine opportunities. This proved costly because Anstiss opened the scoring for Vale in the thirteenth minute by thundering in a shot from a Kirkham flick-on. Shortly afterwards, heavy rain began to fall, which turned the pitch into a quagmire, and controlling the ball became exceedingly difficult. Nevertheless, Page skimmed a post for the visitors, whilst Johnson spurned a marvellous opportunity to equalise by completely missing his kick!

After the interval, Vale gained the ascendancy and several times went close before Wilson struck their bar with a header from a corner. Nevertheless, the visitors extended their lead in the seventieth minute when Kirkham fired in an acute-angled shot and almost immediately afterwards Stoke were reduced to ten men as Williams limped off. Thereafter, the home defence became very hard pressed and Anstiss hit a post five minutes from time.

THE AFTERMATH
Stoke dropped a place in the division as a result of their defeat, whilst Vale moved up to twelfth. Although Stoke's league form was rather mixed, they remained in the promotion hunt well into the spring and reached the sixth round of the F.A. Cup, knocking out First Division Bolton Wanderers en route. Vale continued their own good form, making the fifth round of the same competition and climbing to sixth position in the league by Christmas.

110: SATURDAY 17 MARCH 1928, FOOTBALL LEAGUE, SECOND DIVISION

PORT VALE (0) 0, STOKE CITY (0) 0.

VALE: Matthews, Maddock, Oakes, H. Smith, Connelly, Rouse, Lowe, Fishwick, Kirkham, Page, Briscoe.
STOKE: Dixon, McGrory, Spencer, Armitage, Williamson, Sellars, J. Williams, Bussey, Wilson, Davies, Archibald.

Venue: The Old Recreation Ground, Hanley.
Attendance: 21,071.
Referee: T. Crew (Leicester).

THE SETTING
Vale were eighth in the Second Division and had won 3-1 at sixth from the bottom Southampton on the Saturday before the local Derby. Stoke were two places above their rivals, but just four points adrift of second place with a match in hand, although they had only managed to draw 2-2 at home to the penultimate club, Wolverhampton Wanderers, a week prior to the Derby. Vale's manager, Joe Schofield, made five team changes for the local contest, four of these being for tactical reasons in the forward line, which included the newly-signed sharpshooter, Albert Fishwick. Stoke's side showed three alterations and Armitage and Bussey returned after injury. The clash attracted an immense crowd and thousands were unable to gain admission, whilst those inside the ground were 'packed like sardines'.

THE MATCH
The match was notable for the stark contrast in styles adopted by the two teams, with Vale preferring short passes, whilst Stoke used the long ball. Much of the initial play was in midfield, although in due course Davies forced the Vale keeper into a full-length save. The home side retaliated and Kirkham fired a shot on the turn just over the bar, but Stoke then twice went close with Matthews making a magnificent save to deny Wilson and Oakes trapping a Davies shot on the goal line! Vale gradually increased the pressure, although Archibald rolled an effort agonisingly close to an unguarded net for the visitors just before the interval.

The second half opened quietly, but Stoke eventually got into their stride and Armitage put a forty-yard drive only just over the bar, whilst a Wilson cross-shot brought an excellent save out of the home custodian. Both centre-halves were towers of strength and the crowd became increasingly subdued as the attacking play continued to falter, although just before the end Bussey struck the bar for Stoke and then dithered too long when presented with a wonderful opportunity to poach the winner.

THE AFTERMATH
Vale remained in eighth position, but Stoke moved up to fifth and both clubs were cheered by the £1,297 taken at the gate. Vale produced mediocre league form until the completion of the season and finished in ninth place, whilst Stoke could only remain fifth, despite winning six of their final ten games.

111: SATURDAY 15 SEPTEMBER 1928, FOOTBALL LEAGUE, SECOND DIVISION

STOKE CITY (2) 2 (Bussey, Davies), PORT VALE (0) 1 (Griffiths).

STOKE: Dixon, McGrory, Spencer, Armitage, Jackson, Sellars, Cull, Bussey, Wilson, Davies, Archibald.
VALE: Prince, Maddock, Oakes, Briscoe, Connelly, Rouse, Griffiths, Page, Littlewood, Anstiss, Simms.

Venue: The Victoria Ground, Stoke-upon-Trent.
Attendance: 35,288.
Referee: I. Caswell (Blackburn).

THE SETTING
Stoke were fifth in the Second Division and had made a promising start to the 1928-1929 season with three straight victories, but had suffered their first defeat, by 1-0 at lowly Clapton Orient, on the Saturday prior to the local Derby. Vale were in thirteenth place, having taken four points from their opening four games, but had hammered struggling Millwall 5-2 at home in their last match a week before the Derby. Stoke made two team changes for the local clash, losing their regular centre-half, Williamson, to a leg injury, but welcoming back Cull, their right winger, after an illness. Vale likewise showed two alterations in their line-up, with their keeper Bennett feeling unwell, whilst Simms was brought back on to the left wing. The contest attracted a new record local Derby crowd.

THE MATCH
Stoke exerted intense pressure from the outset and Prince was forced to make fine saves from both Wilson and Armitage, but he was unable to prevent Bussey firing the home team in front in the eighteenth minute, following a corner. Vale remained under the cosh and eight minutes later, Davies extended Stoke's lead with a thumping shot after being set up by Bussey. Vale's defence continued to work overtime, although the home side were unable to increase their score.

After the interval, Vale finally started to get to grips with their opponents, although only a timely block by the visiting keeper prevented Davies from compounding their problems. The play became increasingly scrappy, but in the seventy-second minute Vale finally reduced the arrears when a long-range centre from Griffiths drifted into the net. The visitors then pressed strongly for an equaliser, but Stoke hung on until the end.

THE AFTERMATH
Although Stoke moved into fourth position as a consequence of their victory, three defeats in their next four games put the brakes on their challenge to the leading teams and they drifted into midtable. Vale remained thirteenth despite their local Derby defeat, but they slipped into the relegation battle through two successive reverses which followed and a dire sequence of results in December left them fourth from the bottom of the division.

112: SATURDAY 26 JANUARY 1929, FOOTBALL LEAGUE, SECOND DIVISION

PORT VALE (0) 1 (Mandley), STOKE CITY (1) 2 (Shirley 2).

VALE: Prince, Maddock, Briscoe, Smith, Connelly, Rouse, Mandley, Fishwick, Kirkham, Pynegar, Simms.
STOKE: R. Williams, McGrory, Spencer, Armitage, Williamson, Sellars, Cull, Bussey, Shirley, Davies, Archibald.

Venue: The Old Recreation Ground, Hanley.
Attendance: 18,869.
Referee: I. Caswell (Blackburn).

THE SETTING
Vale were struggling at fourth from the bottom of the Second Division and were just two points clear of the relegation places. They had lost seven of their last eight league matches, which had included a 2-1 defeat at Millwall on the Saturday before the local Derby. In contrast, Stoke were eleventh and had beaten the penultimate team, Clapton Orient, 3-1 at home a week prior to the Derby. However, both clubs had exited from the F.A. Cup at the first hurdle. Vale named an unchanged side for the local clash, whilst Stoke's secretary-manager, Tom Mather, made two alterations to his line-up, with Armitage and Shirley returning to the team. However, only the most strenuous efforts by a small army of workers enabled the pitch, which 'resembled a ploughed field', to become playable.

THE MATCH
The match was strongly contested and full of incident from the outset. The Vale keeper diverted a shot from Shirley to deny the visitors an early lead, but the home side soon began to dominate the exchanges. Nevertheless, it was Stoke who went in front when a Davies pass enabled Shirley to run clear on his own, round the home custodian and place the ball into an empty net. Vale then pressed hard for an equaliser, but both Fishwick and Kirkham missed good chances, whilst the visiting keeper made a splendid save from Simms.

Vale attacked with a vengeance after the interval, although Kirkham wasted another fine opportunity by shooting wide and was then thwarted by a magnificent save by Williams. However, Stoke extended their lead in the sixty-sixth minute when Shirley fired the ball home after a scramble, although almost immediately Mandley hurtled in to convert a Simms cross to reduce the deficit. Vale then penned the visitors into their own half for lengthy spells, but were unable to effect a further breakthrough.

THE AFTERMATH
Vale dropped to third from the bottom of the table as a result of their defeat, whilst Stoke climbed to fifth place. Vale gained thirteen points from their final eight home games and scored twenty-four goals in the process, but still finished in penultimate position and were relegated to the Third Division (North). However, Stoke ended up sixth and beat Wolverhampton Wanderers 3-2 to win the North Staffordshire Royal Infirmary Cup after Vale had scratched because of their inability to field a team!

113: MONDAY 5 MAY 1930, NORTH STAFFORDSHIRE ROYAL INFIRMARY CUP

PORT VALE (1) 1 (Jennings), STOKE CITY (1) 2 (Bussey, Kirkham).

VALE: Davies, Shenton, Wootton, O'Grady, Briscoe, Jones, Griffiths, Pynegar, Jennings, Anstiss, Baxter.
STOKE: Beswick, McGrory, Spencer, Armitage, Jackson, Scrimshaw, Cull, Bussey, Kirkham, Crichton, Archibald.

Venue: The Old Recreation Ground, Hanley.
Attendance: 6,343.
Referee: T. Greaves (Burslem).

THE SETTING

Vale resumed their rivalry with Stoke in this charity competition after Wolverhampton Wanderers had stood in for them the previous year. The Hanley team had secured the Third Division (North) championship, with a then record number of points, and had thereby gained promotion to the Second Division. They had won all their final five league matches, which had included a 2-0 victory at Crewe Alexandra two days before the Potteries Derby. Stoke had finished eleventh in the Second Division and had ended their league campaign by beating Tottenham Hotspur 1-0 at home on the Saturday prior to the Derby. Both clubs selected very strong teams for the local clash, although Vale fielded two reserves, O'Grady and Briscoe, whilst their former centre-forward, Kirkham, was recalled by Stoke, who also gave a trial to John Crichton, an amateur.

THE MATCH

Vale took the lead in the tenth minute in the first incident of real note when Jennings fought off two defenders and squeezed in an acute-angled drive. The home side continued to press forward and the Stoke centre-half miskicked an intended clearance against his own bar. However, the visitors rallied and Kirkham twice shot just wide before Bussey headed the equaliser from a corner in the thirty-seventh minute. Kirkham then fired inches over, whilst the Stoke keeper made a marvellous save to deny Griffiths.

Although Stoke opened the second period brightly, the play soon became desultory. Nevertheless, the visitors went in front after sixty-five minutes when Crichton struck the bar and Kirkham tapped in the rebound. Both goals had narrow escapes afterwards and Griffiths missed an excellent chance to level the score, whilst Crichton ran the ball out of play with only Davies to beat.

THE AFTERMATH

Gross gate receipts of £348 were taken and after the game the players, directors and officials of both clubs dined together at the Grand Hotel in Hanley. Vale announced a profit of £363 17s. 1d. on the season, but there was little transfer activity at the club during the summer, with Harry Roberts, an inside-right who cost £100 from Lincoln City, being the only new signing of note. The close season was also quiet at Stoke, who essentially chose to keep faith with their existing players, although John Crichton was signed permanently, whilst their goalkeeper, Dick Williams, was sold to Reading for £250.

114: SATURDAY 13 DECEMBER 1930, FOOTBALL LEAGUE, SECOND DIVISION

STOKE CITY (0) 1 (Robertson), PORT VALE (0) 0.

STOKE: Lewis, McGrory, Spencer, Robertson, Jackson, Sellars, Liddle, Bussey, Wilson, Mawson, Archibald.
VALE: Slater, Shenton, Oakes, Cope, Round, Jones, Anstiss, Fishwick, Jennings, Marshall, Baxter.

Venue: The Victoria Ground, Stoke-upon-Trent.
Attendance: 26,609.
Referee: A.E. Fogg (Bolton).

THE SETTING
Stoke were tenth in the Second Division and had drawn 1-1 at Bristol City a week before the local Derby. Vale were three places higher and only three points adrift of a promotion spot. They had won four of their previous five matches and had beaten Southampton 1-0 at home on the Saturday prior to the Derby. Stoke were unchanged for the local clash, whilst Vale were forced to include Anstiss at outside-right instead of Griffiths, who was suffering from a severe cold.

THE MATCH
Accompanied by a constant roar from the crowd, Stoke tested the visiting keeper a number of times early in the match and Slater made a tremendous save from a hard Mawson drive. Although Bussey was outstanding for Stoke, spraying the ball around majestically, both defences essentially held command. The play became increasingly congested in midfield, but Anstiss and Jennings forced the home custodian to make two vital saves and towards the interval the Stoke forwards kept Slater on his toes.

Stoke attacked more aggressively at the start of the second half, but the visiting centre-forward was only thwarted when Lewis dived at his feet to smother the ball. Then Marshall spurned a fine chance for Vale, which proved costly because Robertson headed the home side into the lead from a corner in the sixty-fifth minute and the crowd went 'wild with excitement'. Shortly afterwards, Liddle twice hit the bar as Stoke piled on the pressure, but, following a marvellous solo effort by Round, Vale desperately fought for an equaliser and Jennings had a goal disallowed for offside. Then, remarkably, as Wilson was about to extend Stoke's lead by thumping the ball into the net, the final whistle sounded!

THE AFTERMATH
As a result of their victory, Stoke moved up to eighth place, on level points with Vale, who remained seventh. However, Stoke's triumph did not prove a launch pad for success because they won none of their following seven league and cup games and were eliminated from the F.A. Cup at the first hurdle. Vale produced inconsistent form after the local Derby, although they remained in the top half of the table and survived one round of the F.A. Cup before being knocked out.

115: SATURDAY 18 APRIL 1931, FOOTBALL LEAGUE, SECOND DIVISION

PORT VALE (0) 0, STOKE CITY (0) 0.

VALE: Davies, Shenton, Oakes, Cope, Round, Jones, Griffiths, Roberts, Littlewood, Jennings, Henshall.
STOKE: Lewis, McGrory, Spencer, Armitage, Turner, Robertson, Liddle, Bussey, Kirkham, Sale, Archibald.

Venue: The Old Recreation Ground, Hanley.
Attendance: 13,403.
Referee: A.E. Fogg (Bolton).

THE SETTING

Vale were eighth in the Second Division, but could no longer gain promotion after suffering two consecutive defeats, the second of which had been by 2-0 at Southampton on the Saturday before the local Derby. Stoke were a single place below their rivals, but had the same number of points.They had staged a mini-revival from midtable mediocrity with three victories on the trot, which had culminated in a 3-1 home win against Bristol City a week prior to the Derby. Oakes resumed at left-back for Vale after recovering from a leg injury, but otherwise both teams were unchanged from their previous matches. The lowest ever crowd for a Football League Potteries Derby assembled, with its size being adversely affected by continuous rain which had left pools of water down the centre of the pitch.

THE MATCH

Although Stoke won the toss and kicked with the advantage of a strong wind, the game opened quietly. However, the visiting keeper made a wonderful save from a Round free kick as the tempo increased, whilst Kirkham hit a thirty-yard pile-driver inches over the bar for Stoke. Also, Sale twice went close, but generally both defences were on top, with the play being rather scrappy.

After the interval, Vale attacked more vigorously and Jones fired in a tremendous shot which Lewis was hard-pushed to save, but then Kirkham broke clear, only to be denied by the home custodian. In another Stoke breakaway shortly afterwards, Kirkham shot just wide of a post with Davies stranded almost forty yards out of his goal! Nevertheless, Vale continued to dominate the exchanges and Round almost put them in front, although Bussey headed against the bar for the visitors as the deadlock failed to broken.

THE AFTERMATH

The draw proved to be relatively satisfactory because both teams moved up one position in the table as a result of it. Later in the month, Vale undertook a profitable two-match tour of the Netherlands, during which they had the interesting experience of playing under artificial lighting, and they returned to end the season on a particularly high note by finishing fifth, the club's best ever Football League placing. Stoke, however, gained only one point from their remaining two games and fell away to end up eleventh.

133

116: SATURDAY 26 SEPTEMBER 1931, FOOTBALL LEAGUE, SECOND DIVISION

STOKE CITY (1) 4 (Bussey 3, Sale), PORT VALE (0) 0.

STOKE: Lewis, McGrory, Beachill, Robertson, Turner, Sellars, Liddle, Bussey, Mawson, Sale, Archibald.
VALE: Slater, Shenton, Wootton, Cope, Round, Jones, York, Easton, Littlewood, Marshall, Dorrell.

Venue: The Victoria Ground, Stoke-upon-Trent.
Attendance: 28,292.
Referee: T. Crew (Leicester).

THE SETTING

Stoke were fifth in the Second Division and had gained seven points from their last four matches, the most recent of which had resulted in a 2-0 victory at fourth-placed Southampton a week before the local Derby. Vale were in a comfortable tenth position, but had lost their previous game 4-0 at home to fifth from the bottom Swansea Town five days prior to the Derby. Stoke were unchanged for the local contest, but Vale's manager, Tom Morgan, brought in Slater, Round and Easton following his team's midweek drubbing.

THE MATCH

Vale, playing in blue jerseys, began briskly, but Dorrell missed a glorious opportunity to put them in front by miskicking a centre from York. This proved costly because shortly afterwards, in the nineteenth minute, Bussey slotted in a rebound with the aid of a slight deflection to give Stoke the lead. The home side then piled on the pressure, with Mawson a constant danger, but the Vale keeper kept them at bay by making a series of fine saves.

After the interval, the play became more even, although the Stoke custodian was obliged to tip a looping shot by York over the bar. However, the home team regained command in due course and Sale slashed the ball hopelessly wide from two yards out, whilst Bussey headed against the bar before he put Stoke further in front with a snap-shot following a corner after sixty-four minutes. Three minutes later, Bussey completed his hat trick with a sharp, low drive from a partial clearance by the Vale keeper and the visitors then made a series of positional changes without appreciable improvement. Indeed, Sale latched on to a long free kick in the seventy-fourth minute to fire in a fourth goal, whilst Mawson had a further effort disallowed for handling, as Stoke completed the biggest ever victory in a full Football League Potteries Derby.

THE AFTERMATH

In spite of their fine victory, Stoke remained in fifth position, although they won their next two matches to become the league leaders temporarily and maintained a firm promotion challenge thereafter. As a bonus, they also reached the fifth round of the F.A. Cup before being eliminated. In contrast, Vale dropped to fifteenth after their local Derby defeat, were trounced 9-3 by midtable Tottenham Hotspur in November and had slumped to third from the bottom of the table by the end of the year.

117: SATURDAY 6 FEBRUARY 1932, FOOTBALL LEAGUE, SECOND DIVISION

PORT VALE (0) 3 (Marshall 2, Henshall), STOKE CITY (0) 0.

VALE: Davies, Shenton, Oakes, Cope, Connelly, Izon, Henshall, Marshall, Tippett, Kirkham, Dorrell.
STOKE: Lewis, McGrory, Beachill, Robertson, Turner, Sellars, Liddle, Ware, Mawson, Sale, Taylor.

Venue: The Old Recreation Ground, Hanley.
Attendance: 21,089.
Referee: T. Crew (Leicester).

THE SETTING
Vale were fourteenth in the Second Division, but were only four points clear of the relegation zone and had lost 2-0 at fifth-placed Bury in their last match a week before the local Derby. In contrast, Stoke were strongly challenging for promotion in fourth place and boasted a fourteen-game unbeaten run, which included a 2-1 victory against First Division Sunderland in an F.A. Cup fourth round second replay five days prior to the Derby. Vale's manager, Tom Morgan, made four team changes for the local clash, bringing in Oakes, Connelly and Henshall, whilst Wilf Kirkham made his return debut, having been signed from Stoke a week earlier. The visitors were unchanged and the crowd was so large that many spectators scaled the railings and sat behind the touchlines, whilst others climbed on to the hoardings at the back of the goals.

THE MATCH
Both sides began brightly and the play soon became end to end. However, Vale gradually gained the ascendancy and Kirkham had a shot rather fortunately kicked clear by the visiting keeper, who also made a fine save from an acute-angled strike by Tippett. The latter further made his presence felt by shooting just wide and forcing Lewis to save a header brilliantly, but the Stoke defence held firm.

The contest became more even after the interval and Sale went close for Stoke before a superb first-time shot by Marshall put the home team in front in the sixty-fifth minute. Vale extended their lead just six minutes later when Henshall rushed in to convert a precise pass from Tippett and then the Stoke custodian brilliantly denied Marshall. As Vale piled on the pressure, Marshall added a third goal ten minutes from time following a marvellous solo run.

THE AFTERMATH
Vale not only triumphed on the pitch, but also took a magnificent £1,350 at the gate, although the team remained fourteenth in the table in spite of their success. They then began an almost disastrous sequence of results which took them to the brink of relegation before two consecutive victories at the death enabled them to finish third from the bottom on goal average only. Stoke stayed in fourth position despite their local Derby defeat and finally missed promotion by just one place and two points.

118: MONDAY 9 MAY 1932, NORTH STAFFORD-SHIRE ROYAL INFIRMARY CUP

STOKE CITY (2) 7 (Mawson 2, Matthews 2, Sale, Round o.g., Taylor), PORT VALE (0) 0.

STOKE: Lewis, McGrory, Beachill, Buller, Turner, Sellars, Matthews, H. Davies, Mawson, Sale, Taylor.
VALE: B. Davies, Shenton, Oakes, Cope, Round, McGrath, Henshall (Baker), Easton, Littlewood, Kirkham, Tippett.

Venue: The Victoria Ground, Stoke-upon-Trent.
Attendance: Unknown.
Referee: Unknown.

THE SETTING
This charity competition between the two rival clubs resumed after a one-year gap. Stoke had ended up third in the Second Division, two points adrift of promotion, and had beaten sixth-placed Bradford Park Avenue 1-0 at home in their final league game on the Saturday before the local Derby. Vale had escaped relegation from the same division on goal average by winning their last match 2-0 at second-placed, but already promoted, Leeds United two days prior to the Derby! Both clubs selected strong line-ups for the local clash, with Cope returning for Vale, who also gave their new left-half, Jimmy McGrath, his debut, whilst Lewis, Matthews and Mawson replaced John, Ware and Johnson for Stoke.

THE MATCH
The match was a generally poor affair and Vale seemed to make little effort so the home side won with ease. From the outset, there was a lack of passion and the score was still goalless when Henshall was carried off with a badly twisted ankle after twenty-five minutes. For a while, Vale continued with ten men and Sale put Stoke in front before Baker came on as a substitute for the injured right winger. Nevertheless, the home team extended their lead a minute before the interval when Round diverted a Taylor shot into his own net.

The game 'developed into an exhibition' in the second half and Stoke 'scored almost at will'. In the fifty-second minute, Mawson made a magnificent run through the Vale defence to put the home team further ahead and Taylor, Mawson and Matthews (twice—with his first senior goals) were all on target to complete the rout. Although Stoke played some fine football and Matthews was outstanding, the score more reflected the visitors' lacklustre efforts.

THE AFTERMATH
A loss of £1,332 6s. 10d. on the season and a total debt of £8,551 16s. 11d. went a long way to explain Stoke's sale of their winger, Harry Taylor, to Liverpool and their lack of major close season signings to boost a further promotion bid. In June, the Vale directors appointed their trainer, Tom Holford, as their new manager to replace Tom Morgan, who was demoted to the post of assistant secretary! Despite Vale's £873 profit on the campaign, the new boss was forced to recruit on the cheap, so that the only noteworthy new signing was Bob Morton, a left winger from Bradford Park Avenue.

119: SATURDAY 22 OCTOBER 1932, FOOTBALL LEAGUE, SECOND DIVISION

STOKE CITY (1) 1 (Johnson), PORT VALE (0) 0.

STOKE: John, Spencer, Beachill, Robertson, Turner, Sellars, Liddle, Ware, Mawson, Davies, Johnson.
VALE: Leckie, Shenton, Poyser, Sherlock, Round, Jones, McGrath, Mills, Nolan, Page, Morton.

Venue: The Victoria Ground, Stoke-upon-Trent.
Attendance: 29,296.
Referee: L. Boulstridge (Tamworth).

THE SETTING
Stoke were top of the Second Division on goal average, having suffered only one league defeat, and were unbeaten in eight matches. Indeed, they had overcome their nearest rivals, Plymouth Argyle, by 2-0 at home a week before the local Derby. Vale were also faring well in fifth place, but had lost 7-0 and 5-0 in their previous two away games, the latter thrashing having been received at fourth from the bottom Notts County on the Saturday prior to the Derby! Stoke were unchanged for the occasion, whilst Tom Holford, Vale's manager, made just one alteration in his line-up, with the usual right-back, Shenton, returning after an injury.

THE MATCH
Stoke opened forcefully and, although chances were at a premium, Turner shot just wide. After fifteen minutes, Vale's centre-half picked up a groin injury and then went to play on the right wing, which increased the home side's advantage. Stoke took the lead just seven minutes later when Johnson struck in a rebound and shortly afterwards, Round was forced to retire for treatment. The home team consequently pressed strongly, but spurned several good opportunities before the Vale pivot returned, although only as a passenger. Stoke produced some brilliant football, but Leckie made a series of inspired saves.

Vale resumed the second period without Round, but pushed for an equaliser, although the match became rather bad-tempered. Stoke gradually regained the ascendancy and Mawson fired a tremendous shot just wide, whilst the ball later hit the home bar during a frantic goalmouth melee. Nevertheless, Stoke remained the more dangerous side and the visiting keeper saved superbly from Johnson before Mawson curled an effort inches outside a post.

THE AFTERMATH
Stoke remained as the league leaders as a result of their victory and Roy John, their goalkeeper, was capped for Wales against Scotland the following Wednesday. Although Stoke failed to progress beyond the fourth round of the F.A. Cup and hit a spell of poor form in midwinter, they recovered to continue their challenge for promotion. Vale were unable to regain their earlier form, dropped to eighth place after their local Derby defeat and were sixth from the bottom by the beginning of December, whilst their involvement in the F.A. Cup ended at the first hurdle.

120: SATURDAY 4 MARCH 1933, FOOTBALL LEAGUE, SECOND DIVISION

PORT VALE (0) 1 (McGrath), STOKE CITY (2) 3 (Johnson, Matthews, Ware).

VALE: Leckie, Sherlock, Poyser, Birks, Armitage, Jones, McGrath, Mills, Littlewood, Page, Morton.
STOKE: John, Spencer, Beachill, Robertson, Turner, Sellars, Matthews, Davies, Ware, Liddle, Johnson.

Venue: The Old Recreation Ground, Hanley.
Attendance: 19,625.
Referee: L. Boulstridge (Tamworth).

THE SETTING
Vale were fifteenth in the Second Division, but had won only one of their previous five matches and had lost 2-0 at fifth-placed Swansea Town in their last game a fortnight before the local Derby. In contrast, Stoke were a point clear at the top of the table, but had been defeated 1-0 at Plymouth Argyle on the Saturday prior to the Derby. Vale's team was unchanged for the clash, whilst Stoke's secretary-manager, Tom Mather, preferred to make a single alteration to his line-up and included Davies following his recovery from an injury. Fine weather attracted a large crowd, which became so compressed that many youngsters were allowed to sit beyond the perimeter barriers.

THE MATCH
The match began at a furious pace and after five minutes, Johnson swerved the ball straight into Vale's net from a corner, with Leckie unable to get more than his fingertips to it. Although the home keeper was then forced to make a magnificent save from Robertson, Vale fought back strongly and a shot from Littlewood skimmed the bar. However, Matthews extended Stoke's lead in the thirty-second minute with a ferocious narrow-angled shot following a breakaway. The visitors then held control for much of the remainder of the first half and produced some immaculate football.

After the interval, Vale increased the tempo and Spencer cleared a goal-bound header by McGrath from under the crossbar, although Davies powered a tremendous thirty-yard drive against the home bar shortly afterwards. Nevertheless, Ware put Stoke further in front in the fifty-eighth minute with a remarkable hook shot which looped over the home custodian, but Vale continued to press and Sellars kicked a Littlewood shot off the line. Finally, McGrath reduced the arrears in heading in a Morton centre after sixty-eight minutes, although the Stoke defence held firm in the face of a further onslaught.

THE AFTERMATH
In spite of their defeat, Vale only dropped one place in the table, whilst Stoke extended their lead at the top to two points. Vale's form was fairly steady for the rest of the season and they finished four points clear of relegation in seventeenth position. Stoke, however, secured the Second Division championship with a point to spare, despite losing four of their last eleven matches.

121: MONDAY 30 SEPTEMBER 1935, FRIENDLY

PORT VALE (0) 2 (Birks 2), STOKE CITY (3) 6 (Johnson 2, Sale, Westland, Matthews, Robson).

VALE: Potts, Shenton, Breeze, Curley, Hayward, Jones, Birks, Rhodes, Baker, Mitcheson, Caldwell.
STOKE: Wilkinson, McGrory, Spencer, Tutin, Turner, Sellars, Matthews, Robson, Sale, Westland, Johnson.

Venue: The Old Recreation Ground, Hanley.
Attendance: 4,600.
Referee: E. Adams (Hanley).

THE SETTING
This match was played as a benefit for Vale's long-serving right-back, George Shenton. Vale were thirteenth in the Second Division, but had lost 5-2 at sixth-placed Tottenham Hotspur two days before the local Derby and the board had released Tom Holford from his role as the manager so that he could concentrate on being the coach and chief scout! Stoke were in ninth position in the First Division and had also fared badly the previous Saturday in losing 3-0 at home to Arsenal. Vale's team was entirely unchanged for the local clash, but Stoke preferred to make three alterations from their last game, with Wilkinson and Robson replacing Lewis and Steele and their manager, Bob McGrory, standing in for the injured Scrimshaw.

THE MATCH
The match was played in a highly sporting manner and was open and free flowing, with some wonderful football exhibited by Stoke. Matthews was in brilliant form and his mazy dribbling runs caused havoc in the Vale defence. Stoke went in front in the fifteenth minute when Johnson lashed in a tremendous shot from a seemingly impossible angle and the same forward doubled the visitors' tally eighteen minutes later when he converted from a pass by Westland. Just before half-time, Sale further extended Stoke's lead.

Westland put Stoke 4-0 up with a header from a corner only two minutes after the interval, but the home side fought back strongly, inspired by the probing of Curley. As a result, Birks netted twice within the space of five minutes to put Vale back into contention. He first struck in a hard drive, after being set up by Baker, and then headed in from a Caldwell cross. However, in the sixty-third minute, Matthews thumped the ball home for Stoke after a dazzling solo run and Robson completed a rout by heading in from a corner.

THE AFTERMATH
Vale continued for the rest of the season without a manager and won only one of their following thirteen league matches. Although they remarkably beat the First Division leaders and eventual champions, Sunderland, to reach the fourth round of the F.A. Cup, a financial crisis developed in the spring at a time when relegation seemed likely. After a poor spell of form in November, Stoke made steady progress up the First Division table until they were third at the beginning of April, whilst they also reached the fifth round of the F.A. Cup.

139

122: MONDAY 27 APRIL 1936, FRIENDLY

STOKE CITY (1) 3 (Westland, Matthews, Steele), PORT VALE (0) 2 (Caldwell, Dean).

STOKE: Wilkinson, Winstanley, Scrimshaw, Tutin, Turner, Soo, Matthews, Liddle, Steele, Westland, Johnson.
VALE: Todd, Shenton, Gunn, Curley, Griffiths, Jones, Dean, Rhodes, Roberts, Stabb, Caldwell.

Venue: The Victoria Ground, Stoke-upon-Trent.
Attendance: Between 8,000 and 9,000.
Referee: E. Adams (Hanley).

THE SETTING

This game was played in aid of Vale's 40,000 Shillings Fund, which had been launched in the throes of a financial crisis, and was the result of a kind offer by the Stoke directors to help their old rivals. Stoke were fourth in the First Division with only one match remaining and had drawn 0-0 at Middlesbrough on the Saturday before the local Derby. In contrast, Vale were in penultimate position in the Second Division, two points adrift of safety with just one away game to play, and had lost 3-2 at home to third-placed West Ham United two days prior to the Derby. Bob McGrory, Stoke's manager, made just a single change to his team for the local clash, bringing in Westland for Davies, whilst Vale's line-up was altered by the inclusion of Todd and Dean. The match was preceded by a march of four jazz bands to Stoke from the Old Recreation Ground.

THE MATCH

The match was performed more as an exhibition than as a competitive encounter, with neither set of players risking injury, although there was plenty of skilful football on show. Stoke preferred a methodical style of play, whilst the visitors relied mainly on breakaways to trouble their opponents who were generally in command. Stoke attacked with great precision and the visiting keeper was forced to make fine saves from Westland and Steele, although Roberts missed a glorious opportunity for Vale. Westland netted the only goal of the first half, after thirty minutes, to put Stoke in front from a Johnson pass.

A quarter of an hour into the second period, Matthews burst inside to flash a shot in to double Stoke's lead and Steele added a third goal following a thrilling solo run in the sixty-fifth minute. Although Vale then rallied strongly and Caldwell and Dean both pulled goals back, the home side ended up worthy winners.

THE AFTERMATH

£528 2s. was taken at the gate, which netted around £500 for Vale's fund, and the directors, officials and players of the two clubs had supper together at the Grand Hotel in Hanley after the game. Unfortunately, Vale were relegated in penultimate position to the Third Division (North) after drawing their final league match 1-1 at second-placed Charlton Athletic on the following Saturday. On the same day, Stoke beat struggling Liverpool 2-1 at home to finish fourth in the First Division and attain their highest ever league position.

123: SATURDAY 23 SEPTEMBER 1939, FRIENDLY

STOKE CITY (2) 3 (Sale, Ormston, Baker), PORT VALE (0) 2 (Jones, Beresford).

STOKE: Martin, Brigham, Oldham, Massey, Mould, Soo, Matthews, Peppitt, Sale, Ormston, Baker.
VALE: Jepson, Rowe, Cumberlidge, Hannah, Griffiths, Smith, Triner, Roberts, Jones, Nolan, Beresford.

Venue: The Victoria Ground, Stoke-upon-Trent.
Attendance: 4,512.
Referee: E.V. Gough (Penkhull).

THE SETTING

As a result of the outbreak of the Second World War earlier in the month, the Football League competition had been abandoned. Subsequently, the government had given permission for friendly matches to be played and, a week before the local Derby, Stoke had beaten Coventry City 3-1 at home, whilst Vale had lost 3-0 at Shrewsbury Town. Both clubs made two team changes for the Derby, with Martin being given a trial in goal and Massey returning after injury for Stoke, whilst Roberts and Jones were selected for Vale.

THE MATCH

The match got off to a pulsating start when Sale prodded the ball into a corner of the Vale net from a Matthews centre after only thirty seconds' play! Stoke's skill and the wonderful talents of Matthews quickly became apparent, although the visitors battled ruggedly and launched speedy raids. Sale miskicked with only the Vale keeper to beat and Beresford squandered an excellent opportunity for the visitors before Ormston doubled Stoke's lead with a twenty-five-yard shot in the thirty-sixth minute. The home side continued to press and Soo twice put good chances wide, whilst Roberts cleared an effort from Sale off the line.

After the interval, Stoke bombarded the visitors' goal, which witnessed several close calls, but on the hour Jones reduced the arrears by turning in a cross from Triner during a Vale breakaway. However, Baker restored Stoke's advantage just three minutes later when he completed a beautiful flowing move by flashing a low drive into a corner of the net. A determined solo run by Peppitt nearly added a fourth goal for the home team, but Beresford made the score more respectable for Vale when he crashed in a shot off an upright two minutes from time.

THE AFTERMATH

Both sides played several further friendly games before the Football League resumed in late October with a wartime competition, in which Stoke and Vale were placed in the Western Regional Tournament. Stoke quickly found this to their liking, scoring four goals in each of their opening four matches and losing only two of their first thirteen games, as they made a strong bid for the championship. Vale also settled in nicely and by the middle of March were fifth out of twelve teams.

124: MONDAY 25 MARCH 1940, FOOTBALL LEAGUE, WESTERN REGIONAL TOURNAMENT

STOKE CITY (3) 5 (Ormston 2, H. Griffiths 2 o.g.s, Sale), PORT VALE (0) 1 (Roberts).

STOKE: Jones, Brigham, Scrimshaw, Massey, Mould, Soo, Peppitt, Liddle, Sale, Steele, Ormston.
VALE: Jepson, Rowe, J. Griffiths, Smith, H. Griffiths, Cumberlidge, P. Griffiths, Higgins, Roberts, Pursell, Tunnicliffe.

Venue: The Victoria Ground, Stoke-upon-Trent.
Attendance: 9,450.
Referee: G. Dutton (Warwick).

THE SETTING
Stoke were second in their twelve-club wartime league and being kept off the top spot by goal average, but had only drawn 3-3 at fourth from the bottom Chester on the Saturday before the local Derby. Vale were in fifth position, although they had been beaten 3-1 at home by the league leaders, Manchester United, two days prior to the Derby. Stoke welcomed back Steele in the forward line for the local clash, but were without the unavailable Matthews, whilst Vale drafted in Pursell and Jack Griffiths (of Manchester United) guested for them at left-back. The good form of the two teams attracted a very large crowd.

THE MATCH
Both sides began briskly and goalmouth action was abundant. There was a series of near misses at both ends and Brigham kicked the ball off the line during a melee in the Stoke goal. On the half-hour, Stoke went in front when Ormston fired in a strong, low shot after being set up by Steele and Peppitt then missed a sitter, whilst Ormston had a second effort disallowed for offside. Vale's goal remained under siege and in the thirty-ninth minute the home side extended their lead when Harry Griffiths turned a Sale shot into his own net. Worse befell the visiting centre-half thirty seconds before the interval when he converted another effort from Sale in identical circumstances!

Although Vale resumed brightly, the home team soon regained command, but in the fifty-seventh minute Roberts reduced the arrears from a tap-in after the Stoke keeper had dropped the ball. This stung the home side into further action and only Jepson kept them at bay until Ormston increased Stoke's lead with a tremendous effort after seventy minutes. Sale then had a goal overruled because of offside, although the same player added a fifth for Stoke ten minutes from time.

THE AFTERMATH
More than £500 was collected at the gate, an excellent amount for wartime, and Stoke had further joy in that they took over as the tournament leaders as a result of their victory, whilst a seven-league and cup match unbeaten run followed. Although Vale initially remained fifth in the league, they had dropped to eighth by the beginning of May and exited from the Football League (War) Cup in the preliminary round.

125: MONDAY 6 MAY 1940, FOOTBALL LEAGUE, WESTERN REGIONAL TOURNAMENT

PORT VALE (1) 1 (Roberts), STOKE CITY (1) 2 (Sale, Steele).

VALE: Jepson, Pursell, Oakes, Smith, Ware, Cumberlidge, Triner, P. Griffiths, Roberts, Blunt, Bellis.

STOKE: Jones, Brigham, Scrimshaw, Tutin, Mould, Soo, Matthews, Peppitt, Steele, Sale, Ormston.

Venue: The Old Recreation Ground, Hanley.
Attendance: 3,053.
Referee: G. Dutton (Warwick).

THE SETTING

Vale were fifth from the bottom of the twelve-team wartime competition, despite having won two more matches than they'd lost! They had defeated struggling Chester 3-1 at home two days before the local Derby, but had crashed out of the Football League (War) Cup in their previous game, losing 6-0 at Walsall in a preliminary round replay! Stoke, in contrast, were the Western Regional league leaders and a point clear of the field. In addition, they had won 2-0 at Barrow in the first leg of their second round cup tie on the Saturday prior to the Derby. Vale made three changes in their line-up for the local clash, with Oakes, Ware and Triner returning to the side, whilst Stoke's manager, Bob McGrory, brought in Scrimshaw and Tutin.

THE MATCH

Vale were the more forceful and dangerous team in the first half, but three times had shots charged down, whilst Blunt squandered a golden opportunity and Bellis hit the bar. However, Stoke went in front in the thirty-third minute when a brilliant move led to Sale shooting past the advancing keeper following a precise through ball by Steele. Nevertheless, Vale gained some reward for their spirited efforts when Roberts headed an equaliser three minutes from the interval.

Stoke regained the lead just five minutes after the restart when Steele stroked the ball in from a clever pass back from Sale. Almost immediately afterwards, Sale shot against a post and later Oakes cleared a goal-bound effort off the line, but Vale also had their moments and near to the death Jones made a wonderful save to deny Bellis an equaliser.

THE AFTERMATH

The result ensured that both teams remained in their respective positions in the league and Vale finished the season fifth from the bottom after conceding twelve goals in two defeats by Manchester City in their remaining three matches. The club then became inoperative until 1944, other than running an amateur junior side, because of the insurmountable costs of continuing to function in the Football League. In contrast, Stoke became the Western Regional Tournament champions and trounced Barrow 6-0 in the second leg of their cup tie, although they were then eliminated by Everton in the next round.

143

126: SATURDAY 18 NOVEMBER 1944, FOOTBALL LEAGUE NORTH

STOKE CITY (0) 2 (Bowyer 2), PORT VALE (0) 0.

STOKE: Foster, Watkin, McCue, F. Mountford, Franklin, Jackson, Matthews, Bowyer, Steele, Sale, Mannion.
VALE: H. Prince, J. Griffiths, Sproson, Smith, H. Griffiths, Wright, E. Prince, Lane, Pursell, Bellis, W. Pointon.

Venue: The Victoria Ground, Stoke-upon-Trent.
Attendance: 16,163.
Referee: W.H. Clinton (Wolverhampton).

THE SETTING

Stoke were in midtable in the wartime league, having won and lost an equal number of matches, but they had been beaten 3-2 at home by West Bromwich Albion a week before the local Derby. Vale were not doing nearly so well and had lost seven of their opening twelve league games, which included a 4-0 defeat at Aston Villa on the Saturday prior to the Derby. Bob McGrory, Stoke's manager, made two changes in his line-up for the local clash, with the junior players Watkin and Jackson being drafted in, whilst Vale welcomed back Sproson, Pursell and Billy Pointon to the ranks. The struggle was witnessed by an excellent crowd and long queues formed well before the kickoff.

THE MATCH

The start of the match was delayed for almost a quarter of an hour as the teams awaited the arrival of Vale's right-back, Jack Griffiths, but when it began, Stoke attacked strongly. Although Vale fought back, Steele headed against the woodwork and several exciting melees occurred in the visitors' goalmouth. Steele twice went close with further headers, whilst Bowyer ballooned a marvellous opportunity over the bar, but Stoke were unable to break the deadlock.

After the interval, Vale pressed vigorously, although Pursell and Pointon both squandered opportunities to open the scoring. Stoke then responded and only fine goalkeeping by Harry Prince prevented them from taking the lead before the fifty-sixth minute when Bowyer smashed in an unstoppable shot following an intricate build-up. The same player made the game safe fifteen minutes later, although Stoke continued to spurn chances to add to their score.

THE AFTERMATH

As well as recording their ninth consecutive victory against Vale, Stoke took an excellent £1,465 at the gate. They moved up to twenty-second out of an astonishing fifty-four sides in the tournament as a result of their success, whilst Vale slumped to seventh from the bottom of the table. Nevertheless, Vale had an opportunity to reverse their fortunes the following Saturday in the return Derby.

127: SATURDAY 25 NOVEMBER 1944, FOOTBALL LEAGUE NORTH

PORT VALE (2) 3 (McDowell, Bellis, P. Griffiths), STOKE CITY (0) 0.

VALE: H. Prince, J. Griffiths, Sproson, Martin, H. Griffiths, Wright, Lane, McDowell, P. Griffiths, Bellis, Maudsley.

STOKE: Foster, Brigham, McCue, F. Mountford, Franklin, Jackson, G. Mountford, Bowyer, A. Basnett, Sale, Mannion.

Venue: The Old Recreation Ground, Hanley.
Attendance: 9,618.
Referee: E.R. Varney (Derby).

THE SETTING

Vale were seventh from the bottom of a remarkable fifty-four-team wartime league and had lost eight of their thirteen matches, which included a 2-0 defeat at Stoke the previous Saturday. Their local rivals were comfortably placed in twenty-second position, but were well adrift of the most consistent sides. Vale's team manager, Jack Diffin, made four changes in his line-up for the return Derby, with Martin, McDowell and Maudsley returning to the fray, whilst Phil Griffiths, the thirty-nine-year old "A" team coach, was also pressed into action. Stoke were without both Matthews and Steele, who were unavailable, and brought in Brigham, George Mountford and Fred Basnett.

THE MATCH

Bowyer was presented with an early opening for Stoke, but struck the ball well wide and then the visiting keeper made two magnificent saves from McDowell. Nevertheless, Vale went in front in the twenty-fourth minute when McDowell headed a free kick from Martin into the net. Lane wasted an opportunity to extend Vale's lead, but Bellis made amends after thirty-five minutes when he finished off a breakaway by planting the ball into the far corner of the goal. Stoke then pressed strongly, although both Mannion and Basnett spurned clear-cut chances to reduce the arrears.

After the interval, Vale took command and, inspired by McDowell, threatened the visitors' goal several times. However, after Phil Griffiths had put Vale further in front, they concentrated on preserving their lead. As the home side fell back on defence, the Stoke players poured forwards, but squandered numerous opportunities in the final twenty-five minutes. Therefore, although the visitors finished the more cohesive outfit, Vale comfortably secured their first local Derby victory since 1932.

THE AFTERMATH

Although Vale took a healthy £836 in gate receipts, they gained just one point from their remaining four league games, but still finished with nine teams below them in the table. From Christmas, their efforts became concentrated on the Football League North Cup, but they lost four out of their first five matches in the qualifying group. Stoke won all their last four league games, scoring sixteen goals in the process, to end the tournament in eleventh position, although they began the Football League North Cup competition indifferently.

128: SATURDAY 17 FEBRUARY 1945, FOOT-BALL LEAGUE NORTH CUP, QUALIFYING COMPETITION

STOKE CITY (5) 8 (G. Mountford 5, Soo 2, A. Basnett), PORT VALE (1) 1 (Cardwell).

STOKE: Herod, Brigham, McCue, F. Mountford, Franklin, Jackson, G. Mountford, Peppitt, Sale, Soo, A. Basnett.
VALE: H. Prince, H. Griffiths, Bateman, Hannah, Cardwell, Lane, E. Prince, McDowell, Booth, Sproson, McShane.

Venue: The Victoria Ground, Stoke-upon-Trent.
Attendance: 12,644.
Referee: F.S. Milner (Wolverhampton).

THE SETTING

The main competition for the local clubs this season was the Football League North, which had been completed in December 1944. The ten-match League North Cup, Qualifying Competiton, had begun thereafter and Stoke had taken seven points from their five games played thus far, but Vale had lost four of their seven matches contested. Stoke had trounced Chester 7-0 at home on the Saturday before the local Derby, whilst Vale had completed a double over Wolverhampton Wanderers by gaining a 2-1 away victory on the same day. Stoke's manager, Bob McGrory, made two changes to his line-up for the local clash, owing to the unavailability of Matthews (for whom George Mountford deputised) and the arrival of Soo on leave. Bellis, Vale's usual left winger, did not turn up for the game and was replaced by Harry McShane, a guest from Blackburn Rovers.

THE MATCH

Stoke took control from the outset and 'outplayed, outschemed and outpaced' their opponents, scoring 'almost at will'. George Mountford and Soo both went close before Basnett headed Stoke in front in the fourteenth minute. Vale became penned in their own half and after Basnett had struck the bar, George Mountford sent a tremendous drive into the net in the twenty-third minute. Although the Vale keeper excelled, Soo added a third with a low twenty-yard shot three minutes later and the same player prodded Stoke further in front ten minutes from the break. Cardwell reduced the arrears five minutes afterwards when his free kick was deflected over Herod, but George Mountford hit an upright and then made it five for Stoke following a solo run just before the interval.

Two minutes into the second period, George Mountford cut inside to complete his hat trick and struck again after sixty-three minutes. Although McDowell ran through in a rare Vale breakaway and hit the bar midway through the half, the home side remained in command and George Mountford completed the rout ten minutes from time in scoring his fifth goal. Thus Stoke equalled the all-time record victory in a Potteries Derby.

THE AFTERMATH

A pleasing £1,165 was taken at the gate and there was the prospect of more invaluable funds to come from the return Derby the following Saturday.

146

129: SATURDAY 24 FEBRUARY 1945, FOOT-BALL LEAGUE NORTH CUP, QUALIFYING COMPETITION

PORT VALE (1) 2 (McShane, W. Pointon), STOKE CITY (3) 6 (Steele 3, Sale 2, Soo).

VALE: H. Prince, Lane, Sproson, F. Pointon, Cardwell, Cooper, Clunn, McDowell, W. Pointon, Bellis, McShane.

STOKE: Herod, Brigham, McCue, F. Mountford, Franklin, Soo, Matthews, G. Mountford, Sale, Steele, A. Basnett.

Venue: The Old Recreation Ground, Hanley.
Attendance: 17,040.
Referee: F.S. Milner (Wolverhampton).

THE SETTING

Vale had lost five of their eight matches played thus far in the wartime Football League North Cup, Qualifying Competition, and in the last of these, a week before this return local Derby, they had been annihilated 8-1 at Stoke! This victory had given Stoke their fourth win in six games in the tournament and kept them on target for qualification for the later stages of the competition. Vale's team manager, Jack Diffin, made numerous changes in his line-up for the local clash, with Frank Pointon, Cooper, Clunn, Billy Pointon and Bellis being brought back into the side and two positional alterations being preferred. Worryingly for Vale, Matthews and Steele returned to Stoke's team, which boasted four England internationals (Franklin, Soo, Matthews and Steele).

THE MATCH

A tremendous crowd gathered to see Stoke give a 'stimulating and high quality exhibition' after taking the lead in the first minute when Sale ran through and placed the ball into the net. Eleven minutes later, a George Mountford shot hit a post, but Vale battled hard and, after Steele had struck the woodwork for Stoke, McShane cut inside to equalise in the twenty-fifth minute. However, Stoke went in front again after thirty-five minutes when Steele headed in from a Matthews cross. Towards the end of the half, George Mountford again struck a post, although Steele extended Stoke's lead two minutes before the interval when he once more headed home a perfect centre from Matthews.

Sale shot Stoke further in front two minutes into the second period, but the home side reduced the arrears in the fifty-seventh minute when Billy Pointon tapped in a rebound. Bellis then had a marvellous goal disallowed for offside, although Soo made the game safe for Stoke after sixty-five minutes, while Steele completed his hat trick five minutes from time.

THE AFTERMATH

Vale collected excellent gate receipts of £1,464, but their defeat ensured their exit from the cup competition. Although Stoke only gained three points from their remaining three qualifying matches, they progressed into the knockout stages of the tournament, but were eliminated in the second round by 10-2 on aggregate over two legs by Manchester United.

147

130: SATURDAY 5 MAY 1945, FOOTBALL LEAGUE NORTH, SECOND CHAMPIONSHIP

STOKE CITY (3) 6 (G. Mountford 4, Sellars, Sale), PORT VALE (0) 0.

STOKE: Herod, Brigham, Watkin, F. Mountford, Cowden, Kirton, G. Mountford, Sellars, Sale, Jackson, A. Basnett.
VALE: H. Prince, Bateman, Lane, F. Pointon, H. Griffiths, Cooper, Birks, Roden, Wilshaw, Bailey, Clunn.

Venue: The Victoria Ground, Stoke-upon-Trent.
Attendance: Just over 1,000.
Referee: E. Adams (Ash Bank).

THE SETTING
Oddly, a second championship had been launched following the completion of the initial wartime Football League North tournament in December 1944 and Stoke and Vale were once again both included in the same section. Stoke had won one and lost one of their opening two matches in this competition and had been defeated 2-0 at Aston Villa in the qualifying round of the Midland Cup a week before the local Derby. Vale were also faring badly, with only a single victory in their initial five Second Championship games, and had lost 1-0 at home to Tranmere Rovers on the Saturday prior to the Derby. Stoke were without their four England internationals, Franklin, Soo, Matthews and Steele, and made four changes in their line-up for the local contest, as did Vale, who featured the Wolverhampton Wanderers' forward, Dennis Wilshaw, as a guest.

THE MATCH
A mere 500 spectators saw the match get off to a leisurely start, but the tempo gradually increased and Bateman headed a Jackson effort off the line, whilst Wilshaw spurned a golden opportunity for Vale by dithering. George Mountford put Stoke in front in the twentieth minute with a fierce drive following a solo run and then doubled their lead twelve minutes later when he intercepted a weak back pass by Griffiths and stroked the ball in. Mountford completed his hat trick just before the interval by slotting home from a through ball by Sale.

Stoke continued to dominate in the second half, although Herod made a marvellous save from Clunn to prevent Vale from reducing the arrears. Nevertheless, Sellars extended Stoke's lead and George Mountford then notched his ninth goal within three months against Vale! The visitors battled gamely and Wilshaw produced some neat touches, but Sale later completed the rout by adding a sixth goal for Stoke.

THE AFTERMATH
Stoke's crushing victory considerably improved their chances of attaining a good final position in the Second Championship, whilst the result condemned Vale to finishing in the lower reaches of the league table, even though they still had one game left to play. This was the return Derby against their local rivals, scheduled for the following Wednesday, which was also planned to celebrate the end of the war in Europe.

131: WEDNESDAY 9 MAY 1945, FOOTBALL LEAGUE NORTH, SECOND CHAMPIONSHIP/STAFFORDSHIRE VICTORY CUP

PORT VALE (0) 2 (Isherwood, H. Griffiths)**, STOKE CITY (0) 4** (Sellars 2, Kirton, Jackson).

VALE: H. Prince, Bateman, Sproson, McKay, Hughes, Bray, Roden, H. Griffiths, Isherwood, Cooper, Allen.
STOKE: Herod, Brigham, Watkin, F. Mountford, Cowden, Kirton, Windsor, Sellars, Sale, Jackson, A. Basnett.

Venue: The Old Recreation Ground, Hanley.
Attendance: 5,550.
Referee: Unknown.

THE SETTING
This match was officially a fixture in the Football League North, Second Championship, but was also played 'to commemorate the cessation of hostilities in Europe' and consequently carried the Staffordshire Victory Cup as a prize. It was Vale's last game in the Second Championship and gave them the chance to avenge their 6-0 drubbing at Stoke the previous Saturday. Vale's line-up for the return Derby showed six new faces from their previous match, with Sproson and Allen returning to the fray, whilst four guest players (William McKay of Manchester United, Stephen Hughes of Crewe Alexandra, Jackie Bray of Manchester City and Dennis Isherwood of Wrexham) made their debuts for the club. Stoke remained without several of their big stars and the only alteration to their team was the replacement of George Mountford with Windsor.

THE MATCH
Vale began brightly, but the visitors took control after the opening ten minutes and frequently threatened danger. Sellars and Basnett went very close to putting Stoke in front, although Vale also had their moments and Allen and Roden squandered clear goalscoring opportunities. Nevertheless, by the interval, neither side had managed to break the deadlock.

The position was transformed during the first thirty minutes of the second period as Stoke raced into a four-goal lead, thanks to successful strikes by Sellars (twice), Kirton and Jackson. This achievement was the result of Stoke's fine teamwork and sharpness, although Kirton was instrumental in breaking up many of the home side's attacks. However, Vale rallied strongly in the later stages and scored twice, through Isherwood and Griffiths, in the last six minutes to make the final outcome much closer than had once seemed likely.

THE AFTERMATH
Although it was unknown at the time, this proved to be the final Potteries Derby to be played in Hanley. The match raised £464 and the Staffordshire Victory Cup was presented to the winning team in the Vale boardroom afterwards. As a consequence of their defeat, Vale finished seventh from the bottom of the league, whilst Stoke lost two of their remaining three games to end up seventeenth out of sixty sides.

132: THURSDAY 16 AUGUST 1945, FRIENDLY

STOKE CITY (3) 6 (A. Basnett 3, Steele, Sellars, Sale), PORT VALE (0) 0.

STOKE: Leigh, Brigham, Topham, F. Mountford, Cowden, Kirton, Matthews, Sellars, Steele, Sale, A. Basnett.
VALE: H. Prince, Bateman, Potts, F. Pointon, Turner, Cooper, Clunn, Birks, Green, H. Johnson, Allen.

Venue: The Victoria Ground, Stoke-upon-Trent.
Attendance: Nearly 3,000.
Referee: A. Mayer (Stoke-on-Trent).

THE SETTING
The match was arranged as a pre-season friendly in celebration of V-J Day, although the agreement to stage it was only reached twenty-four hours beforehand. Consequently, the clubs appealed through the "Evening Sentinel" for all their players in the area to report to the Victoria Ground an hour before the kickoff! Stoke were successful in assembling almost their entire first team and included three internationals (Kirton, Matthews and Steele) in their line-up. In contrast, Vale struggled to field a representative eleven and were missing five key players, although Arthur Turner (a former Stoke stalwart) of Birmingham City and Arthur Bateman of Crewe Alexandra guested in their side. The size of the crowd was not surprisingly limited by the short notice and a wealth of alternative events.

THE MATCH
The outcome of the match was strongly contested for the first quarter of an hour, but thereafter Stoke took command and 'won in a canter'. Although Vale fought hard throughout, they were unable to test seriously the home defence and Stoke swept their opponents aside through fine interplay. Matthews exhibited his marvellous skill as usual and only an excellent display from the Vale keeper prevented an even heavier beating. By half-time, Stoke were already 3-0 up, thanks to two goals from Basnett and another from Steele. Basnett completed his hat trick in the second period and Sellars and Sale added to the score before Vale's ordeal finally ended.

THE AFTERMATH
Stoke's triumph against their local rivals did not prove a harbinger of success in the 1945-1946 regional Football League North because they began the tournament indifferently, were annihilated 9-1 at Newcastle United on 22 September and finished thirteenth out of twenty-two teams. However, they reached the sixth round of the F.A. Cup before being eliminated by Bolton Wanderers on 9 March at Burnden Park, where, tragically, thirty-three spectators died in a crush. Vale competed in the Third Division (South) North Region and generally performed well to end up third in an eleven-club league, although they could only manage eighth place in the divison's cup competition. However, they did fight their way through to the third round of the F.A. Cup.

150

133: SATURDAY 6 JANUARY 1951, F.A. CUP, THIRD ROUND

STOKE CITY (0) 2 (Mullard 2), PORT VALE (1) 2 (Bennett, Pinchbeck).

STOKE: Wilkinson, Mould, McCue, Sellars, Beckett, Kirton, Ormston, Bowyer, Brown, Mullard, Oscroft.
VALE: King, Hamlett, Turner, McGarry, Cheadle, Polk, Hulligan, Aveyard, Pinchbeck, Martin, Bennett.

Venue: The Victoria Ground, Stoke-upon-Trent.
Attendance: 49,500.
Referee: R.A. Mortimer (Huddersfield).

THE SETTING
This was the first local Derby since 1945. Stoke were eighth in the First Division, although they had drawn too many times to be in contention for the championship. However, they were unbeaten for four matches and had gained a useful point from a 1-1 draw at Derby County a week before the local contest. Vale were in sixteenth position in the Third Division (South) and had had their previous game, at home against Plymouth Argyle on the same day, abandoned because of a blizzard. Vale had beaten both Third Division (North) New Brighton and Lancashire Combination Nelson 3-2 in earlier rounds to qualify for this F.A. Cup clash with their rivals. Although Sellars and Ormston returned to action for Stoke after illness and injury respectively, the home side were handicapped by the absence of three of their mainstays: Herod, Frank Mountford and Johnston. Vale had no such problems and were represented at full strength.

THE MATCH
The match quickly developed into a fierce struggle on a pudding of a pitch and Bennett put Vale in front after only six minutes when the home keeper failed to hold his shot. Stoke then piled on the pressure and King made a wonderful save from a Bowyer thunderbolt, but the visitors weathered the storm and Polk and Martin both went close to doubling Vale's lead in the latter stages of the first half. However, Bennett was badly injured just before the interval and had to be carried off.

Bennett returned to the fray in the second period and Vale went further in front within a minute of the re-start when Pinchbeck steered a superbly-placed header into the net from a long McGarry punt. Although the Vale supporters 'rose to fever pitch', the home team reduced the arrears just four minutes later when Mullard flashed the ball in from an Oscroft pass. Martin then struck the bar for Vale, but Mullard equalised on the hour with a shot that stopped dead in the mud just over the line! Thereafter Stoke largely held control, although neither side was able to grab the winner.

THE AFTERMATH
The all-time record crowd for a Potteries Derby produced gate receipts of £5,800. However, the replay, on the following Monday, was switched to the Victoria Ground because of major drainage problems with the Vale Park pitch, especially as a result of heavy rain which accompanied a thaw of lying snow.

151

134: MONDAY 8 JANUARY 1951, F.A. CUP, THIRD ROUND REPLAY

PORT VALE (0) 0, STOKE CITY (0) 1 (Bowyer).

VALE: King, Hamlett, Hayward, McGarry, Cheadle, Polk, Hulligan, Aveyard, Pinchbeck, Martin, Griffiths.
STOKE: Herod, Mould, McCue, Sellars, F. Mountford, Kirton, Ormston, Bowyer, Brown, Johnston, Oscroft.

Venue: The Victoria Ground, Stoke-upon-Trent.
Attendance: 40,977.
Referee: R.A. Mortimer (Huddersfield).

THE SETTING
Although Vale were the home team in this replay of the tie drawn 2-2 at Stoke two days previously, the match was switched to the Victoria Ground because of the dire state of the new Vale Park pitch following the combined effects of heavy rain and melting snow. Both clubs made changes in their line-ups, with Hayward and Griffiths replacing Turner and the injured Bennett for Vale and the experienced Herod, Frank Mountford and Johnston returning for Stoke. Queues of thousands of people gathered well before the kickoff, despite the game being played in the afternoon, and many industrial workers were given time off to attend providing that they completed their tasks before or afterwards.

THE MATCH
The pitch proved to be less heavy than had been feared and the play quickly became end to end. However, Vale came the closer to scoring, with Hulligan grazing the bar with a tremendous shot and Herod scrambling a free kick from Polk off the line. Stoke were increasingly forced on to the defensive and Griffiths spurned a golden opportunity to put Vale ahead when he aimed a kick at the ball but completely missed it.

Although the Vale supporters were elated by their team's showing, Stoke attacked strongly at the start of the second period and Brown and Bowyer both went near to giving them the lead. However, their impetus faltered when McCue was injured and became a passenger on the left wing, whilst heavy rain made the pitch a mud bath and the light began to fail. Vale then pressed hard for the winner and Herod made wonderful saves from Hulligan and Aveyard before Bowyer shot fractionally over the bar as Stoke replied. The outcome of the titanic struggle was finally settled in Stoke's favour two minutes from time when Bowyer cut in and struck a fine shot into the net.

THE AFTERMATH
Another £4,660 was taken in match receipts, which left the two clubs with a profit of around £2,800 each after the deduction of tax. Stoke progressed to the fifth round of the cup, but were then eliminated 2-1 at home by their First Division rivals, Newcastle United. Stoke finished the season in thirteenth position in the league, whilst Vale ended up one place higher in the Third Division (South).

152

135: MONDAY 1 OCTOBER 1951, FRIENDLY

STOKE CITY (0) 2 (Woodall, Beckett pen.), PORT VALE (1) 1 (Cunliffe).

STOKE: Yoxall, Mould, Bourne, Hampson, Beckett, Giblin, G. Mountford, Bevans, Brown, Whiston, Woodall.
VALE: King, Hamlett, Hayward, Turner, Cheadle, Sproson, Askey, Polk, Pinchbeck, Mullard, Cunliffe.

Venue: The Victoria Ground, Stoke-upon-Trent.
Attendance: 4,447.
Referee: A. Hughes (Hanford).

THE SETTING
This game had been arranged as a benefit for the dependants of Gordon Hodgson, the former Vale manager, who had died of cancer whilst still in office on 14 June. Stoke were three points adrift at the foot of the First Division, but had won for the first time in twelve attempts by beating third from the bottom Burnley 2-1 at home on the Saturday before the local Derby. Vale were also struggling at sixth from the bottom of the Third Division (South), having won only two matches, and had lost 4-2 at Gillingham two days prior to the Derby. Although Stoke fielded entirely a reserve side apart from George Mountford for the local clash, all Vale's selected players were from their first team squad.

THE MATCH
Vale attacked vigorously from the outset and produced skilful football, with a series of flowing moves that threatened to take their opponents apart. Although they created numerous chances, the visitors' finishing was woeful and several excellent opportunities were wasted, with Pinchbeck the main culprit. Nevertheless, Cunliffe put Vale in front in the twenty-eighth minute when he picked up a miskick from the home keeper and struck the ball just inside a post.

Vale remained well in command in the second half, although inept finishing continued to ruin their fine approach play. On one occasion, Pinchbeck dribbled past the Stoke custodian, but inexplicably then failed to tap the ball into the empty net! Nevertheless, Stoke's Woodall surpassed this blunder by shooting wide of a post when faced with an open goal two yards in front of him! However, even greater shocks were in store because Woodall headed an equaliser from a Mountford centre in the seventy-third minute and then Beckett gave Stoke an undeserved winner from a disputed penalty five minutes from time.

THE AFTERMATH
The Gordon Hodgson Dependants Fund benefited from the gate receipts of £383, whilst Stoke won their next four league matches following the local Derby to climb out of the relegation zone. They eventually finished the season third from the bottom, which ensured their First Division survival. Vale failed to record any victories in their next nine league and F.A. Cup games, although they later recovered to end up thirteenth in their division.

136: MONDAY 4 MAY 1953, FRIENDLY

STOKE CITY (0) 2 (Bowyer, Brown), PORT VALE (0) 0.

STOKE: Elliott, Doyle, McCue, F. Mountford, Thomson, Sellars, Malkin, Bowyer, Brown, Martin, Oscroft.
VALE: Hancock, Turner, Potts, Mullard, Cheadle, Sproson, Askey, Leake, Hayward, Griffiths, Hulligan.

Venue: The Victoria Ground, Stoke-upon-Trent.
Attendance: 9,981.
Referee: W. Ratcliffe (Leek).

THE SETTING
This charity match had been arranged to celebrate the impending coronation of Elizabeth II. Stoke had finished the 1952-1953 season second from the bottom of the First Division and had been relegated. They had lost their final game 2-1 at home to Derby County, the only team beneath them in the league, nine days before the local Derby. In stark contrast, Vale had gained the runners-up spot in the Third Division (North), although four victories in their last five matches (including a 4-0 hammering of fifth-placed Grimsby Town at home four days prior to the Derby) had failed to secure the championship and the promotion it would have entailed. Both sides were unchanged from their previous games for the local contest.

THE MATCH
The clash featured much 'laboured effort' as the intense rivalry of the two clubs created a physical rather than skilful contest. The play in the first half was fairly even and whilst Hayward lobbed the ball against a Stoke upright in the twentieth minute, the visiting keeper produced an excellent save from Oscroft just two minutes later. Hulligan then went close for Vale, as did Brown for the home side, but the defences were largely in command.

The second period continued in the same vein, although after Mullard had almost given Vale the lead, their custodian stood rooted to the line in the fifty-ninth minute as a free kick from Bowyer rolled directly into the net. Hulligan then almost equalised, but a quarter of an hour from the end, Brown swivelled to crash the ball in from an Oscroft centre to extend Stoke's lead. Although Mullard went close to reducing the deficit, the home defence held firm to secure the victory.

THE AFTERMATH
The match raised £1,053 10s., which was divided between the King George VI Memorial Fund, the National Playing Fields Association and the Central Council of Physical Recreation. Following their relegation, Stoke sold their centre-forward, Roy Brown, to Watford for £5,500; their inside-left, Les Johnston, to Shrewsbury Town for £2,000 and their goalkeeper, Dennis Herod, to Stockport County for £750. The club announced the adoption of a youth policy and no major new signings were made in the close season. Likewise, Vale preferred to resist a plunge into the transfer market and intended to rely on their current team to better their efforts the following season.

137: SATURDAY 4 SEPTEMBER 1954, FOOTBALL LEAGUE, SECOND DIVISION

STOKE CITY (0) 0, PORT VALE (0) 0.

STOKE: Robertson, Short, McCue, Mountford, Thomson, Sellars, Malkin, Hutton, J. King, Cairns, Oscroft.
VALE: R. King, Turner, Potts, Mullard, Cheadle, Sproson, Askey, Leake, Hayward, Griffiths, Cunliffe.

Venue: The Victoria Ground, Stoke-upon-Trent.
Attendance: 46,777.
Referee: J.H. Clough (Bolton).

THE SETTING

This was the first full league clash between the two rivals for over twenty-one years. Not surprisingly, the all-ticket game produced a record Potteries Derby league crowd, with special trains and buses in operation and tickets changing hands on the black market. Nevertheless, the atmosphere was rather constrained, although the Stoke-on-Trent Special Constabulary Band provided pre-match entertainment. Stoke were at the top of the Second Division on goal average and had opened their league campaign with four straight victories, the most recent of which had been by 2-0 at home to the bottom club, Nottingham Forest, five days before the local Derby. Vale were in tenth position and had drawn 1-1 at second from the bottom Notts County on the Thursday prior to the Derby. Malkin returned to Stoke's side after injury, whilst Vale were unchanged from their previous game for the local contest.

THE MATCH

Although Stoke looked more dangerous initially, the players appeared to be tense and there was little pattern to the game. Nevertheless, Stoke went close to scoring when Potts headed just over his own bar and then Oscroft thundered a thirty-yard shot slightly above the woodwork. However, Vale countered and Mullard struck the ball inches wide before the home keeper made a flying save to deny Cunliffe. The visitors piled on the pressure and Cunliffe hooked the ball narrowly over the bar and then forced Robertson to pull off a magnificent one-handed save.

Stoke began the second period on the offensive, although there was little constructive football. Nevertheless, Malkin fired fractionally over the bar, but heavy rain began to make the struggle even more dour. Oscroft punted the ball wide when presented with a glorious opportunity and then the Stoke custodian superbly tipped a cross-shot from Cunliffe round a post, but the defences could not be breached.

THE AFTERMATH

In spite of their failure to win, Stoke remained at the top of the division on goal average, although they lost three consecutive league games later in the month and their form became rather inconsistent. In contrast, Vale dropped to twelfth place, twice conceded seven goals (at Swansea Town and Birmingham City) before the autumn was out and steadily slipped down the table.

155

138: MONDAY 25 APRIL 1955, FOOTBALL LEAGUE, SECOND DIVISION

PORT VALE (0) 0, STOKE CITY (0) 1 (Bowyer).

VALE: King, Turner, Potts, Mullard, Cheadle, Sproson, Askey, Griffiths, Done, Stephenson, Cunliffe.
STOKE: Robertson, Bourne, McCue, Mountford, Thomson, Sellars, Malkin, Bowyer, Finney, Ratcliffe, Oscroft.

Venue: Vale Park, Burslem.
Attendance: 41,674.
Referee: J.H. Clough (Bolton).

THE SETTING
This was the first ever Potteries Derby played at Vale Park. Vale were fourth from the bottom of the Second Division, only four points clear of the drop, and had lost 4-2 at fourth-placed Luton Town on the Saturday before the local Derby. In contrast, Stoke were in third position, a single point behind the leaders, and had beaten Bristol Rovers 2-0 at home on the same day. Both clubs made one change to their line-ups for the local clash, with Stephenson and Thomson returning after injury for Vale and Stoke respectively. The importance of the occasion helped to attract an all-time record crowd for a Potteries Derby game staged by Vale.

THE MATCH
In the first half, Stoke kicked with the advantage of a strong wind, but both sides found it difficult to control the ball on a hard pitch. The play was generally dreary and marred by 'faulty passing, wild clearances and innumerable back passes'. Although Done looked dangerous for Vale, scoring chances were at a premium in the first period and invariably the result of defensive mistakes. Nevertheless, Ratcliffe headed a Malkin centre just wide for Stoke and then the latter curled a shot past an upright.

After the interval, Oscroft appeared with a bandage around his right leg and was merely a passenger for the rest of the match. The contest was frequently halted by a series of fouls, although in one inspired moment, Malkin produced a terrific goal-bound drive which unluckily struck the Vale centre-half and was cleared. However, on the hour, Stoke unexpectedly took the lead when Bowyer brilliantly hooked the ball into the corner of the net. The goal finally succeeded in livening up the exchanges and Done headed just wide for Vale, who became handicapped when Cunliffe was injured and left limping. However, there was little further incident of note other than a 'wild scramble' in the home goal-mouth near the end, which Vale survived.

THE AFTERMATH
Despite their defeat, Vale remained fourth from the bottom of the division, but consecutive victories in their final two games ensured their safety from relegation and they finished seventeenth. Stoke went to the top of the table on goal average, although on the following Saturday they lost their remaining match 2-0 at relegation-threatened Plymouth Argyle and ended up in a disappointing fifth position.

139: SATURDAY 8 OCTOBER 1955, FOOTBALL LEAGUE, SECOND DIVISION

PORT VALE (1) 1 (Done), STOKE CITY (0) 0.

VALE: R. King, Potts, Hayward, Mountford, Cheadle, Sproson, Smith, Conway, Done, Stephenson, Cunliffe.

STOKE: Robertson, Short, McCue, Cairns, Thomson, Sellars, Ratcliffe, Bowyer, Lawton, J. King, Oscroft.

Venue: Vale Park, Burslem.
Attendance: 37,261.
Referee: E. Crawford (Doncaster).

THE SETTING
Vale were fifth in the Second Division, two points behind the leaders with a match in hand. They had lost just one of their opening nine games, but had surprisingly only drawn 1-1 at home to third from the bottom Bury a week before the local Derby. Stoke were even better placed, one point ahead of their rivals in third position, although they had played two more matches and had been defeated 3-1 at Leicester City on the Saturday prior to the Derby. The Vale manager, Freddie Steele, made two changes in their line-up from their previous game, with Cunliffe returning from injury and Stephenson being preferred to Leake, whilst Stoke were forced to replace the injured Mountford and Malkin with Cairns and Ratcliffe, as well as selecting Short at right-back. For the first time, over a thousand patients in four local hospitals were able to listen to a radio commentary on the match.

THE MATCH
Only five minutes had elapsed when Done tapped in a rebound from the visiting keeper to give Vale the lead. Almost immediately afterwards, Johnny King grazed the home bar and then Oscroft shot just wide. However, Vale created the better chances, but Cunliffe lobbed a good opportunity behind the wood-work, Conway hooked the ball across the goalmouth when well positioned and Smith shot weakly after being set up by Done.

After the interval, Stoke attacked strongly, although the home team dropped their famous "Iron Curtain" to keep them at bay. The Vale keeper made a string of splendid saves to deny Johnny King three times and Lawton, whilst Done fired inches over the bar in a rare raid by the home side. Stoke twice almost equalised at the death, as firstly Sellars had a goal-bound shot trapped on the line by Potts and then Cheadle made a last-ditch tackle to halt finally a marvellous Johnny King solo run.

THE AFTERMATH
As a result of their first Derby victory since 1944, Vale moved up to third place, but were unable to sustain their promotion challenge, especially by failing to win any of their following nine matches, and slipped to fifteenth by the middle of December. Stoke dropped to seventh position following their local Derby defeat and likewise drifted into midtable, although they did reach the fifth round of the F.A. Cup.

140: SATURDAY 31 MARCH 1956, FOOTBALL LEAGUE, SECOND DIVISION

STOKE CITY (1) 1 (Oscroft), PORT VALE (0) 1 (Griffiths).

STOKE: Robertson, Whiston, McCue, Cairns, Thomson, Sellars, Coleman, Bowyer, Graver, J. King, Oscroft.
VALE: R. King, Turner, Potts, Leake, Hayward, Sproson, Cunliffe, Baily, Smith, Griffiths, Bennett.

Venue: The Victoria Ground, Stoke-upon-Trent.
Attendance: 37,928.
Referee: E. Crawford (Doncaster).

THE SETTING
Stoke were twelfth in the Second Division and had lost 2-0 at West Ham United the day before the local Derby. Vale were fourth, a single point adrift of second position, and had beaten promotion rivals Bristol City 2-0 at home in a vital match the same day. Stoke were unchanged from their last game, whilst Vale brought in Griffiths to replace Stephenson who had injured a thigh. Bright sunshine attracted a bumper crowd to witness an encounter crucial to the visitors' promotion chances played on a hard, dry pitch.

THE MATCH
The match began at a furious pace and Stoke made the early running, although mistakes were frequent. Only a brilliant save by the Vale goalkeeper prevented Coleman from scoring before the home side took the lead in the seventeenth minute with a finely-placed shot by Oscroft. This success stirred Stoke into even greater efforts and the visiting custodian flung himself at the feet of Graver to save an otherwise certain second goal shortly afterwards. Nevertheless, Vale's defence proved resilient and Cunliffe almost equalised towards the end of the first half when he struck a post in a breakaway.

The play in the second period became more end to end and the Vale keeper made a second magnificent save to deny Coleman before the visitors drew level after seventy minutes. Baily, who had hitherto done little of note, lobbed the ball forward for Griffiths to run on to and place a shot into a corner of the net. The equaliser inspired Vale, who then took command, but they were unable to gain the victory which would have put them into second place in the division.

THE AFTERMATH
Despite picking up a point, Stoke dropped a place in the table to thirteenth, which was where they eventually finished. Vale also slipped down one position and, by losing three of their following four games, fell out of contention for promotion, ending up a disappointing twelfth.

158

141: WEDNESDAY 10 OCTOBER 1956, FOOTBALL LEAGUE, SECOND DIVISION

STOKE CITY (3) 3 (Coleman 2, Kelly), PORT VALE (0) 1 (Smith).

STOKE: Robertson, Mountford, McCue, Sellars, Thomson, Cairns, Coleman, Bowyer, J. King, Kelly, Oscroft.
VALE: R. King, Turner, Potts, H. Poole, Hayward, Sproson, Askey, Smith, Done, Stephenson, Cunliffe.

Venue: The Victoria Ground, Stoke-upon-Trent.
Attendance: 39,446.
Referee: K. A. Collinge (Sale).

THE SETTING
Stoke were third in the Second Division and had trounced second from the bottom Rotherham United 6-0 at home on the Saturday before the local Derby. Vale were in sixteenth position and had lost 3-1 at Middlesbrough on the same day. Stoke's line-up was unchanged from their previous match, but Done returned to centre-forward for Vale for the first league game to be played under Stoke's newly-installed £15,000 floodlights.

THE MATCH
Although Stoke produced a magnificent 'harmonised' display in the first half, with 'sharp, fluent attacks', it was the visitors who should have opened the scoring in the first minute when Smith shot wide from a glorious position. This proved costly because just a minute later Coleman rifled Stoke in front. The home side doubled their lead after seventeen minutes when Johnny King provided a pinpoint low cross for Kelly to strike the ball out of the Vale keeper's reach. However, Stoke were indebted to Robertson in retaining their advantage as he made two fine saves, one from a Cairns deflection and the second from Stephenson's header. Nevertheless, Coleman put Stoke 3-0 up in the thirty-first minute as the visiting defence waited in vain for an offside flag to be raised.

The play in the second period was more even, especially because Vale's defenders tightened up their marking, but a dense mist made the events increasingly difficult for the spectators to follow. Coleman and Johnny King squandered clear-cut opportunities to extend Stoke's lead, although Smith made no mistake in converting a Done cross to reduce the arrears twelve minutes from the end. However, there still remained time for Johnny King to balloon the ball towards the floodlights when presented with an open goal!

THE AFTERMATH
As a result of their victory, Stoke went to the top of the table, although Vale's position remained unaltered. Nevertheless, Stoke were unable to maintain their momentum and a dreadful sequence of six successive defeats without scoring a goal in the spring finally put paid to their promotion chances. Vale lost all six matches following their local Derby defeat and slumped to second from the bottom of the division in mid-November as a result.

142: MONDAY 29 APRIL 1957, FOOTBALL LEAGUE, SECOND DIVISION

PORT VALE (1) 2 (Cunliffe, Steele), STOKE CITY (1) 2 (Asprey, Graver).

VALE: J. Poole, Potts, Hayward, Whalley, Sproson, H. Poole, Askey, Steele, Leake, Cunliffe, Miles.
STOKE: Robertson, Mountford, McCue, Asprey, Thomson, Sellars, Coleman, Bowyer, Graver, King, Oscroft.

Venue: Vale Park, Burslem.
Attendance: 22,395.
Referee: K.A. Collinge (Sale).

THE SETTING
Vale were bottom of the Second Division and had already been relegated regardless of the outcome of the local Derby, which was the final league match of the 1956-1957 season for both clubs. Vale had beaten sixth from the bottom Rotherham United 2-1 at home two days before the Derby to end a dreadful sequence of results, during which just a single point had been gained from ten games! In contrast, Stoke were in sixth position and, although they had got no chance of promotion, they had beaten third from the bottom Bury 2-0 in their final home match a week before the local clash. Both teams showed one change for the Derby, with Potts returning to Vale's defence and Thomson to that of the visitors.

THE MATCH
Stoke began in determined mood and Graver shot just over the bar before Asprey put the visitors in front with a slick drive in the twenty-fifth minute. This was the hundredth league goal conceded by Vale that season. However, the home side were far from deflated and Cunliffe hooked the ball against the angle of the woodwork within a minute. He then equalised for Vale in the thirty-sixth minute when he drilled in an Askey centre and, just before the interval, three home players impeded one another as they vainly attempted to tap in Miles' perfectly placed corner kick.

In the opening fifteen minutes of the second half, Vale were in complete command and only fine saves from the visiting keeper prevented them from taking the lead before Steele seized on a defensive error in the fifty-fifth minute and placed the ball into the net. Cunliffe then squandered an excellent chance to make the game safe and Stoke rallied and drew level from a Graver header a quarter of an hour from the end. The visitors pressed strongly for the winner and King netted three minutes later, but the goal was disallowed for offside.

THE AFTERMATH
The draw made no difference to Vale's position in the division and they were relegated in bottom place with a mere twenty-two points. Stoke moved up one position to finish fifth, six points adrift of a promotion spot. In the close season, Vale had a major clear-out of players, although there was no significant transfer activity at Stoke.

143: MONDAY 13 OCTOBER 1958, FRIENDLY

PORT VALE (2) 2 (Steele 2), STOKE CITY (1) 1 (Ratcliffe).

VALE: Jones, Pritchard, Martin, Kinsey, Leake, Miles, Jackson, H. Poole, Wilkinson, Steele, Cunliffe.
STOKE: Robertson, T. Ward, McCue, Asprey, Thomson, Ratcliffe, Howitt, Bullock, King, Bowyer, Oscroft.

Venue: Vale Park, Burslem.
Attendance: 11,356.
Referee: F. Dearden (Endon).

THE SETTING
Vale were third in the Fourth Division and were unbeaten for four matches, but had only drawn 0-0 at home to fourth from the bottom Oldham Athletic two days before the local Derby. Stoke were also faring well and were in fourth position in the Second Division. They had won 2-1 at sixth-placed Charlton Athletic on the Saturday prior to the Derby to extend their undefeated sequence to seven matches. Vale made just one team change from their previous game, with Jackson returning from injury, whilst Frank Taylor, the Stoke manager, called up two reserves, Terry Ward and Bullock, to replace the injured Wilshaw and the unavailable Allen, who was on England under 23 international duty.

THE MATCH
Stoke opened at a tremendous pace and threatened to overwhelm their opponents. Howitt hit the bar with a terrific shot, but Kinsey then did likewise for Vale from twenty-five yards. Stoke were rewarded for their pressure in the twenty-fifth minute when Ratcliffe shot them in front, although Steele equalised eight minutes later with a clever, glancing header from a Jackson corner. Before the interval, Vale unexpectedly took the lead when Steele perfectly placed the ball in the net from twenty-five yards.

The play gradually slowed down in the second half, but Vale forced the issue more strongly than their opponents. Nevertheless, Stoke had the better chances, although Oscroft and then Howitt were valiantly denied by the home keeper when looking certain to score. Stoke's rhythm was disrupted by an injury to McCue, who was forced on to the left wing as a passenger late in the match, whilst Vale's efforts in turn were upset as Wilkinson limped through the final minutes.

THE AFTERMATH
Their victory seemed to inspire Vale to greater efforts and they won four of their following five league games to move to the top of the Fourth Division. Defeat by their old rivals appeared to have done Stoke no harm because they were victorious in their next two Second Division matches, although three successive defeats then followed.

144: MONDAY 3 NOVEMBER 1958, FRIENDLY

STOKE CITY (3) 4 (Howitt 2, Oscroft, Asprey), PORT VALE (0) 0.

STOKE: Hall, McCue, Allen, Asprey, Thomson, Cairns, Ratcliffe, Howitt, Wilshaw, King, Oscroft.
VALE: Jones, Pritchard, Martin (Whalley), Miles, Higgs, Sproson, Jackson, H. Poole, Wilkinson, Steele, Cunliffe.

Venue: The Victoria Ground, Stoke-upon-Trent.
Attendance: 11,576.
Referee: P.J. Mason (Stafford).

THE SETTING
Stoke were third in the Second Division, although they were five points adrift of a promotion spot and had lost 2-0 at home to Liverpool two days before the return local Derby. Vale were also in third position, in the Fourth Division, a single point behind the leaders, and were undefeated in seven matches. They had won 2-0 at Gillingham on the Saturday prior to the Derby. Stoke made two team changes from their previous game, with Cairns and Wilshaw replacing the injured Bowyer and Bullock, whilst Vale's manager, Norman Low, selected Higgs instead of Leake, who had taken a knock.

THE MATCH
Stoke quickly found their feet and Oscroft slotted the ball in from a Howitt cross in the third minute to put them in front. The home side were altogether sharper, passed the ball more accurately and cleverly interchanged positions, whilst Vale's centre-half was hesitant and twice made errors which almost proved costly. First he let in Wilshaw, who shot wide, and then allowed Oscroft the space to balloon the ball over an open goal. Although Wilkinson shot just over the bar for Vale, Howitt ran clear and unleashed a tremendous drive into the net in the thirty-third minute to extend Stoke's lead. Just two minutes later, Howitt superbly put Asprey through to make it 3-0 and then Martin was carried off with a leg injury, although Whalley substituted.

The contest became more even in the second period and Vale were unlucky not to be given a penalty when Cunliffe was upended, whilst the Stoke keeper twice produced excellent saves from the same player. At the other end, Jones brilliantly denied both Wilshaw and Oscroft, but Stoke sealed their victory nineteen minutes from time when Howitt finely placed the ball in to round off a flowing move.

THE AFTERMATH
Stoke continued to do well in the league, but were unable to put together a sufficiently consistent run of good results to test the top two sides and eventually finished fifth, eleven points short of a promotion place. Vale rarely put a foot wrong for the rest of the season and became the first ever Fourth Division champions, with four points to spare, scoring 110 league goals in the process.

145: MONDAY 5 OCTOBER 1959, SUPPORTERS' CLUBS' TROPHY, FIRST LEG

STOKE CITY (1) 3 (King 2, Newlands pen.), PORT VALE (0) 1 (Jackson pen.).

STOKE: Robertson, McCue, Allen, Asprey, Andrew, Skeels, Newlands, Bowyer, Bentley, King, Cunliffe.
VALE: K. Hancock, Raine, Sproson, Leake, Ford, Kinsey, Jackson, Steele, H. Poole, Barnett (March), Oscroft.

Venue: The Victoria Ground, Stoke-upon-Trent.
Attendance: 9,065.
Referee: E.J. Goodwin (Penkhull).

THE SETTING
This was the first game in a new competition to be contested by the two clubs. Stoke were fifteenth in the Second Division and had extended their sequence without a victory to five matches in being hammered 4-0 at Ipswich Town two days before the local Derby. Vale were not faring too well either and were in eighteenth position in the Third Division, although they had beaten sixth from the bottom Southend United 3-1 at home on the Saturday prior to the Derby. Stoke were without the injured Ratcliffe, for whom Skeels deputised in making his debut, and Andrew and Bentley were also drafted into the side for the local clash. In contrast, Vale were unchanged from their previous game, although Leake and Poole swapped positions.

THE MATCH
Stoke got off to a perfect start with King shooting them in front in the first minute from a cross by Newlands. The home side then stroked the ball around with great precision and were in almost complete command during the first half. King caused the Vale defence constant problems and the only surprise was that the home team didn't add to their score before the interval.

Vale made a more determined effort in the second period and Jackson equalised from a penalty after Steele had been felled in the area by Allen. Cunliffe then hit a post for Stoke, whilst Poole missed an opportunity from close in to give the visitors the lead. The play swung from one end to the other and King fired Stoke ahead once more following a brilliant solo run, although Oscroft should have levelled the score again shortly afterwards, but scooped the ball over an unguarded net. The outcome was finally decided two minutes from time when Newlands slotted in a penalty for Stoke after Leake had handled in the area.

THE AFTERMATH
Stoke staged a mini-revival in the league to capitalise on their victory and took five points from their next three matches to rise to eighth place. In addition, their left-back, Allen, made his international debut for England in a home championship clash against Wales twelve days after the local Derby. Vale were far from demoralised by their defeat and won both their following Third Division games, although their efforts remained rather inconsistent overall.

146: MONDAY 26 OCTOBER 1959, SUPPORTERS' CLUBS' TROPHY, SECOND LEG

PORT VALE (2) 2 (Steele, Jackson), STOKE CITY (1) 2 (Wilshaw, Anderson).

VALE: K. Hancock, Raine, Sproson, H. Poole, Ford, Miles, Jackson, Steele, Whalley, Barnett, Oscroft.
STOKE: Robertson, McCue, R. Wilson (D. Wilson, 46), Asprey, Andrew, Ratcliffe, Newlands, Bowyer, King, Wilshaw (Anderson, 46), Cunliffe.

Venue: Vale Park, Burslem.
Attendance: 7,506.
Referee: F. Dearden (Endon).

THE SETTING
Vale were sixteenth in the Third Division, but had won four of their last five matches, which included a 3-1 home victory against the bottom side, Chesterfield, two days before the return local Derby. Stoke were in eighth position in the Second Division and had won 2-1 at fifth-placed Charlton Athletic on the same day. Vale were unchanged from their previous game, whilst Stoke were forced to make one alteration, with Ron Wilson being named for his debut in place of Allen, who was on England international duty.

THE MATCH
Although Vale Park was lashed by wind and rain, the two sides produced an exciting and skilful exhibition of football. Vale exerted considerable pressure from the outset and had the opportunities to have been 2-0 up by the time Stoke went in front in the twenty-second minute. King delivered a through ball and when Raine mistimed his tackle, Wilshaw scored unchallenged. However, Vale equalised just three minutes later when Steele hooked the ball into the net through a crowd of players from a precise Oscroft cross. The home team then pressed even more strongly and were awarded a penalty ten minutes before the interval after Steele had been fouled by Ron Wilson. Although the visiting keeper was able to push Jackson's kick against a post, the latter slotted in the rebound.

Stoke began the second half by introducing two substitutes and made a little more impact, although the home side remained on top. Steele and Whalley both went close, but Stoke came increasingly into contention and King and Bowyer threatened the target before Anderson headed them level from a Denis Wilson cross. In the final few minutes, Vale made a desperate attempt to save the tie and were assisted by the dismissal of McCue for 'improper language', but Robertson made four marvellous saves to deny them.

THE AFTERMATH
The trophy was presented to Stoke afterwards and each player received a gift of china. Vale were unable to strike any consistently good league form thereafter and eventually finished fourteenth in the Third Division, although they were only eliminated from the F.A. Cup in the fifth round by Aston Villa. Stoke gradually slid down the Second Division table and ended up sixth from the bottom, mainly owing to a dreadful sequence of ten consecutive defeats in the spring.

164

147: MONDAY 10 OCTOBER 1960, SUPPORTERS' CLUBS' TROPHY, FIRST LEG

PORT VALE (0) 1 (Steele), STOKE CITY (0) 0.

VALE: K. Hancock, Raine, Sproson, H. Poole, Ford, Miles, Jackson, Portwood, Whalley, Steele, Fidler.

STOKE: O'Neill, T. Ward, Allen, Skeels, Andrew, Asprey, Howitt, Ratcliffe, King, Cairns, Wilshaw.

Venue: Vale Park, Burslem.
Attendance: 7,267.
Referee: E.J. Goodwin (Trent Vale).

THE SETTING

Vale were thirteenth in the Third Division, but had won 4-3 at Bristol City two days before the local Derby, which increased the total goals scored in their last six league games to thirty-two! Although Stoke were in sixteenth position in the Second Division, they were only a point clear of the relegation zone and had lost 2-1 at home to third from the bottom Leyton Orient on the Saturday prior to the Derby. Vale were unchanged from their previous game, whilst Stoke welcomed back Howitt and Cairns after injury.

THE MATCH

The match was 'an incredibly dull and scrappy encounter between two full-strength sides who did little more than exchange courtesies'. It was played at such a frantic pace that skilful football was sadly lacking and a 'near-comedy of errors exhausted the crowd's patience long before the end'! The defences were well on top, especially during the first half, although Ratcliffe spurned several good chances for Stoke and Wilshaw passed the ball to good effect.

Early in the second period, Vale were awarded a penalty when Jackson was upended in the area, but the same player struck his kick over the bar. After that, a goalless draw seemed a most likely outcome, especially as the home defence paid much closer attention to Ratcliffe and bottled him up. However, in the seventieth minute, Steele headed a clearance from Allen straight into the net to put Vale ahead, which jolted the visitors into belatedly exerting strong pressure. Nevertheless, a combination of poor finishing by the Stoke players and fine goalkeeping by Hancock enabled the home team to secure their victory.

THE AFTERMATH

Although their victory did not inspire Vale to put together a consistent run of good results, they steadily moved up the Third Division table until they reached the fringe of the promotion race in the spring. Stoke were unable to drag themselves clear of the relegation struggle, although they annihilated Plymouth Argyle 9-0 at home on 17 December and reached the fifth round of the F.A. Cup before being knocked out by First Division Newcastle United. Nevertheless, the proceeds of the cup run enabled them to buy Jackie Mudie, a Scottish international inside-forward, for £7,000 from Blackpool.

148: TUESDAY 7 MARCH 1961, SUPPORTERS' CLUBS' TROPHY, SECOND LEG

STOKE CITY (0) 1 (Ratcliffe), PORT VALE (0) 0.

STOKE: O'Neill, Asprey, Allen, Howitt, Andrew, Skeels, Anderson, Mudie, Bullock, King, Ratcliffe.
VALE: J. Poole, Raine, Sproson, H. Poole, Ford, Miles, Jackson, Portwood, Llewellyn, Steele, Fidler.

Venue: The Victoria Ground, Stoke-upon-Trent.
Attendance: 9,605.
Referee: R. Capey (Porthill).

THE SETTING

Stoke were struggling in sixteenth position in the Second Division, only three points above the relegation zone, but had beaten Scunthorpe United 2-0 at home three days before the return local Derby. In contrast, Vale were fifth in the Third Division, although they were seven points adrift of second place and had lost 1-0 at the league leaders, Queen's Park Rangers, in a vital match on the Saturday prior to the Derby. Stoke's manager, Tony Waddington, replaced Derek Ward with Anderson, otherwise the two teams were unchanged from their previous games and thus Jackie Mudie, a recent acquisition by the home club, was on show.

THE MATCH

Stoke were generally the more inventive side, but it soon became apparent that no quarter was to be given and the defences consequently held command. However, there was little pattern to the play early on because the exchanges were so furious. Nevertheless, Bullock fired in two terrific shots for Stoke, although they were brilliantly saved by the visiting keeper. The home team were largely dominant, but towards the interval Vale increasingly forced the pace. Portwood squandered a golden opportunity and then forced O'Neill into a 'miraculous' save, which was greeted with thunderous applause.

Stoke went ahead three minutes into the second period when Ratcliffe drifted a twenty-five yard shot over the head of the visiting custodian and into the net! Fidler nearly levelled the score almost immediately afterwards, but the Stoke keeper pushed his rasping drive against a post. However, Vale struggled to exert much pressure until the final few minutes when they bombarded the home goal and Steele nearly lobbed O'Neill with an overhead kick, whilst Fidler put the ball into the net right at the death, but his effort was disallowed for offside.

THE AFTERMATH

As a consequence of Stoke's slender victory, the competition had ended in a tie and so a decider was arranged for late the following month. During the intervening period, Stoke won only three of their eleven matches and dropped to fourth from the bottom of their division. Vale's form was even worse and their Third Division promotion challenge petered out as a result of just two victories being gained in their following nine games.

149: MONDAY 24 APRIL 1961, SUPPORTERS' CLUBS' TROPHY, DECIDER

STOKE CITY (0) 0, PORT VALE (1) 1 (O'Neill o.g.).

STOKE: O'Neill (Hickson, 46), D. Wilson, Allen (R. Wilson, 46), Howitt, Andrew, Skeels, Bridgwood, Matthews, Bullock (Bentley, 46), King (Anderson, 46), Ratcliffe.
VALE: K. Hancock, Lowe, Sproson, Gater, Ford, Miles, Hall, H. Poole, Llewellyn, B. Hancock, Oscroft.

Venue: The Victoria Ground, Stoke-upon-Trent.
Attendance: 4,000.
Referee: E.J. Goodwin (Trent Vale).

THE SETTING
Although Stoke were fourth from the bottom of the Second Division and had lost 3-0 at third-placed Liverpool two days before the deciding local Derby, the retention of their status had been confirmed by Portsmouth's defeat and consequent relegation that same afternoon. In contrast, Vale were in sixth position in the Third Division, although promotion was no longer a possibility, and they had drawn 1-1 at home to Bristol City on the Saturday prior to the Derby. Both clubs took the opportunity to blood young players in the local clash, with Bridgwood and Matthews making their debuts for Stoke and Lowe and Barry Hancock doing likewise for Vale, whilst Gater had only first appeared in the visitors' senior side earlier that month. The two teams were otherwise unchanged for the competition decider for which Stoke had 'secured' the choice of ground.

THE MATCH
Vale opened brightly and in the eighth minute O'Neill remarkably palmed a centre from Hall into his own net! This success put a zip in the play of the visitors and Llewellyn shot just wide shortly afterwards. Although Vale's defence coped with the opposing forwards with relative ease, the home side twice missed chances to equalise towards the interval when Matthews dallied too long and then King shot inches wide.

At the start of the second half, Stoke introduced four substitutes, but if anything the visitors tightened their control and Andrew almost headed a Barry Hancock cross into his own net. The play then began to get rather rough and in the final twenty-five minutes Stoke made a determined effort to save the tie. The Vale defenders several times scrambled the ball away, Bentley fired over the bar from a glorious position and a bombardment of shots nearly levelled the score in the last minute.

THE AFTERMATH
Vale's captain, Peter Ford, was presented with the trophy after the match by the president of the Stoke City Supporters' Club. Vale completed their season with two away draws in the league and finished in seventh place, thirteen points adrift of a promotion spot. Stoke won one and lost one of their two remaining Second Division matches (both at home) and ended up fifth from the bottom, three points clear of relegation.

150: FRIDAY 1 MAY 1970, FRIENDLY

STOKE CITY (0) 2 (Elder, Sproson o.g.), PORT VALE (2) 3 (Morris, McLaren, Gough).

STOKE: Farmer, Marsh, Pejic, Bernard, Smith, Stevenson, Greenhoff (Elder, 46), Mahoney, Ritchie, Dobing, Haslegrave.
VALE: Ball, Boulton, Wilson, King, Sproson, Green, Morris, Lacey, James, McLaren, Gough.

Venue: The Victoria Ground, Stoke-upon-Trent.
Attendance: 11,725.
Referee: A.W.S. Jones (Ormskirk).

THE SETTING
This long-awaited clash, which officially launched the Stoke-on-Trent Festival, was the first local Derby for over nine years. Stoke had completed their 1969-1970 league programme with a 3-2 home win against West Bromwich Albion on 15 April and had finished ninth in the First Division. Vale had drawn their final Fourth Division match 1-1 at home to Colchester United six days before the Derby and had gained promotion by securing fourth place following a nine-game unbeaten run. Stoke made four changes in their team from their previous match, with Farmer, Stevenson, Mahoney and debutant Haslegrave replacing the rested Banks, the unfit Bloor, the absent Conroy and the injured Burrows. In contrast, Vale were at full strength, with King returning to the side.

THE MATCH
Thirty-four free kicks were awarded in a distinctly unfriendly encounter in which the teams 'declared war on each other'. Stoke's Pejic and Greenhoff were booked and Vale's Lacey required stitches in a gashed eye as the two sides fought for local pride in a contest dominated by the visitors' resilient defence. At the very outset, Lacey forced the home keeper to make a brilliant save and, with Green controlling the midfield, Vale pressed strongly. After only ten minutes, the latter floated over a free kick for Morris to head the visitors in front and they extended their lead just five minutes later when McLaren intercepted an under-hit Stevenson back-pass and rolled it into the net. Stoke then fought back and Ritchie headed against the bar, although the visiting defence held firm.

Greenhoff retired injured at half-time, but his replacement, Elder, reduced the arrears with a curling shot. However, in the seventieth minute, Gough restored Vale's advantage with a twelve-yard thunderbolt. Nevertheless, Stoke rallied and Ball saved magnificently from Stevenson before Sproson slashed a bobbling ball into his own net two minutes from time.

THE AFTERMATH
No new major signings were made by Stoke during the close season and the club preferred to pin its hopes on the squad that had performed so well during the 1969-1970 campaign. Vale issued free transfers to six fringe players and signed only three replacements to bolster the team for the challenge of the Third Division: full-back, Mick Hopkinson; centre-half, Roy Cross, and midfielder, Brian Horton.

151: MONDAY 26 APRIL 1976, FRIENDLY

PORT VALE (0) 1 (Tartt), STOKE CITY (1) 1 (Greenhoff).

VALE: Connaughton, Griffiths, Dulson, Ridley, Lees, Beech, Tartt, Williams (Harris, 46), Brownbill, Bailey (Morris, 40), McLaren.
STOKE: Shilton, Marsh, Bowers, Mahoney, Dodd, Bloor, Robertson, Greenhoff, Moores, Crooks, Salmons.

Venue: Vale Park, Burslem.
Attendance: 9,825.
Referee: R. Capey (Madeley Heath).

THE SETTING
This game, the first local Derby for almost six years, was played in celebration of Vale's centenary. Vale had completed their 1975-1976 league fixtures with a 3-0 defeat at Preston North End two days before the Derby and had finished twelfth in the Third Division. Stoke had secured the same position in the First Division, despite losing their final match of the season 2-0 at home to Norwich City on the Saturday prior to the local clash. Vale fielded an unchanged team from their previous game, but Tony Waddington, the Stoke manager, made six alterations to his line-up, three because of injury, one through absence and two by choice, so that Marsh, Bowers, Mahoney, Robertson, Moores and Crooks were all drafted in.

THE MATCH
Although for much of the first half the match was relatively uneventful, Greenhoff produced some beautiful passes and orchestrated the Stoke midfield. Indeed, it was Greenhoff who put the visitors in front on the half-hour when he received the ball from a Robertson free kick and thumped it just inside a post. Vale had the opportunity to equalise two minutes later, but Shilton dived to save a shot from Williams who had been put clean through. The home side were then handicapped by the loss of Bailey to an injury five minutes before the interval, whilst Williams retired hurt at the end of the first period.

Stoke dominated most of the second half, but the home keeper made excellent saves from Salmons and Crooks, whilst Robertson was inches wide with a thunderbolt. Having ridden their luck, Vale stormed back in the final ten minutes and equalised seven minutes from time when Tartt reacted decisively to a loose ball in the visitors' penalty area and turned sharply to fire home.

THE AFTERMATH
Vale were not only delighted at matching their distinguished opponents, but also ecstatic because their rivals allowed them to keep the entire £6,500 takings. That was generous indeed because Stoke were forced to sell their winger, Sean Haslegrave, to Nottingham Forest for £35,000 during the close season and their striker, Ian Moores, to Tottenham Hotspur for £75,000 at the end of August to help offset a £134,127 debt. Vale also had financial problems and attempted to solve them by transferring the versatile Terry Lees to Sparta Rotterdam of the Netherlands for £25,000 in August.

152: TUESDAY 18 OCTOBER 1977, FRIENDLY

STOKE CITY (2) 3 (Crooks 2 [1 pen.], Conroy), PORT VALE (2) 2 (Beamish, Bentley).

STOKE: Jones, Pejic, Bowers (Scott), Johnson, D. Smith, M. Smith, Waddington (Draper), Richardson, Gregory, Conroy, Crooks.
VALE: Connaughton, McGifford, Bentley, Harris, Dulson, Brownbill, Sutcliffe, Lamb, Beech, Beamish, Bailey (Cullerton).

Venue: The Victoria Ground, Stoke-upon-Trent.
Attendance: 5,017.
Referee: R.N. Perkin (Stafford).

THE SETTING
Stoke were seventh in the Second Division and had beaten third-placed Brighton & Hove Albion 1-0 at home three days before the local Derby. Vale were struggling at third from the bottom of the Third Division and, although they had picked up a creditable 1-1 draw at Swindon Town on the same day, Roy Sproson had subsequently been 'relieved of his duties' as manager and offered instead an 'executive position dealing with the club's youth policy'. The player-coach, Colin Harper, had temporarily taken the reins while the managerial position was being advertised. Stoke made five team changes from their previous match, selecting Pejic, Bowers, Johnson and Mike Smith to replace the injured Kendall and Dodd and the rested Marsh and Lindsay, whilst Conroy returned upon regaining full fitness. Vale were unchanged apart from Connaughton replacing Dance in goal.

THE MATCH
Although Vale matched their opponents for most of the game, the home side got off to a lightning start. Conroy put Stoke in front with a pile-driver following a clever interchange with Crooks in only the fifth minute and the former netted again just four minutes later, but had the goal disallowed. Nevertheless, Vale weathered the storm and in the twenty-third minute Beamish equalised by prodding in a free kick. Just seven minutes afterwards, the visitors surprisingly took the lead when a speculative effort by Bentley drifted over the line with the aid of a deflection.

Although Bailey cleared a goal-bound strike by Mike Smith off the line before the interval, Vale took command and seemed to be coasting towards victory until Crooks converted a penalty fifteen minutes from time, after having been felled by Harris. Vale continued to press strongly, but Crooks stabbed in the winner for Stoke in the last minute.

THE AFTERMATH
£3,700 was raised from a disappointing crowd and divided between the Staffordshire F.A. Centenary Fund and the Queen's Silver Jubilee Appeal Fund. The victory failed to inspire Stoke, who lost their following three league matches, although they later staged a recovery to finish the season in seventh place. Vale were unable to win any of their next ten Third Division games, ended up fourth from the bottom and were thus relegated.

170

153: MONDAY 30 JULY 1979, FRIENDLY

PORT VALE (0) 0, STOKE CITY (0) 2 (Doyle, Ursem).

VALE: Dance, Keenan, Bentley, Beech, Delgado, Hawkins, Tully, Farrell, Wright, Owen, Healy.
STOKE: Jones, Pejic, Scott, Irvine, Smith (Dodd, 46), Doyle, Ursem, Busby (Randall, 73), O'Callaghan, Crooks, Richardson.

Venue: Vale Park, Burslem.
Attendance: 8,860.
Referee: M.J. Heath (Blurton).

THE SETTING
Vale had just returned undefeated from a three-match tour of the West Country and had won their final friendly game 2-0 at Western League Saltash United two days before the local Derby, which had been arranged to give further pre-season practice before their impending Fourth Division campaign. Stoke were also warming up for the 1979-1980 league season and had drawn 1-1 at their First Division rivals, Wolverhampton Wanderers, on the Friday prior to the Derby. Both clubs fielded their strongest available line-ups for the local clash and Vale included their new striker, Terry Owen (later the father of the English international, Michael Owen), signed from Rochdale, whilst Stoke selected their Dutch under 21 international midfielder, Loek Ursem, recently acquired for approximately £58,000 from AZ 67 Alkmaar.

THE MATCH
Vale dominated the opening half and the visitors were indebted to their keeper, who produced a magnificent save from Healy just before the interval to keep them on level terms. Also, Beech hit the bar and Owen miskicked when presented with a good chance, although Stoke seemed content to remain on the defensive and absorb the pressure.

Vale continued to dominate in the second period and Farrell, Bentley, Tully and Healy all went close before Stoke made a decisive substitution in the seventy-third minute by introducing Randall into the fray. Their play livened up immediately and Doyle put them in front just two minutes later with a tremendous thirty-yard drive which rocketed into the net. The crowd rose in applause and this success inspired Stoke to take complete control of the game. The visitors' victory was confirmed seven minutes from the end when Ursem poked in a second goal following fine work by Crooks and Randall.

THE AFTERMATH
The warm-up didn't help Vale a great deal because they opened their Fourth Division campaign with four straight defeats and also found themselves eliminated from the League Cup in the first round. Their whole season proved a struggle and they avoided finishing in the re-election zone only by virtue of their number of goals scored. Stoke found life in the First Division to be almost as tough and also ended up fifth from the bottom, although they preserved their top flight status by five points.

154: TUESDAY 5 AUGUST 1980, FRIENDLY

PORT VALE (0) 1 (Bromage), STOKE CITY (1) 1 (Ursem).

VALE: Harrison (Dance, 46), Keenan (Brissett), Griffiths, Beech, Harwood, Sproson, Jones (Woolfall), Farrell, Allen, N. Chamberlain, Bromage.
STOKE: Fox, Evans, P. Johnson (Cook), Doyle, Bradley (Smith), Ursem, Richardson, P.A. Johnson, Chapman, Heath, Randall (Bracewell).

Venue: Vale Park, Burslem.
Attendance: 4,302.
Referee: M.J. Heath (Blurton).

THE SETTING
Vale had failed to win any of their three pre-season friendly matches played thus far and had only an own goal to their credit in terms of scoring. Indeed, they had lost 2-1 at Alliance Premier League Stafford Rangers in their previous game three days before the local Derby. Stoke had fared just as badly on a three-match Welsh tour, but after two defeats had at least drawn 1-1 at Third Division Newport County the night prior to the Derby. Both clubs fielded very strong sides for the local clash, although Vale were without their injured centre-half, Bowles, whilst Dodd and O'Callaghan were likewise indisposed for Stoke. Although the crowd was a respectable enough size by friendly standards, it was disappointingly under half of that which had attended the previous Derby.

THE MATCH
The match got off to a slow start, but Stoke took the lead in the tenth minute when Ursem raced on to a long ball from Doyle and squeezed it past the advancing Harrison. Although Ursem later shot just wide, Vale gradually gained in confidence and Griffiths, Allen and Farrell all went close.

Although a Chapman header grazed the bar after the interval, Vale pressed strongly and Doyle kicked a goal-bound shot from Chamberlain virtually off the line before the latter had a goal disallowed for offside. There was further action at both ends, but Vale equalised in the seventy-fourth minute when Bromage applied the final touch to a flick-on by Farrell from a free kick. Stoke were stung into retaliation and Chapman forced the home keeper into a magnificent save, although Fox then denied Chamberlain. However, only a vital last-minute clearance off the line by Farrell prevented Cook from snatching victory for Stoke.

THE AFTERMATH
Vale's creditable draw proved not to have been an auspicious sign for their forthcoming season because they were knocked out of the League Cup in the first round, lost five of their opening seven league games and finished sixth from the bottom of the Fourth Division. They also suffered a humiliating 3-0 defeat at Berger Isthmian League Enfield in an F.A. Cup third round replay in front of TV cameras. Although Stoke conceded five goals in each of their first two league away matches, they then staged a recovery and ended up in a respectable eleventh position in the First Division.

155: FRIDAY 14 AUGUST 1981, FRIENDLY

PORT VALE (1) 1 (Bowles), STOKE CITY (3) 6 (Cook 3, Chapman, Griffiths, Maguire pen.).

VALE: Harrison, Keenan, Deakin, Armstrong (Bennett), Bowles, Higgins, Miller, Moss, N. Chamberlain, Bromage, M. Chamberlain.
STOKE: Fox, Johnson, Hampton, Dodd, O'Callaghan, Doyle (Bould), Bracewell, Griffiths, Chapman (Heath), Cook, Maguire.

Venue: Vale Park, Burslem.
Attendance: 4,500.
Referee: M.J. Heath (Blurton).

THE SETTING
Vale had restricted First Division Manchester United to a 1-0 win in a pre-season friendly match at Vale Park three days before the local Derby. Stoke had warmed up for their 1981-1982 campaign with victories in friendlies against Rotherham United and Crewe Alexandra, but on the Wednesday prior to the Derby, they had lost 2-1 at Second Division Shrewsbury Town. Vale fielded a strong side for the local clash and paraded their recent signings, Ray Deakin from Everton and £12,000 striker, Ernie Moss, secured from Chesterfield, but their central defender, Sproson, was out injured. Richie Barker, the Stoke manager, selected virtually his first-choice team, although the game failed to attract a crowd of any great size.

THE MATCH
Vale had announced with jubilation to the crowd that they had signed the former Stoke striker, Jimmy Greenhoff, but then the team were trounced by their deadly rivals in a 'nightmare of embarrassment'. Stoke exhibited a new pattern of play by passing into space and went in front in the third minute when Harrison and Bowles collided with one another, allowing Cook to thump the ball into an empty net. Bowles headed the equaliser from a Miller free kick twenty-three minutes later, although Vale were effectively reduced to ten men in the thirty-fourth minute when Armstrong was injured but continued as a passenger. He could therefore only watch as Chapman restored Stoke's lead by slotting in the rebound after Cook had struck the bar and then Griffiths scored with a twenty-yard shot. With the damage done, Armstrong limped off!

Five minutes after the interval, Cook smashed the ball into the net from a long cross to put Stoke 4-1 up and, although Neville Chamberlain hit a post for Vale, the visitors remained in command. Maguire belted home a dubiously-awarded penalty in the sixty-fifth minute and Heath struck a post with a lob before Cook ran through to complete his hat trick ten minutes from time.

THE AFTERMATH
In spite of their thrashing, Vale began the new season well and were undefeated in their first six competitive matches. They threatened to join the Fourth Division promotion race at times, but by the following spring had dropped out of contention. Stoke opened their First Division campaign with two consecutive victories, although they then began to struggle and sank to penultimate position in mid-April.

173

156: WEDNESDAY 21 APRIL 1982, WEDGWOOD TROPHY

STOKE CITY (2) 3 (Chapman 3), PORT VALE (1) 2 (M. Chamberlain, Moss).

STOKE: McManus, Evans, Hampton, Dodd, Johnson (Lumsden), McAughtrie (Bould), McIlroy, Biley (Ford), Chapman, Bracewell (Griffiths), Maguire.
VALE: Harrison (Farrell, 51), Tartt, Bromage, Hunter (Bright), Sproson, Bowles, N. Chamberlain, Moss, Deakin, Keenan, M. Chamberlain.

Venue: The Victoria Ground, Stoke-upon-Trent.
Attendance: 3,729.
Referee: M.J. Heath (Blurton).

THE SETTING

The two teams met to contest the new Wedgwood Trophy in a game which doubled as a testimonial for the long-serving Stoke defender, Alan Dodd. Stoke were second from the bottom of the First Division, a point adrift of safety with seven matches to play, as a result of a disastrous sequence of eight defeats and one draw in their previous nine games. These had culminated in a 2-0 reverse at second-placed Ipswich Town four days before the local Derby. In contrast, Vale were in seventh position in the Fourth Division and, although they had beaten third from the bottom Scunthorpe United 2-1 on the Saturday prior to the Derby, they had no real hope of promotion. Stoke were forced to make three alterations in their line-up from their previous match, with McManus, Evans and McAughtrie replacing Fox, Watson and O'Callaghan, all of whom were injured, whilst Vale were unchanged apart from Neville Chamberlain standing in for the unfit Greenhoff.

THE MATCH

Vale took a surprise lead in the fifth minute when Mark Chamberlain shot them in front and his pace and dribbling skills troubled the home defence for the rest of the match. Nevertheless, Chapman headed an equaliser to crown a flowing move, although the Stoke keeper proved a saviour to his side, twice denying Neville Chamberlain and also Moss. The home team rode their luck and Chapman put them in front with another header just before the interval.

Chapman completed his hat trick in the fifty-first minute with a tremendous volley and the Vale custodian was then forced to retire with a groin injury, being replaced in goal by Neville Chamberlain. Nevertheless, Moss reduced the arrears by heading in a Farrell cross in the fifty-fifth minute and the same player almost put Vale level, but Hampton cleared his effort off the line.

THE AFTERMATH

The "Player of the Match" awards were given to Chapman and Bromage, who received three bottles of champagne each. The victory proved a turning point for Stoke who gained eleven points from their final seven First Division matches and finished fifth from the bottom, two points clear of the drop. Vale's form in their remaining league games was mediocre, but they managed to end up in seventh place regardless.

157: FRIDAY 13 AUGUST 1982, WEDGWOOD TROPHY

PORT VALE (0) 0, STOKE CITY (1) 1 (Griffiths).

VALE: Harrison, Tartt, Bromage, Hunter, Sproson (Armstrong), Cegielski, Ridley, Moss, Lawrence (Earle), Greenhoff, M. Chamberlain.
STOKE: Fox, Bould, Hampton, Bracewell, McAughtrie, Berry, Heath, McIlroy, Maguire (O'Callaghan), Griffiths, Maskery.

Venue: Vale Park, Burslem.
Attendance: 3,195.
Referee: T.J. Holbrook (Wightwick).

THE SETTING
Vale had played two pre-season warm-up matches against non-league opposition without defeat and, in the second of these, four days before the local Derby, had won 5-2 at Parkway of the Potteries & District Sunday League. Stoke had undertaken a two-game tour of Norway and had won two of their four friendly matches played in total before losing 2-0 at Irish League Linfield on the Tuesday prior to the Derby. John McGrath, the Vale manager, included his new signings, Wayne Cegielski (from Wrexham), John Ridley (from Chesterfield) and Les Lawrence (from Torquay United) in a strong line-up for the local clash, but Stoke were without their main marksman, Lee Chapman, who had signed for Arsenal, whilst their regular full-back, Parkin, was injured and long-serving central defender Dodd was in dispute with the club. This enabled the apprentices, Heath and Maskery, to gain selection and the newly-signed George Berry (from Wolverhampton Wanderers) was also included.

THE MATCH
Although the two teams could not match the intense rivalry of the supporters, the players made a surprisingly determined effort in a game dominated by Stoke's long ball tactics, which troubled the opposing defence. Maguire had already shot just wide when Sproson was forced to retire with an ankle injury, which further unsettled Vale's back four. Consequently, when a corner was not properly cleared around the half-hour, Griffiths fired Stoke into the lead.

Vale worked hard to get level during the second period, but they created few chances. On one occasion, the Stoke keeper just beat Lawrence to a through ball, whilst Chamberlain flashed a shot past a post following a solo run. Also, Heath went close for Stoke, but the single goal proved sufficient for the visitors to retain the trophy.

THE AFTERMATH
Vale's goalkeeper, Mark Harrison, and winger, Mark Chamberlain, impressed their rivals to such an extent that Stoke paid a combined fee of £181,000 for their services a week later. Despite their loss, Vale mounted a strong challenge for promotion from the Fourth Division during the 1982-1983 season and were eventually successful in finishing third. Stoke also fared well and enjoyed considerably improved fortunes in ending up in a comfortable thirteenth place in the First Division.

158: TUESDAY 6 AUGUST 1985, WEDGWOOD TROPHY

STOKE CITY (0) 1 (Bertschin), PORT VALE (1) 1 (Jones).

STOKE: Siddall, Mills, Maskery, Hudson, Dyson, Bould, Chamberlain, Beeston, Bertschin, Painter (Saunders), Heath.
VALE: Pearce (Phelan, 46), Webb, Bromage, Hunter, Sproson, W.J. Williams, O. Williams, Earle, Jones, Johnson, Maguire.

Venue: The Victoria Ground, Stoke-upon-Trent.
Attendance: 5,369.
Referee: T.J. Holbrook (Wightwick).

THE SETTING
Stoke had won all four of their pre-season friendly matches before losing to their Second Division rivals, Blackburn Rovers, 1-0 in the final of the Isle of Man Football Festival three days before the local Derby. Vale had only played three warm-up games, but were unbeaten and had drawn 1-1 at home to First Division Birmingham City on the Saturday prior to the Derby. Both clubs fielded their strongest available teams for the local clash, although Stoke were without their injured goalkeeper, Fox, and central defender, Berry, whilst Vale were minus the unfit Brown, their regular centre-forward. Stoke's new player-manager, Mick Mills, selected himself and Vale included four new signings: John Williams (a £12,000 buy from Tranmere Rovers), Andy Jones (who cost £3,000 from Rhyl), Jeff Johnson (from Gillingham) and Paul Maguire (a former Stoke player, from Tacoma Stars of the U.S.A.).

THE MATCH
Stoke took command from the outset, but found the visiting defence difficult to break down, although Pearce was forced to make an excellent save from Mills. However, in the twentieth minute, Vale moved out of their shell and Jones struck home a tremendous cross-shot to complete a flowing move. Maguire caused Stoke trouble from set pieces, but Chamberlain should have equalised just before the interval instead of shooting feebly at the Vale keeper.

Although Pearce was forced to retire because of an ankle injury and replaced at the outset of the second half by Phelan, a trialist, Stoke's moves continued to founder on the rock of the visiting defence. Nevertheless, Bertschin squandered a good chance when put through by Hudson, but Siddall saved magnificently from Jones as Vale sought to make the victory safe. However, Stoke levelled the score with just three minutes remaining when Bertschin fired the ball in from a Bould headed flick-on, which resulted in the trophy being shared.

THE AFTERMATH
Stoke initially found the going rather tough in the Second Division and won only once in their opening ten matches, although their sole victory was remarkably by 6-2 at home to Leeds United! Owing to the severity of Pearce's injury, Vale were forced to sign a replacement goalkeeper, the much-travelled Jim Arnold, and he proved a revelation as a firm promotion bid from the Fourth Division was mounted, based on a tight defence which conceded few goals.

159: SUNDAY 13 APRIL 1986, FRIENDLY

PORT VALE (0) 0, STOKE CITY (0) 1 (Sproson o.g.).

VALE: Pearce, Banks, P. Johnson, Hunter (Bowden), Sproson, W.J. Williams (Kerr), Chamberlain, Earle, Biggins, J. Johnson, Maguire (Ebanks).
STOKE: Fox (Roberts), Callaghan, Hemming, Mills (Beeston), Bould, Berry, Painter (Adams), Saunders, Bertschin (Sutton), Shaw, Heath.

Venue: Vale Park, Burslem.
Attendance: 1,528.
Referee: G.L. Wilkes (Baddeley Green).

THE SETTING
This game was played as a testimonial for the long-serving Vale left-back, Russell Bromage. Vale were third in the Fourth Division, with a six-point cushion against fifth-placed Hartlepool United. They had won a vital match 2-1 at promotion-chasing Stockport County on the Friday before the local Derby to extend their unbeaten league run to sixteen games. Stoke were in eleventh position in the Second Division, but had only managed to draw 0-0 at home to second from the bottom Carlisle United on the day prior to the Derby. John Rudge, the Vale manager, chose to rest five first teamers (Arnold, Ebanks, Jones, Brown and Bowden) for the local clash, but the side included Paul Johnson, of Shrewsbury Town, and Vale's former forward, Neville Chamberlain, of Mansfield Town, as guests. However, Bromage was unfortunately sidelined with damaged ankle ligaments and unable to play. Stoke selected a very strong line-up and made just two changes from their previous match, with Callaghan and Shaw replacing Bonnyman and Adams.

THE MATCH
The main match was preceded by a short 'golden oldies' contest between former players of the two clubs and was reduced to thirty minutes each way. Rain helped to limit the crowd to the smallest gathered at a local Derby since 1945, but the spectators saw plenty of action. Vale exerted the early pressure and the visiting keeper made a splendid save from an effort by Earle, whilst Sproson headed just wide from a corner. However, Pearce was the busier overall of the two custodians and magnificently denied Heath, Berry, Shaw and Sutton. The issue was finally decided in the second period when Sproson glided the ball past his own keeper whilst intercepting a knock-down by Shaw.

THE AFTERMATH
Russell Bromage collected just under £3,000 from the proceeds of the match and returned to Vale's side before the end of the season in time to celebrate the club's promotion in fourth place to the Third Division, even though only two of the final five games were won. Stoke took seven points from their last five matches, which was a sufficient tally to secure tenth place for them in the Second Division. Although this achievement hardly set the world alight, the team's fortunes had at least been stabilised following their ignominious relegation in the previous campaign.

160: MONDAY 4 AUGUST 1986, FRIENDLY

PORT VALE (0) 1 (Bould o.g.), STOKE CITY (1) 3 (Saunders, Heath, Shaw).

VALE: Grew, Webb, Bromage, Hunter, Sproson, Williams, Jones (Banks), Earle, O'Kelly, Walker, Maguire.
STOKE: Fox, Dixon, Hemming, Kelly (Bertschin, 60), Bould, Berry, Ford, Maskery, Saunders, Shaw, Heath.

Venue: Vale Park, Burslem.
Attendance: 4,757.
Referee: T.J. Holbrook (Walsall).

THE SETTING
Vale were unbeaten in three pre-season friendlies, the most recent of which had resulted in a 1-0 win at Gola League Nuneaton Borough three days before the local Derby. Stoke had also been undefeated in their three warm-up matches before losing 1-0 to Third Division Wigan Athletic on the Thursday prior to the Derby and thereby being eliminated from the Okells Brewery International Football Festival. Both clubs fielded strong sides for the local clash and Vale paraded three new signings: Mark Grew (from Ipswich Town), Richard O'Kelly (who cost £6,000 from Walsall) and Ray Walker (a £12,000 purchase from Aston Villa). In addition, the Stoke manager, Mick Mills, selected his new players, Lee Dixon (bought from Bury for £40,000) and Tony Ford (acquired for £35,000 from Grimsby Town).

THE MATCH
Stoke made most of the early running and a fine through ball by Shaw in the twenty-eighth minute enabled Saunders to break clear and plant a left-footed shot in the net. The nearest Vale came to equalising before half-time was when Dixon inadvertently struck a back-pass inches wide of his own goal.

Stoke extended their lead ten minutes into the second period when the home defence failed to catch Heath offside and the winger cut inside to curl the ball over the Vale keeper and into the net off the far post. However, the home team then took control of the midfield and reduced the arrears on the hour when Sproson headed on a Maguire corner for the ball to bounce off Bould into the goal. Vale pressed strongly for the equaliser and O'Kelly lobbed fractionally wide of a post before the issue was settled in Stoke's favour nine minutes from the end. The home keeper struck a clearance straight to the feet of Shaw, who then stroked the ball into the unguarded net, which inspired the rain-drenched Stoke fans to dance the conga on the Hamil End!

THE AFTERMATH
The Vale fans found it difficult to forgive their goalkeeper for his untimely error and in their next home game, a friendly against Aston Villa, poor Grew received a 'barrage of abuse'! Nevertheless, Vale consolidated their newly-earned position in the Third Division and finished a respectable twelfth. Stoke began their Second Division campaign with three straight defeats, but recovered to end up in eighth place and also progressed to the fifth round of the F.A. Cup.

178

161: TUESDAY 4 AUGUST 1987, FRIENDLY

STOKE CITY (0) 2 (Saunders, Heath), PORT VALE (0) 0.

STOKE: Fox (Barrett), Dixon, Carr (Parkin, 46), Talbot, Hemming, Berry, Ford, Daly, Morgan, Shaw (Saunders, 45), Allinson (Heath, 46).
VALE: Williams, Banks, Bromage, Walker, Hazell, Webb, Smith (Maguire), Earle, Jones, Beckford, Harper.

Venue: The Victoria Ground, Stoke-upon-Trent.
Attendance: 5,279.
Referee: T.J. Holbrook (Walsall).

THE SETTING

Stoke had begun their preparations for the new season by participating in the Okells Brewery Football Festival and had won the competition. They had remained undefeated in their four matches and had beaten Scottish Premier Division Dundee 1-0 in the final three days before the local Derby. Vale had won two and lost two of their five warm-up games and had gained a 2-1 home victory against Fourth Division Crewe Alexandra on the Friday prior to the Derby. Stoke were without their injured centre-half, Bould, but chose their strongest available side for the local clash, which included their new signings, Cliff Carr (who cost £45,000 from Fulham) and Ian Allinson (from Arsenal). Vale's manager, John Rudge, also committed his full first team to the fray and selected Darren Beckford, a £15,000 capture from Manchester City, whilst Harper made his debut.

THE MATCH

Vale began strongly, with Walker orchestrating the midfield, and looked particularly dangerous from set pieces. However, the outcome was fiercely contested and the Stoke defence was in no mood to concede any advantage. Although both sides created chances, the interval arrived with the score goalless.

A strong run by Talbot, three minutes into the second period, led to the Stoke substitute, Saunders, slotting in a rebound from the visiting keeper to put the home team in front. They doubled their lead just two minutes later when Heath, another substitute, scored with a header after receiving a flick-on by Morgan. Thus the game was remarkably transformed, although Vale fought back determinedly. Beckford headed against the bar, Jones forced Barrett into a magnificent save, Earle steered a header just wide and Berry cleared a corner off the line, but the visitors were unable to effect a breakthrough.

THE AFTERMATH

Stoke performed competently throughout most of the 1987-1988 season, although they were unable to put together a sufficiently consistent run of good results to make any real impact on the Second Division promotion race. Vale found themselves at the top of the Third Division in mid-September, but then sold Andy Jones, their main striker, to Charlton Athletic for £350,000 and plummeted down the table, although their slide was eventually arrested.

162: MONDAY 21 MARCH 1988, FRIENDLY

PORT VALE (1) 1 (A. Heath), STOKE CITY (0) 1 (Shaw).

VALE: Grew, Webb, Hughes, Walker, Hazell (Steggles, 46), Sproson, Maguire (G. Ford, 82), A. Heath, Davies, Earle (Porter, 70), Beckford (Riley, 68).
STOKE: Barrett (Powell, 46), T. Ford, Carr, Daly, Beeston, Hemming, Chamberlain, Henry, Stainrod, Shaw, P. Heath.

Venue: Vale Park, Burslem.
Attendance: 4,419.
Referee: J. Rushton (Dresden).

THE SETTING
This match was played as a testimonial for Vale's long-serving central defender, Phil Sproson. Vale were thirteenth in the Third Division, but had inspired their fans with a marvellous F.A. Cup run before being eliminated in the fifth round and had drawn 0-0 at Gillingham in the league two days before the local Derby. Stoke were in ninth position in the Second Division and had beaten Barnsley 3-1 at home on the same day. Vale made four alterations from their team in the previous match, with Steggles, Ford, Riley and Holdsworth being rested and replaced by Webb, Maguire, Adrian Heath of Everton and Davies. Stoke were without their first-choice half-back line, having lost Bould and Berry to injury and Parkin to England under 21 duty. Their places were taken by Daly, Mark Chamberlain of Sheffield Wednesday and Stainrod and the side was somewhat reshuffled.

THE MATCH
Although the match was a testimonial, the players did not treat it as a friendly and the outcome was vigorously contested. Vale started strongly and Maguire spurned a golden opportunity in the very first minute, whilst Davies fired just wide only a minute afterwards. Stoke retaliated, but Stainrod in turn squandered a fine chance when his twelfth-minute header was cleared off the line and he then hit the rebound against the bar. Adrian Heath headed inches wide of a post after a quarter of an hour, although he made no mistake in giving Vale the lead in the twenty-eighth minute when Beckford flicked the ball on from a corner for him to head into the net.

Although Vale remained in the lead against their old rivals, the home supporters constantly chanted for the return of their former striker, Andy Jones, from Charlton Athletic. Their mood was not improved seven minutes from time when Stainrod set up Shaw to poach the equaliser.

THE AFTERMATH
The proceeds of the game yielded £12,000 for Phil Sproson's testimonial and Vale followed up their success by winning their next three league matches, which helped them to climb to their final position of eleventh. Stoke tasted victory in only two of their remaining seven Second Division games and fell away to end up also in eleventh place.

163: TUESDAY 16 AUGUST 1988, FRIENDLY

PORT VALE (1) 1 (Atkinson pen.), STOKE CITY (0) 0.

VALE: Grew, Webb, Hughes, Walker, Hazell, Sproson (Mills), G. Ford, Earle, Riley, Beckford, Atkinson.
STOKE: Fox, Ware, Carr, Kamara (Saunders, 70), Lewis, Henry, T. Ford, Saunders (Hackett), Stainrod (Morgan), Shaw, Beagrie.

Venue: Vale Park, Burslem.
Attendance: 4,849.
Referee: J. Rushton (Dresden).

THE SETTING
Vale had won four and drawn one of their five pre-season friendly matches to date and had gained a 4-0 victory at G.M. Vauxhall Conference League Kidderminster Harriers three days before the local Derby. Stoke had played no fewer than eight warm-up games, winning six and losing two, the second defeat of which had been by 2-1 at home to Third Division Wolverhampton Wanderers on the Saturday prior to the Derby. Vale's manager, John Rudge, selected his strongest available line-up for the local contest and included Paul Atkinson (a recent £20,000 signing from Sunderland), although new striker, Ron Futcher (who cost £35,000 from Bradford City), was absent with an upset stomach. Although Stoke also took the clash seriously, they had a makeshift defence because of injuries and were forced to field two YTS players, Ware and Lewis. Nevertheless, they did parade their summer signings, Peter Beagrie (purchased for £215,000 from Sheffield United) and Chris Kamara (who cost £27,500 from Swindon Town).

THE MATCH
Vale piled on the pressure in the early stages and Atkinson gave them the lead from the penalty spot in the tenth minute after Lewis had felled Beckford in the area. Stoke's makeshift defence was all at sea and Gary Ford and Earle both went close to doubling the home side's advantage. However, Stoke dug in and Kamara increasingly marked Walker out of the game, which stifled the home team's midfield. The contest became so competitive that Saunders required three stitches in a head wound, whilst Sproson was forced to retire for one of his lips to be stitched.

Stoke largely controlled the second period, with Beagrie supplying a series of dangerous crosses, but their forwards were rather goal shy. Nevertheless, Carr struck the bar, forced the Vale keeper to save magnificently and had two further goal-bound shots hacked away. However, Vale's survival was assisted when Kamara departed with a leg injury in the seventieth minute and they managed to hang on to record their first local Derby victory since 1970.

THE AFTERMATH
Vale carried on their good work when their Third Division campaign opened and they climbed to the top of the table in mid-September. In contrast, Stoke found the going tough in the Second Division and failed to win any of their first six games, although they gradually got into their stride.

164: TUESDAY 18 OCTOBER 1988, FRIENDLY

STOKE CITY (1) 1 (Saunders), PORT VALE (1) 1 (Porter).

STOKE: Fox, Gidman, Carr, Henry, Higgins, Berry, Hackett, Ford, Saunders, Stainrod (Spender), Beagrie.
VALE: Wood, Mills (Hughes), Simpson, Finney, Hazell, Webb, Harper (Booth), Porter, Beckford, Riley (Lomax), Atkinson (Davies).

Venue: The Victoria Ground, Stoke-upon-Trent.
Attendance: 1,686.
Referee: J. Rushton (Dresden).

THE SETTING
This match was played as a testimonial for Stoke's midfielder, Chris Maskery, who had been forced to retire from professional football. Stoke were fifth from the bottom of the Second Division and had lost 2-0 at Leicester City three days before the local Derby. In contrast, Vale were two points clear at the top of the Third Division and had extended their unbeaten run in the league to eight matches in beating fourth-placed Bolton Wanderers 2-1 at home on the Saturday prior to the Derby. Stoke made just two changes in their line-up from their previous game, with Fox replacing the injured Barrett and Ware standing down in favour of Gidman. However, Vale's manager, John Rudge, preferred to select seven reserves, with Wood, Simpson, Finney, Webb, Harper, Porter and Atkinson replacing Grew, Hughes, Walker, Sproson, Ford, Earle and Futcher, as the club did not wish to take unnecessary risks with injury in view of their league position.

THE MATCH
Although the teams had nothing to play for, the game proved yet another typical blood and guts Potteries Derby. Stoke almost went in front in the fourth minute when Henry thumped the ball against the bar from a corner, but it was the visitors who took the lead with a tremendous twenty-five yard drive from Porter which shot just inside a post. However, Stoke equalised three minutes before the interval when Saunders collected a centre from Ford, slipped his marker and stroked the ball into the net.

Despite incessant rain, the second period was just as strongly contested and Hughes was denied by the Stoke keeper before Saunders almost put the home side ahead with an effort that was deflected inches outside a post. Nevertheless, neither team could further break the deadlock so that the match rightly ended as a draw.

THE AFTERMATH
Despite Stoke's failure to beat their under-strength opponents, they took sixteen points from their following six league games, but could not maintain their form and finished the season in thirteenth place. Although Vale gained just one point from their next three matches, they ended the campaign in third place and were promoted via the play-offs to join their old rivals in the Second Division.

165: SATURDAY 23 SEPTEMBER 1989, FOOTBALL LEAGUE, SECOND DIVISION

STOKE CITY (0) 1 (Palin), PORT VALE (0) 1 (Earle).

STOKE: Fox, Butler, Statham, Kamara, Cranson, Beeston, Ware (Hackett, 55), Palin (Saunders, 75), Bamber, Morgan, Beagrie.
VALE: Grew, Webb, Hughes, Mills, Aspin, Glover, Porter, Earle (Walker, 71), Futcher, Beckford (Jepson, 60), Jeffers.

Venue: The Victoria Ground, Stoke-upon-Trent.
Attendance: 27,004.
Referee: T. Simpson (Sowerby Bridge).

THE SETTING
The prospect of the first Football League local Derby for over thirty-two years attracted Stoke's largest crowd in the competition since 1982. However, Stoke were third from the bottom of the Second Division, although they had beaten First Division Millwall 1-0 at home in a second round Littlewoods Cup match four days before the local Derby. Vale were only three places and two points above their rivals in the league, whilst they had lost 2-1 at home to First Division strugglers Wimbledon at the same stage of the Littlewoods Cup on the Monday prior to the Derby. Mick Mills, the Stoke manager, made just a single change in their team from their previous game, with Beeston replacing Higgins, whilst recent signing, Leigh Palin, made his league debut. Vale were without the injured Cross and Walker was rested; their places were taken by Porter and Jeffers.

THE MATCH
Vale began brightly and largely controlled the tempo of the match during the first half, with Mills inspirational in midfield. Jeffers and Hughes repeatedly caused problems on the left for the Stoke defence, but the visiting strikers failed to capitalise on their efforts. Nevertheless, the home keeper pulled off a fine save to deny Webb and Beckford had a goal disallowed for offside in the twenty-fifth minute.

Stoke pressed strongly after the interval, but Vale took the lead in the fiftieth minute when Earle raced on to a pass from Jeffers and planted the ball into the net. Stoke then introduced a second winger, Hackett, into the fray and aimed crosses at Bamber's head. This paid dividends in the sixty-fifth minute when the centre-forward set up Palin to strike the equaliser with the aid of a 'wicked' deflection. Stoke then stormed forward in a determined attempt to snatch the winner, but the visitors came the closer to victory when Jepson headed wide of a gaping goal after Futcher had hit the bar.

THE AFTERMATH
The occasion was marred by the arrest of eighty-five supporters 'during an orgy of destruction' at The Huntsman in Burslem where rival fans confronted one another after the game. Stoke went a further four league matches before recording their first victory and they soon became marooned at the foot of the table. Vale also continued to find the going tough and by the turn of the year they remained only three points clear of the relegation zone.

183

166: SATURDAY 3 FEBRUARY 1990, FOOTBALL LEAGUE, SECOND DIVISION

PORT VALE (0) 0, STOKE CITY (0) 0.

VALE: Grew, Mills, Hughes, Walker, Aspin, Glover, Porter, Earle, Cross (Millar, 80), Beckford, Jeffers.
STOKE: Fox, Butler, Carr, Beeston, Sandford, Berry, Kelly (Hackett, 54), Ellis, Palin, Biggins, Kevan.

Venue: Vale Park, Burslem.
Attendance: 22,075.
Referee: P.A. Tyldesley (Bredbury).

THE SETTING
Vale were tenth in the Second Division and had won their previous three league matches, but had been trounced 6-0 at First Division championship-chasing Aston Villa in the fourth round of the F.A. Cup a week before the local Derby. Stoke were in dire straits, six points adrift at the bottom of the Second Division, and had lost their last three league games. Their most recent failure had been a 3-0 defeat at Blackburn Rovers on the Saturday prior to the Derby. Despite their cup drubbing, Vale were unchanged for the return clash with their local rivals, but Stoke made four alterations in their team from their previous match, with Statham, Holmes, the injured Fowler and Ware standing down in favour of Carr, Berry and debutants Tony Kelly (signed for £20,000 from St. Alban's City) and David Kevan (who was on loan from Notts County). The police made thirty-five arrests as a result of running battles between rival fans in Burslem town centre before the game.

THE MATCH
The match got off to a lively start with the play being quite even, although Cross had a goal disallowed for a foul in the twelfth minute. Vale then gained the ascendancy and forced their opponents to defend desperately. Nevertheless, a looping header over the bar by Porter was the best they could offer in strikes at goal, whilst shortly before half-time, Ellis pulled the ball across the Vale area, but no-one was on hand to convert the chance.

The second period was as doggedly contested as the first and, after Ellis had missed a sitter for Stoke almost immediately following the restart, Cross had a goal ruled out for a second time, on this occasion for handling the ball. As the game progressed, the passing degenerated as the pitch increasingly cut up and Porter spurned a golden opportunity by firing wide. Also, Beckford twice went close to breaking the deadlock near to the end, but Stoke survived to earn a much-needed point.

THE AFTERMATH
Despite their failure to extend their winning sequence in the league, Vale remained tenth, although they finished the season one rung lower. Stoke's immediate position was also unaltered and their hard-earned draw counted for little other than local pride because their league form did not improve and they were eventually relegated in bottom place.

167: TUESDAY 14 AUGUST 1990, FRIENDLY

STOKE CITY (1) 1 (Biggins), PORT VALE (0) 0.

STOKE: Fox, Butler, Statham, Ware, Blake, Berry (Fowler, 30), Sandford, Ellis, Thomas, Biggins, Kelly (Gallimore, 71).
VALE: Wood, S. Mills, Hughes, Walker, Aspin, Glover, Ford (Porter, 63), Earle, Cross (Millar, 39), Beckford, Jeffers (Swan, 84).

Venue: The Victoria Ground, Stoke-upon-Trent.
Attendance: 10,731.
Referee: T.J. Holbrook (Walsall).

THE SETTING

This game was played as a testimonial for Stoke's long-standing central defender, George Berry. Stoke had performed positively in the 1990-1991 pre-season, winning six and drawing two of their eight warm-up matches to date, although they had only won 2-1 at Bass North West Counties League Newcastle Town two days before the local Derby. Vale had done even better, winning all their six pre-season outings thus far, all of which had been played away from home, and they had scored twenty-one goals in the process. Their most recent victory had been by 2-0 at Third Division Crewe Alexandra on the Saturday prior to the Derby. Both clubs fielded their strongest available line-ups for the local clash, although Vale's first-choice goalkeeper, Grew, was absent with a thigh strain. An excellent crowd assembled for the game.

THE MATCH

Stoke showed a tremendous appetite for the contest from the outset and, after only two minutes, Ellis raced through and thumped a shot against the bar. Beckford responded by forcing the home keeper to make a fine save, although Stoke then surged back and Biggins netted, only to have his goal disallowed because of a foul by Ellis. Berry was substituted on the half-hour, but kissed the turf before he departed to stand with the Stoke fans on the Boothen End to watch the rest of the match! Biggins finally put Stoke in front in the thirty-fifth minute with a carefully-placed low drive after latching on to a magnificent through ball from Ellis.

Vale attacked forcefully at the start of the second period and Millar, Beckford, Walker and Jeffers all went close to equalising, but the home side gradually reasserted their grip on the game and the visitors' momentum petered out. The Stoke players hustled their way to victory, with the tight marking of Sandford nullifying the threat of playmaker Walker.

THE AFTERMATH

Stoke began their Third Division campaign strongly, with two successive victories, but gradually fell away and finished fourteenth, the lowest Football League position ever recorded in their history. In contrast, Vale found themselves in difficulty at the outset of their season in the Second Division and lost their opening two matches. However, although they continued to struggle throughout most of the autumn, they eventually rallied to end up in fourteenth place.

168: SATURDAY 24 OCTOBER 1992, FOOTBALL LEAGUE, SECOND DIVISION

STOKE CITY (0) 2 (Cranson, Stein pen.), PORT VALE (0) 1 (Kerr).

STOKE: Sinclair, Butler, Gleghorn, Cranson, Overson, Sandford, Foley, Ware (Russell, 46), Stein, Shaw, Beeston.
VALE: Musselwhite, Sandeman, Sulley, Walker, Swan, Glover, Aspin, Taylor, Cross, Houchen, van der Laan (Kerr, 56).

Venue: The Victoria Ground, Stoke-upon-Trent.
Attendance: 24,334.
Referee: J. Watson (Seaton Sluice).

THE SETTING
Stoke were seventh in the Second Division and just two points adrift of second position. They had stretched their unbeaten run in the league to eight matches with a 2-1 win at Preston North End a week before the local Derby. Vale were below their rivals in the table only as a result of having scored one goal fewer and had extended their own sequence without a defeat to seven games by hammering Plymouth Argyle 4-0 at home on the Saturday prior to the Derby. Both clubs made one team change from their previous matches, with Nigel Gleghorn (a new £100,000 signing from Birmingham City) replacing Harbey for Stoke and Vale preferring the more physical presence of van der Laan to Kerr in midfield. The game was all ticket and had been sold out in advance.

THE MATCH
Stoke exerted most of the early pressure and Musselwhite needed two attempts to save a low drive by Stein in the twentieth minute. Shaw glanced a header across the face of the Vale goal seven minutes later, but chances were at a premium as the visitors defended in depth and relied on breakaways.

Stoke sent on their winger, Russell, for the injured Ware at the start of the second half and almost immediately the former put a shot wide from ten yards to miss a golden opportunity. The momentum of the match increased and more chances began to be created at both ends. Then, in the sixty-seventh minute, Kerr received a pass from Taylor and put Vale ahead with a curling shot. However, Stoke were level within a minute as Cranson powered in to head a free kick from Russell into the top of the net. Both sides then searched for the winner, which went to Stoke four minutes from time as Stein rifled in a penalty after being grounded in the area by the visiting keeper.

THE AFTERMATH
There were twenty-four arrests made during the match from the third-highest crowd recorded in English football that day and brawls between rival fans followed in Hanley at night. Stoke moved up to fourth place as a result of their victory and their promotion challenge intensified as their unbeaten run in the league continued throughout the rest of the autumn. Although Vale dropped one position in the table following their defeat, the setback proved to be temporary and they were soon pushing to regain their First Division status.

169: MONDAY 16 NOVEMBER 1992, F.A. CUP, FIRST ROUND

STOKE CITY (0) 0, PORT VALE (0) 0.

STOKE: Sinclair, Butler, Sandford, Cranson, Overson, Gleghorn, Foley, Russell, Stein, Shaw, Beeston.
VALE: Musselwhite, Sandeman, Sulley, Walker, Swan, Glover, Aspin, Kerr (Jeffers, 70), Cross (Foyle, 80), Houchen, Taylor.

Venue: The Victoria Ground, Stoke-upon-Trent.
Attendance: 24,490.
Referee: V.G. Callow (Solihull).

THE SETTING
Stoke were in second position in the Second Division and being kept off the top spot only by goals scored. They had extended their unbeaten run in the league to twelve matches in winning 2-0 at home to Bournemouth nine days before the local Derby. Vale were also flying high in fifth place in the same division, three points behind their rivals, and had drawn 1-1 at Bolton Wanderers in their last game on the same day. Both teams were unchanged from their previous matches. The event was sold out well in advance and a carnival atmosphere was created for Sky TV's live screening of the clash by the provision of dancing girls and fireworks before the kickoff and giant Sumo wrestlers at half-time!

THE MATCH
Stoke attacked strongly from the outset and forced six corners in the opening twenty minutes. However, Vale absorbed the pressure and only once during this period, when Stein fired wide after a quarter of an hour, did the home side look like scoring. Nevertheless, Stoke preferred to move the ball around at speed, which kept the visitors well occupied so that it took them twenty-three minutes to muster their first shot at goal and a further twenty-one minutes to force the home keeper to make a save.

Vale almost took the lead a minute after the interval, but Shaw cleared Taylor's goal-bound header off the line. Stoke then reasserted their stranglehold on the game and, on the hour, Russell broke away and netted, only to find his effort disallowed for offside. In addition, Stein shot against the bar just a minute later, whilst the same player and Shaw also went close as the match progressed. Vale retaliated and Foyle struck a thirty-yarder inches wide before a magnificent save by the visiting custodian prevented Gleghorn from snatching victory for Stoke three minutes from time. Therefore, the celebrations of the 6,700 assembled Vale fans were not to be denied.

THE AFTERMATH
In addition to the gate receipts, both clubs received £48,000 from Sky TV for the screening of the game and stood to reap the benefit of a further £24,000 each from the company for the right to show the replay. On the intervening Saturday, Stoke gained a 3-1 victory at the bottom side, Blackpool, and took the leadership of the division, but Vale could only draw 1-1 at home to struggling Hull City and consequently dropped two places in the table.

170: TUESDAY 24 NOVEMBER 1992, F.A. CUP, FIRST ROUND REPLAY

PORT VALE (2) 3 (Foyle 2, Porter), STOKE CITY (1) 1 (Sandford).

VALE: Musselwhite, Sandeman, Sulley, Walker, Swan, Glover, Aspin (Jeffers, 15), Porter, Cross, Foyle, Taylor.
STOKE: Sinclair, Butler, Sandford, Cranson, Overson, Gleghorn, Foley, Russell, Stein, Shaw (Regis, 65), Beeston.

Venue: Vale Park, Burslem.
Attendance: 19,810.
Referee: V.G. Callow (Solihull).

THE SETTING
Stoke had moved to the top of the Second Division by winning 3-1 at bottom of the table Blackpool three days before the return local Derby and had thereby lengthened their unbeaten league run to thirteen matches. Vale were also faring well in the same division, but had dropped to seventh position as a result of a 1-1 home draw against sixth from the bottom Hull City on the Saturday prior to the Derby. John Rudge, the Vale manager, made two changes in their line-up from their previous game, replacing Kerr with the more industrious Porter and Houchen with the speedier Foyle. Stoke were unchanged. Before the match, an estimated £20,000 worth of damage was done to the front of Ye Olde Crown in Burslem by a 'mob' of about a hundred Stoke fans who hurled bricks and bottles through its stained glass windows.

THE MATCH
The replay was a pulsating encounter played in atrocious conditions and the competitive edge of the contest was well illustrated in the fifteenth minute when Aspin limped off with a leg injury sustained by a high tackle from Foley. Although Vale did most of the early pressing, Sandford prodded the ball in from an Overson header-on to put the visitors in front in the twenty-third minute. However, Vale roared back to equalise within a minute when Foyle lashed in an acute-angled drive after being set up by Cross. The latter was the provider again on the stroke of half-time when he enabled Porter to strike a tremendous shot to give Vale the lead.

The conditions deteriorated after the interval and the teams 'had to splash through a monsoon'. Vale continued to push forward and Swan had a goal disallowed for offside, although a goal-bound effort by Stoke substitute, Regis, got stuck in the mud six yards from the line! Taylor then squandered a golden opportunity for the home side and Jeffers hit a post before Cross once more supplied the vital pass, to enable Foyle to seal the victory in the final minute.

THE AFTERMATH
Afterwards, it was discovered that £5,000 worth of damage had been done to the Hamil End, which had housed Stoke supporters. Nevertheless, the tie had produced a financial bonanza and Vale progressed to the third round of the competition. Also, both Vale and Stoke intensified their promotion challenges and the Potters did not taste defeat again until 27 February.

188

171: WEDNESDAY 3 MARCH 1993, AUTOGLASS TROPHY, SOUTHERN AREA SEMI-FINAL

STOKE CITY (0) 0, PORT VALE (0) 1 (van der Laan).

STOKE: Sinclair, Butler, Sandford, Cranson, Overson, Gleghorn, Foley (Russell, 80), Ware, Stein, Shaw, Beeston.
VALE: Musselwhite, Aspin, Sulley, van der Laan, Billing, Glover, Kent, Kerr, Cross, Foyle (Porter, 37), Taylor.

Venue: The Victoria Ground, Stoke-upon-Trent.
Attendance: 22,254.
Referee: G.R. Ashby (Worcester).

THE SETTING
Stoke had finally surrendered their remarkable club record twenty-five league match unbeaten run in losing 1-0 at third-placed Leyton Orient four days before the local Derby, but remained seven points clear at the top of the Second Division. Vale were their nearest challengers and had defeated West Bromwich Albion, who were equal third, by 2-1 at home on the Saturday prior to the Derby. Both clubs made one change from their teams in their previous games, with Stoke, the trophy holders, selecting Ware in preference to Russell, whilst van der Laan replaced the injured Walker for Vale.

THE MATCH
Stoke applied their usual pressure game in a frantic battle, during which the visitors were forced to defend for long spells. Stein had a series of chances to put Stoke ahead, but after shooting over the bar from ten yards, he then tamely tapped the ball against a post from the penalty spot in the twelfth minute following a foul on Shaw. Vale later lost Foyle as a result of a knee injury and a brilliant forty-five-yard lob by Beeston was saved under the bar by the visiting keeper. Vale finally forced their first corner in the forty-second minute, although Stein had a goal disallowed for offside on the verge of half-time.

Vale took the lead against the run of play eight minutes after the interval when van der Laan headed in from a Sulley free kick. Stoke then bombarded the visitors' goal in almost relentless fashion, but Stein shot wide from eight yards before Musselwhite made a magnificent save from a Beeston power drive six minutes from time. However, Stein spurned a wonderful opportunity to equalise just two minutes later when he headed a precise centre from Russell wide of the target when a goal seemed a certainty.

THE AFTERMATH
The triumph of Vale's first victory at Stoke in a competitive match since 1927 helped to give them the impetus to emulate their rivals and win the trophy by beating Stockport County 2-1 in the final at Wembley on 22 May. Although Foyle's injury proved to be long term, Vale won four of their following six league games to keep their promotion hopes on the boil. Stoke did even better and collected thirteen points from their next five matches to tighten their grip on the Second Division championship.

172: WEDNESDAY 31 MARCH 1993, FOOTBALL LEAGUE, SECOND DIVISION

PORT VALE (0) 0, STOKE CITY (1) 2 (Stein, Gleghorn).

VALE: Musselwhite, Kent, Sulley (Jeffers, 60), Walker, Swan, Glover, Slaven, van der Laan, Houchen, Billing (Cross, 80), Kerr.
STOKE: Grobbelaar, Butler, Sandford, Cranson, Overson, Gleghorn, Foley, Kevan, Stein, Regis (Shaw, 80), Ware (Russell, 88).

Venue: Vale Park, Burslem.
Attendance: 20,373.
Referee: R.G.Milford (Bristol).

THE SETTING

Stoke held a seven-point lead at the top of the Second Division, but had been surprisingly beaten 1-0 at home by fifth from the bottom Blackpool four days before the local Derby. Vale occupied second position and retained a four-point cushion from their nearest challengers by winning 1-0 at Hull City on the Saturday prior to the Derby. In addition, they held the only unbeaten home record in all four divisions. Vale were without their injured midfielder, Taylor, who was replaced by Houchen, but were otherwise unchanged from their previous match. However, Lou Macari, the Stoke manager, preferred to make two alterations in his team to contest the vital fifth Derby of the season and so Russell and Beeston were omitted in favour of Kevan and Ware.

THE MATCH

Stoke took the lead in only the fourth minute when Butler jinked through three weak challenges and put in a low cross for Stein to turn and fire the ball home in a flash. Vale then pressed strongly and Sulley went close before slashing wide from a Walker centre when a careful side-footer would almost certainly have levelled the score. Although Stein missed narrowly, Vale continued to dictate the play and Grobbelaar had to be alert to save from Slaven right on half-time.

Vale's challenge somewhat faded after the interval and Jeffers was thrown into the fray on the hour to provide more width. However, the substitution did not have the desired effect and the home keeper was forced to make a brilliant save from a Gleghorn shot before the latter headed Stoke further in front from a corner in the sixty-fourth minute. Stein nearly added to the tally as Vale then tamely surrendered their unbeaten home record, although the visiting custodian magnificently turned a fine strike from Slaven round a post a minute before the end.

THE AFTERMATH

The police stated their pleasure that only twenty-five arrests had been made with so much at stake on the game. Stoke extended their lead at the top of the table to ten points and eventually won the championship with three points to spare. Despite their defeat, Vale remained second, but could only finish the season in third position, despite taking thirteen points from their last five matches. Therefore, they were obliged to enter the play-offs, in the final of which at Wembley on 30 May they were beaten 3-0 by West Bromwich Albion.

173: TUESDAY 14 MARCH 1995, FOOTBALL LEAGUE, FIRST DIVISION

PORT VALE (1) 1 (Naylor), STOKE CITY (1) 1 (Sandford).

VALE: Musselwhite, Sandeman, Tankard, Porter, Aspin, Billing, Guppy, van der Laan, L. Glover (Allon, 79), Naylor, Walker (Kent, 70).

STOKE: Sinclair, Butler, Sandford, Cranson, Overson, Orlygsson (Keen, 86), Sigurdsson, Beeston, Carruthers (Scott, 62), Allen, Gleghorn.

Venue: Vale Park, Burslem.
Attendance: 19,510.
Referee: A. Dawson (Jarrow).

THE SETTING

Vale were fifteenth in the First Division, but had beaten fourth from the bottom Bristol City 2-1 at home on the Saturday before the local Derby to extend their cushion against the relegation zone to four points. In doing so, they had leapfrogged above Stoke, who had dropped to eighteenth position, a point behind their old rivals, by losing 1-0 at fifth from the bottom Sunderland three days prior to the Derby. John Rudge, the Vale manager, made two team changes from the previous match, with Billing and Lee Glover replacing the unavailable Kevin Scott and the injured Foyle, whilst Stoke opted for just one alteration, with Keith Scott standing down in favour of Orlygsson.

THE MATCH

The match was a typical hard-fought Derby with finesse at a premium on a heavy pitch. However, there was great excitement in only the third minute when Naylor finished a flowing Vale move by lashing a Walker cross straight into the net. Guppy caused continual problems for the visiting defence, but Stoke gradually gained more possession and Sandford headed the equaliser from a Gleghorn free kick in the thirty-third minute. Nevertheless, Glover and van der Laan went close for Vale, whilst Orlygsson twice nearly put the visitors in front.

Vale exerted the early pressure after the interval, although Stoke eventually succeeded in restricting their free play. The home keeper did not have to make a single save in the second half and in the latter stages of the game, Vale almost stole a victory. Tankard struck a tremendous shot against the Stoke bar six minutes from time, whilst four minutes later, Naylor appeared to be impeded as he ran through on goal.

THE AFTERMATH

Both sides remained in their existing positions in the table as a result of the draw, but both edged a point closer to safety from relegation. Although Vale lost four of their following five matches, they retained a relatively comfortable advantage over their main relegation rivals. Stoke dropped to sixth from the bottom and within two points of the relegation zone through being defeated in their next two games, but then staged a major revival by gaining fourteen points from the seven outings that followed.

174: SATURDAY 22 APRIL 1995, FOOTBALL LEAGUE, FIRST DIVISION

STOKE CITY (0) 0, PORT VALE (0) 1 (Foyle).

STOKE: Sinclair, Butler, Wallace, Cranson, Overson, Sigurdsson, Allen, Keen, Peschisolido, Carruthers (Gayle, 58), Gleghorn.
VALE: Musselwhite, Sandeman, Tankard, Porter, Aspin, D. Glover, Bogie, van der Laan, Foyle, Naylor, Guppy.

Venue: The Victoria Ground, Stoke-upon-Trent.
Attendance: 20,408.
Referee: S.W. Dunn (Bristol).

THE SETTING
Stoke were fifteenth in the First Division and had virtually guaranteed their survival from relegation by winning 1-0 at fourth from the bottom Swindon Town on the Monday before the local Derby. Vale had crept closer to safety by beating third from the bottom Burnley 1-0 at home on the same day and had moved up to sixteenth position as a result. Lou Marcari, the Stoke manager, made three alterations in their line-up from their previous match, with Wallace, Cranson and Peschisolido replacing the suspended Clarkson, Orlygsson (who was on international duty with Iceland) and the injured Angola, whilst Vale were unchanged.

THE MATCH
The match was contested at a frantic pace and Stoke attacked strongly from the outset. Peschisolido shot fractionally over the bar in the fourteenth minute and headed wide from a good position twelve minutes later, but chances were few and far between in the first half despite the intensity of Stoke's pressure game.

Vale finally settled into their stride after the interval and began to get a grip of midfield. The first danger sign occurred for Stoke in the fiftieth minute when Naylor broke clear and forced the home keeper to save his shot at the second attempt. Gleghorn missed a fine chance seventeen minutes later, which proved costly because Foyle magnificently headed a corner from Guppy into the net to give Vale the lead in the following minute. Naylor almost made the game safe for the visitors eleven minutes from time, but shot fractionally over the bar, whilst Peschisolido was denied the equaliser by a post just two minutes afterwards. However, Cranson was sent off for a foul on Sandeman in the eighty-fourth minute, which was decisive in Vale holding on to record their first league win at Stoke for over sixty-seven years.

THE AFTERMATH
As a result of their defeat, Stoke dropped two places in the table, although their First Division status was confirmed because relegation-threatened Swindon Town also lost. With the pressure off, Stoke took seven points from their final three matches to finish eleventh. Vale's local Derby success also ensured their survival and pushed them up to fourteenth place. However, they completed the season with two draws and ended up seventeenth.

175: SUNDAY 27 AUGUST 1995, FOOTBALL LEAGUE, FIRST DIVISION

STOKE CITY (0) 0, PORT VALE (0) 1 (Bogie).

STOKE: Muggleton, Clarkson, Sandford, Sigurdsson, Overson, Orlygsson (Sturridge, 66), Keen, Wallace, Peschisolido, Scott, Gleghorn (Potter, 79).
VALE: Musselwhite, Hill, Tankard, Bogie, Griffiths, D. Glover, McCarthy, Porter, Mills, L. Glover (Naylor, 85), Guppy.

Venue: The Victoria Ground, Stoke-upon-Trent.
Attendance: 14,270.
Referee: G. Singh (Wolverhampton).

THE SETTING
Stoke were tenth in the First Division, having played just two matches, and had won 3-2 at Leicester City eight days before the local Derby. Vale were second from the bottom, although they had played one game fewer than most of the other teams in the division. In addition, they had lost 3-1 at home to First Division rivals Huddersfield Town in the first round of the Coca-Cola Cup on the Tuesday prior to the Derby. In doing so, they had thrown away a 2-1 lead from the first leg and thus found themselves eliminated from the competition. Stoke's team was unchanged from their previous match, but Vale replaced Sandeman, Walker and the injured Foyle with debutant Andy Hill (recently signed from Manchester City for £150,000), Griffiths and Lee Glover.

THE MATCH
The match was an unusually slow-paced affair for a Potteries Derby and Stoke's normal hustle and bustle was noticeably lacking. Vale quickly gained control of the midfield and, although Peschisolido's movement was excellent, the home side were unable to exert any sustained pressure. Indeed, only on two occasions, when Guppy cleared Overson's header off the line and when Gleghorn shot just over, did Stoke seriously threaten to take the lead.

Vale went in front three minutes into the second period when Bogie beautifully squeezed a low drive between the home keeper and a post to round off an incisive move. Guppy then had an opportunity to put the visitors further ahead, but Muggleton saved impressively. Stoke belatedly woke up, although Peschisolido shot too near to the visiting custodian after breaking away, whilst substitute Sturridge lobbed the ball wide of a post with only Musselwhite to beat five minutes from the end.

THE AFTERMATH
Stoke dropped four places in the table as a consequence of losing to their rivals and three consecutive league defeats followed. However, they then staged a major recovery and lost only once in their next fifteen First Division games to set up a major challenge for promotion. Vale's third successive victory at Stoke pushed them up to eighteenth place, but the improvement was temporary and a dreadful sequence of just one more victory in their following fifteen league matches plunged them to the foot of the table.

176: TUESDAY 12 MARCH 1996, FOOTBALL LEAGUE, FIRST DIVISION

PORT VALE (1) 1 (Bogie), STOKE CITY (0) 0.

VALE: Musselwhite, Hill, Stokes, Bogie (Walker, 85), Griffiths, Aspin, McCarthy, Porter, Foyle, L. Glover (Naylor, 85), Guppy.
STOKE: Prudhoe, Clarkson, Sandford, Sigurdsson, Cranson, Wallace, Beeston (Potter, 64), Keen (Gayle, 82), Sheron, Sturridge, Gleghorn.

Venue: Vale Park, Burslem.
Attendance: 16,737.
Referee: E. Lomas (Manchester).

THE SETTING

Vale were in penultimate position in the First Division, but had won their first league match since 13 January by 2-1 at home against Southend United on the Saturday before the local Derby. In addition, they had recently beaten Premier League Everton 2-1 at home in the fourth round of the F.A. Cup before being knocked out after a replay by Leeds United. Stoke had extended their undefeated league run to six games with a 0-0 draw at Sheffield United three days prior to the Derby, which was sufficient to retain their promotion-challenging fourth place. Vale were unchanged from their previous match, whilst Lou Macari, the Stoke manager, preferred to make just one alteration in his line-up, with Wallace returning after suspension to replace Potter.

THE MATCH

Bogie put Vale in front after only twelve seconds when he ran on to a through ball from Hill and lashed an unstoppable shot into the top corner of the net. The goal equalled the quickest scored in the entire Football League all season. Vale were inspired by their success and controlled the midfield for most of the first half, whilst their wingers continually caused problems for the visiting defence. The home side created a series of chances, but Stoke came closer to scoring when Sheron shot against the inside of a post in the twenty-ninth minute.

After the interval, Stoke took command and pumped a succession of high balls into their opponents' penalty area, which caused danger, although Vale's defence held firm. Sturridge, Sheron and Gleghorn (twice) all went close for the visitors, but Vale almost extended their lead in the final minute when Prudhoe made a magnificent save from a rocket shot by Hill. Nevertheless, Vale completed their first league double over their local rivals since 1925.

THE AFTERMATH

As a result of their victory, Vale moved up four places and out of the relegation zone. Their success also proved the springboard for four successive league wins which followed and they eventually finished the season in a comfortable twelfth position, although they were beaten 5-2 in the final of the Anglo-Italian Cup at Wembley on 17 March. Stoke's promotion charge continued despite their local Derby setback and they ended up fourth, but were then eliminated from the play-offs in a two-legged semi-final 1-0 on aggregate by Leicester City.

177: SUNDAY 13 OCTOBER 1996, FOOTBALL LEAGUE, FIRST DIVISION

PORT VALE (0) 1 (Mills), STOKE CITY (0) 1 (Keen).

VALE: van Heusden, Hill (Foyle, 87), Tankard, Bogie (Mills, 46), Griffiths, Aspin (Glover, 83), McCarthy, Porter, Talbot, Naylor, Guppy.
STOKE: Prudhoe, Pickering, Worthington, Dreyer, Sigurdsson, Forsyth, Devlin (Whittle, 82), Wallace, McMahon (Keen, 45), Sheron (M. Macari, 90), Kavanagh.

Venue: Vale Park, Burslem.
Attendance: 14,396.
Referee: K.A. Leach (Wolverhampton).

THE SETTING
Vale were sixth from the bottom of the First Division and had lost 3-0 at Oldham Athletic (who were stranded at the foot of the table) eight days before the local Derby. In contrast, Stoke were eighth and had at least one match in hand over all the teams above them. They had drawn 1-1 at Bolton Wanderers, the league leaders, in their last game fifteen days prior to the Derby. Vale made three changes to their line-up from the Oldham debacle, with Bogie, Griffiths and Porter replacing Walker, Glover and Foyle, whilst Stoke were forced to include Prudhoe and McMahon instead of Muggleton, who was ill, and the injured Gayle.

THE MATCH
The contest was a scrappy affair, adversely affected by a strong wind, and chances were few and far between. Naylor struck the bar with a twenty-yard shot for Vale, whilst the home keeper produced a fine save to touch over an acute-angled drive from McMahon. However, most of the play in the first half was fought out in the midfield.

McMahon retired at half-time after being tackled by Porter and Bogie was carried off with an ankle injury shortly after the resumption of play. Nevertheless, with the introduction of substitute Mills, Vale went on the offensive, although the visitors eventually gained control. Sheron headed just wide and Aspin cleared an under-struck Wallace effort off the line before Keen put Stoke in front with a looping header from a Pickering centre in the sixty-fifth minute. Vale then bombarded the visitors' goal with high balls and Tankard and Guppy both went close before the home side seemed to have run out of steam ten minutes from the end. However, Mills rose majestically to head one final cross from Guppy into the net to equalise three minutes into injury time!

THE AFTERMATH
Vale climbed one position in the table as a result of the draw and steadily improved so that they mounted a serious promotion challenge in the new year. Stoke remained eighth after the local Derby, but their bid for the Premiership steadily fell away from the end of January.

178: SUNDAY 20 APRIL 1997, FOOTBALL LEAGUE, FIRST DIVISION

STOKE CITY (1) 2 (Sheron 2), PORT VALE (0) 0.

STOKE: Muggleton, Pickering, Griffin, Sigurdsson, Whittle, Forsyth, Flynn (McMahon, 72), Wallace, M. Macari, Sheron, Beeston (Mackenzie, 89).
VALE: Musselwhite, Hill, Tankard, Bogie, Aspin, Glover, McCarthy (Talbot, 70), Porter, Mills, Naylor, Koordes (Corden, 70).

Venue: The Victoria Ground, Stoke-upon-Trent.
Attendance: 16,209.
Referee: D.B. Allison (Lancaster).

THE SETTING
This was the last ever local Derby at the Victoria Ground before Stoke moved to their purpose-built new Britannia Stadium. Stoke were fourteenth in the First Division and had lost 2-0 at Crystal Palace on the Tuesday before the local Derby. Vale were faring rather better in a promotion-chasing sixth position and had won 3-2 at home to second from the bottom Oldham Athletic in their last match eight days prior to the Derby to chalk up their fourth consecutive league victory. Stoke made two alterations to their line-up from their previous game, with Sigurdsson returning from suspension and Sheron from injury to replace McMahon and Mackenzie, whilst Vale were unchanged. Stoke were still reeling from the announcement by their manager, Lou Macari, the day before the clash, that he was intending to quit his job at the end of the season. Thus circumstances combined to provide a tense setting for the televised match.

THE MATCH
The first half was closely contested and the tightness of the play meant that chances were at a premium. Vale's midfield was unable to flow as the Stoke players constantly harried their visitors and tempers threatened to boil over after Koordes made a wild tackle on Pickering. The home team finally broke the deadlock a minute before the interval when Sheron dribbled past three opponents and saw his shot deflect off Glover into the net.

The contest became more open in the second period as Vale searched for an equaliser, but Macari almost doubled the home side's lead in the fifty-sixth minute when he struck the bar from an overhead kick. Nevertheless, Muggleton came to Stoke's rescue by brilliantly saving a McCarthy shot ten minutes later and Sheron made the game safe six minutes from time by thumping in a loose ball to score his last ever goal for the club, as the Vale defence appealed in vain for a foul. There still remained time for Wallace to slash wide in the last minute after being put clean through and Vale finished a well-beaten team.

THE AFTERMATH
That night, a brawl developed in Burslem town centre between about thirty rival supporters, as a result of which a man from Bradwell sustained a fractured skull. Nevertheless, Stoke moved up a place in the table and seriously dented their rivals' promotion aspirations. Stoke eventually finished the season in twelfth position, whilst Vale disappointingly ended up eighth.

179: SUNDAY 12 OCTOBER 1997, FOOTBALL LEAGUE, FIRST DIVISION

STOKE CITY (2) 2 (Forsyth, Keen), PORT VALE (1) 1 (Naylor).

STOKE: Muggleton, Pickering, Griffin, Sigurdsson, Tweed, Keen, Forsyth, Wallace, Thorne, Andrade (Crowe, 85), Kavanagh.
VALE: Musselwhite, Hill (Bogie, 86), Tankard, Talbot, Aspin, Snijders, Ainsworth, Porter, Mills (Foyle, 76), Naylor, Koordes (Corden, 76).

Venue: The Britannia Stadium, Sideway.
Attendance: 20,251.
Referee: C.R. Wilkes (Gloucester).

THE SETTING
This was the first local Derby to be played at Stoke's new Britannia Stadium. Stoke were twelfth in the First Division and had beaten Bury 3-2 at home in their last match eight days before the Derby. Vale had accumulated the same number of points as their rivals, but were two positions above them by virtue of more goals scored. However, Vale had lost 4-2 at sixth-placed Swindon Town in their last outing on 4 October. Stoke had hired a private aircraft at a cost of £5,000 to fly their central defender, Sigurdsson, back from international duty in Iceland and this enabled them to name an unchanged team for the local clash. However, John Rudge, the Vale manager, selected Porter to replace Bogie and Hill to stand in for Glover, who had broken a leg in training.

THE MATCH
The play was very open in what was arguably the most entertaining local Derby in recent years. Stoke attacked strongly from the outset and Forsyth headed them in front from a centre by Keen in only the fourth minute. The home side continued to exert most of the pressure and Forsyth took the ball around the Vale keeper, but then managed to shoot wide of a gaping goal! Vale took advantage of their luck to equalise in the twenty-first minute when Naylor floated a wonderful header from distance into the net. However, Stoke regained the lead thirteen minutes later when Kavanagh broke away and laid the ball off at the vital moment for Keen to stroke it in. Vale retaliated and had loud appeals for a penalty denied shortly before the interval.

Both teams continued to push forward in the second period and Stoke had strong claims for a third goal disallowed eight minutes after the interval when Musselwhite palmed away a Forsyth header, possibly from behind the line. Nevertheless, as the game progressed, Vale fought desperately to level the score and almost succeeded near to the death through Foyle, but the home custodian produced a magnificent save to deny him.

THE AFTERMATH
Stoke climbed five places in the division as a result of their victory, but the following month they embarked on a disastrous run of ten games without a win which culminated in a club record 7-0 home defeat by Birmingham City as they plummeted down the table. Vale dropped one position following their local Derby failure and gradually slipped towards the relegation zone.

180: SUNDAY 1 MARCH 1998, FOOTBALL LEAGUE, FIRST DIVISION

PORT VALE (0) 0, STOKE CITY (0) 0.

VALE: van Heusden, Carragher, Tankard (Snijders, 57), Bogie, Glover, Hill, Ainsworth, Porter, Mills (Naylor, 88), Foyle, Jansson.
STOKE: Southall, Pickering, Tiatto, Sigurdsson, Whittle, Tweed (Crowe, 71), Forsyth, Wallace, Thorne, Lightbourne, Kavanagh.

Venue: Vale Park, Burslem.
Attendance: 13,853.
Referee: P. Rejer (Tipton).

THE SETTING

Vale were struggling at the foot of the First Division, two points from the safety zone, and had lost 2-1 at Bradford City on the Tuesday before the local Derby. Stoke were just one position and a single point ahead of their old rivals and had extended their sequence without a league victory to seven matches by being defeated 2-1 at home by fifth-placed Charlton Athletic four days prior to the Derby. Vale made only one change to their team from their previous game, with Bogie standing in for the injured Talbot, whilst Stoke's line-up showed four alterations. New loan signing, Neville Southall (from Everton), Tweed, Forsyth (who had returned to fitness) and Thorne replaced Muggleton, Tony Scully (who had returned to Manchester City), Keen and Crowe. The contest was staged in front of the lowest crowd for a Football League Potteries Derby since 1931.

THE MATCH

Stoke's five-man defensive system shaped the pattern of the match that neither side could afford to lose and restricted genuine scoring opportunities to a minimum. Nevertheless, Foyle almost put Vale in front in only the second minute, but Sigurdsson courageously threw himself in the way of his shot. Although the home side dominated the play, Thorne went close for Stoke, but the most memorable incident of the first half was a melee of jostling players near to the visitors' dugout.

Vale continued to force the pace in the second period, with Jansson providing most of the creativity on view, although he was fortunate not to be dismissed following a knee-high challenge on Pickering. Nevertheless, he nearly broke the deadlock with a tremendous twenty-five yard drive, whilst Ainsworth took the ball around the Stoke keeper, but then stroked it wide of the target! When the visitors substituted Crowe for centre-back Tweed, the play opened up somewhat, although neither team proved capable of stealing the victory.

THE AFTERMATH

Both sides remained in their respective positions as a consequence of the draw, although both edged a point closer to their relegation rivals. As it transpired, the point was critical in maintaining Vale's First Division survival and they therefore finished sixth from the bottom rather than being relegated along with Stoke, who ended up in penultimate position, three points adrift of the safety zone.

The Statistics

Stoke's Total Playing Record

HOME AND AWAY RECORD

	P	W	D	L	F	A	P	W	D	L	F	A
Football League	20	9	5	6	20	15	20	7	7	6	21	20
F.A. Cup	2	0	2	0	2	2	2	1	0	1	2	3
English Cup	1	1	0	0	1	0	1	1	0	0	4	2
Football League, Lanc. Reg. Section	3	2	1	0	7	3	3	3	0	0	12	2
Football League, Lanc. Reg. Sec. Sub. T.	3	2	1	0	10	2	3	1	0	2	5	7
Football League, West. Reg. Tournament	1	1	0	0	5	1	1	1	0	0	2	1
Football League North	1	1	0	0	2	0	1	0	0	1	0	3
Football League North, Second Champ.	1	1	0	0	6	0	1	1	0	0	4	2
Football League North Cup, Qual. Comp.	1	1	0	0	8	1	1	1	0	0	6	2
Autoglass Trophy	1	0	0	1	0	1	0	0	0	0	0	0
Birmingham Cup	4	2	2	0	5	3	7	3	1	3	13	13
Staffordshire Cup	6	5	0	1	18	11	6	2	2	2	9	7
Staffordshire Charity Cup	1	0	0	1	0	2	0	0	0	0	0	0
North Staffs. Charity Challenge Cup	1	1	0	0	1	0	0	0	0	0	0	0
North Staffs. (Royal) Infirmary Cup	5	3	2	0	15	1	4	3	0	1	8	7
Supporters' Clubs' Trophy	3	2	0	1	4	2	2	0	1	1	2	3
Wedgwood Trophy	2	1	1	0	4	3	1	1	0	0	1	0
Friendlies	27	18	7	2	54	23	35	20	4	11	80	48
Total	**83**	**50**	**21**	**12**	**162**	**70**	**88**	**45**	**15**	**28**	**169**	**120**

NEUTRAL VENUES RECORD

	P	W	D	L	F	A
North Staffs. Charity Challenge Cup	1	0	1	0	1	1

Stoke Reserves' Total Playing Record

HOME AND AWAY RECORD

	P	W	D	L	F	A	P	W	D	L	F	A
North Staffs. And District League	2	1	0	1	3	3	2	1	0	1	4	3
Hanley Cup	1	1	0	0	2	0	1	1	0	0	4	2
May Bank Cup	1	1	0	0	2	1	0	0	0	0	0	0
North Staffs. Nursing Society's Cup	1	1	0	0	2	1	0	0	0	0	0	0
Total	**5**	**4**	**0**	**1**	**9**	**5**	**3**	**2**	**0**	**1**	**8**	**5**

Stoke's Overall Playing Record

	P	W	D	L	F	A
Home Matches	88	54	21	13	171	75
Away Matches	91	47	15	29	177	125
Neutral Venues	1	0	1	0	1	1
Total	**180**	**101**	**37**	**42**	**349**	**201**

Vale's Total Playing Record

HOME AND AWAY RECORD

	P	W	D	L	F	A	P	W	D	L	F	A
Football League	20	6	7	7	20	21	20	6	5	9	15	20
F.A. Cup	2	1	0	1	3	2	2	0	2	0	2	2
English Cup	1	0	0	1	2	4	1	0	0	1	0	1
Football League, Lanc. Reg. Section	3	0	0	3	2	12	3	0	1	2	3	7
Football League, Lanc. Reg. Sec. Sub. T.	3	2	0	1	7	5	3	0	1	2	2	10
Football League, West. Reg. Tournament	1	0	0	1	1	2	1	0	0	1	1	5
Football League North	1	1	0	0	3	0	1	0	0	1	0	2
Football League North, Second Champ.	1	0	0	1	2	4	1	0	0	1	0	6
Football League North Cup, Qual. Comp.	1	0	0	1	2	6	1	0	0	1	1	8
Autoglass Trophy	0	0	0	0	0	0	1	1	0	0	1	0
Birmingham Cup	7	3	1	3	13	13	4	0	2	2	3	5
Staffordshire Cup	6	2	2	2	7	9	6	1	0	5	11	18
Staffordshire Charity Cup	0	0	0	0	0	0	1	1	0	0	2	0
North Staffs. Charity Challenge Cup	0	0	0	0	0	0	1	0	0	1	0	1
North Staffs. (Royal) Infirmary Cup	4	1	0	3	7	8	5	0	2	3	1	15
Supporters' Clubs' Trophy	2	1	1	0	3	2	3	1	0	2	2	4
Wedgwood Trophy	1	0	0	1	0	1	2	0	1	1	3	4
North Staffs. And District League	2	1	0	1	3	4	2	1	0	1	3	3
Hanley Cup	1	0	0	1	2	4	1	0	0	1	0	2
May Bank Cup	0	0	0	0	0	0	1	0	0	1	1	2
North Staffs. Nursing Society's Cup	0	0	0	0	0	0	1	0	0	1	1	2
Friendlies	35	11	4	20	48	80	27	2	7	18	23	54
Total	**91**	**29**	**15**	**47**	**125**	**177**	**88**	**13**	**21**	**54**	**75**	**171**

NEUTRAL VENUES RECORD

	P	W	D	L	F	A
North Staffs. Charity Challenge Cup	1	0	1	0	1	1

Vale's Overall Playing Record

	P	W	D	L	F	A
Home Matches	91	29	15	47	125	177
Away Matches	88	13	21	54	75	171
Neutral Venues	1	0	1	0	1	1
Total	**180**	**42**	**37**	**101**	**201**	**349**

Note that in both Stoke and Vale's playing records:
1. The details of two abandoned matches (26 January 1884 and 23 April 1910) have been included;
2. The 9 May 1945 Football League North, Second Championship, match also incorporated the Staffordshire Victory Cup;
3. Vale's home game in the F.A. Cup on 8 January 1951 was played at the Victoria Ground.

Big Crowds

CROWD	DATE	VENUE	COMPETITION
49,500	6 January 1951	The Victoria Ground, Stoke	F.A. Cup
46,777	4 September 1954	The Victoria Ground, Stoke	Football League
41,674	25 April 1955	Vale Park, Burslem	Football League
40,977	8 January 1951	The Victoria Ground, Stoke	F.A. Cup
39,446	10 October 1956	The Victoria Ground, Stoke	Football League
37,928	31 March 1956	The Victoria Ground, Stoke	Football League
37,261	8 October 1955	Vale Park, Burslem	Football League
35,288	15 September 1928	The Victoria Ground, Stoke	Football League
31,493	5 November 1927	The Victoria Ground, Stoke	Football League
Nearly 30,000	24 September 1921	The Victoria Ground, Stoke	Football League
29,296	22 October 1932	The Victoria Ground, Stoke	Football League
28,292	26 September 1931	The Victoria Ground, Stoke	Football League
27,455	2 October 1920	The Victoria Ground, Stoke	Football League
27,004	23 September 1989	The Victoria Ground, Stoke	Football League
Approx. 27,000	13 March 1920	The Victoria Ground, Stoke	Football League
26,609	13 December 1930	The Victoria Ground, Stoke	Football League
24,490	16 November 1992	The Victoria Ground, Stoke	F.A. Cup
24,334	24 October 1992	The Victoria Ground, Stoke	Football League
22,747	20 September 1924	The Victoria Ground, Stoke	Football League
22,697	6 March 1920	The Old Recreation Ground, Hanley	Football League

Small Crowds

CROWD	DATE	VENUE	COMPETITION
Perhaps 300	9 April 1900	The Victoria Ground, Stoke	Friendly
400	28 April 1900	The Athletic Ground, Cobridge	Friendly
About 500	24 April 1899	The Victoria Ground, Stoke	Friendly
A few hundred	26 April 1897	The Athletic Ground, Cobridge	Friendly
A few hundred	25 September 1905	The Victoria Ground, Stoke	Staffordshire Cup
800	26 September 1904	The Victoria Ground, Stoke	Birmingham Cup
Never more than 800 or 1,000	17 February 1894	The Athletic Ground, Cobridge	Friendly
About 1,000	7 May 1892	The Victoria Ground, Stoke	Staffordshire Charity Cup
Just over 1,000	5 May 1945	The Victoria Ground, Stoke	Football League North, Second Championship
Between 1,000 and 1,500 when the game started	27 March 1894	The Athletic Ground, Cobridge	Friendly
Under 1,500	6 October 1902	The Victoria Ground, Stoke	Staffordshire Cup
Not more than 1,500	27 April 1891	The Victoria Ground, Stoke	Friendly
1,500	24 September 1900	The Victoria Ground, Stoke	Birmingham Cup
1,500	7 October 1901	The Athletic Ground, Cobridge	Birmingham Cup
1,528	13 April 1986	Vale Park, Burslem	Friendly
1,600 'besides ticket-holders and supernumeraries'	27 November 1897	The Athletic Ground, Cobridge	Friendly
1,686	18 October 1988	The Victoria Ground, Stoke	Friendly

Big Scores

SCORE	DATE	VENUE	COMPETITION
Vale 1, Stoke 8	12 October 1918	The Old Recreation Ground, Hanley	Football League, Lanc. Reg. Sec.
Stoke 8, Vale 1	17 February 1945	The Victoria Ground, Stoke	Football League North Cup, Qual. Comp.
Vale 0, Stoke 7	17 February 1894	The Athletic Ground, Cobridge	Friendly
Stoke 7, Vale 0	9 May 1932	The Victoria Ground, Stoke	North Staffs. Royal Infirmary Cup
Stoke 6, Vale 0	1 April 1918	The Victoria Ground, Stoke	Football League, Lanc. Reg. Sec., Sub. Tournament
Stoke 6, Vale 0	5 May 1945	The Victoria Ground, Stoke	Football League North, Second Championship
Stoke 6, Vale 0	16 August 1945	The Victoria Ground, Stoke	Friendly
Vale 1, Stoke 6	14 August 1981	Vale Park, Burslem	Friendly
Vale 2, Stoke 6	30 September 1935	The Old Recreation Ground, Hanley	Friendly
Vale 2, Stoke 6	24 February 1945	The Old Recreation Ground, Hanley	Football League North Cup, Qual. Comp.
Stoke 0, Vale 5	25 September 1905	The Victoria Ground, Stoke	Staffordshire Cup
Vale 0, Stoke 5	25 December 1918	The Old Recreation Ground, Hanley	Friendly
Vale 5, Stoke 0	6 October 1919	The Old Recreation Ground, Hanley	Friendly
Stoke 5, Vale 0	5 May 1927	The Victoria Ground, Stoke	North Staffs. Royal Infirmary Cup
Stoke 5, Vale 1	9 December 1882	The Victoria Ground, Stoke	Staffordshire Cup
Vale 1, Stoke 5	16 February 1889	The Athletic Ground, Cobridge	Friendly
Vale 1, Stoke 5	14 December 1914	The Old Recreation Ground, Hanley	Birmingham Cup
Stoke 5, Vale 1	25 March 1940	The Victoria Ground, Stoke	Football League, West. Reg. Tourn.
Stoke 5, Vale 2	14 September 1903	The Victoria Ground, Stoke	Staffordshire Cup
Vale 2, Stoke 5	28 September 1903	The Athletic Ground, Cobridge	Birmingham Cup
Vale 3, Stoke 5	22 March 1884	Westport Meadows, Westport	Friendly
Stoke 5, Vale 3	6 October 1902	The Victoria Ground, Stoke	Staffordshire Cup
Vale 3, Stoke 5	9 May 1921	The Old Recreation Ground, Hanley	North Staffs. Infirmary Cup

Hat Trick Heroes

SCORER & GOALS	TEAM	DATE	VENUE	COMPETITION
George Mountford 5	Stoke	17 February 1945	The Victoria Ground, Stoke	Football League North Cup, Qual. Comp.
George Shutt 4	Stoke	9 December 1882	The Victoria Ground, Stoke	Staffordshire Cup
Arty Watkin 4	Stoke	14 December 1914	The Old Recreation Ground, Hanley	Birmingham Cup
Bob Whittingham 4	Stoke	12 October 1918	The Old Recreation Ground, Hanley	Football League, Lanc. Reg. Sec.
George Mountford 4	Stoke	5 May 1945	The Victoria Ground, Stoke	Football League North, Second Championship
Lewis Ballham 3	Stoke	7 May 1887	The Athletic Ground, Cobridge	Friendly
Willie Dickson 3	Stoke	8 October 1894	The Athletic Ground, Cobridge	Friendly
Mart Watkins 3	Stoke	6 October 1902	The Victoria Ground, Stoke	Staffordshire Cup
Peplow 3	Vale	11 September 1909	The Athletic Ground, Cobridge	North Staffs. And District League
Aaron Lockett 3	Vale	6 October 1919	The Old Recreation Ground, Hanley	Friendly
Arty Watkin 3	Stoke	7 January 1922	The Old Recreation Ground, Hanley	English Cup
Wilf Kirkham 3	Vale	7 September 1925	The Victoria Ground, Stoke	Football League
Harry Davies 3	Stoke	5 May 1927	The Victoria Ground, Stoke	North Staffs. Royal Infirmary Cup
Wattie Bussey 3	Stoke	26 September 1931	The Victoria Ground, Stoke	Football League
Freddie Steele 3	Stoke	24 February 1945	The Old Recreation Ground, Hanley	Football League North Cup, Qual. Comp.
Fred Basnett 3	Stoke	16 August 1945	The Victoria Ground, Stoke	Friendly
Jeff Cook 3	Stoke	14 August 1981	Vale Park, Burslem	Friendly
Lee Chapman 3	Stoke	21 April 1982	The Victoria Ground, Stoke	Wedgwood Trophy

Most Appearances

PLAYER	FIRST DERBY	LAST DERBY	Football League	F.A. Cup/ English Cup	Other Leagues	Other Cups	Friendlies	Stoke	Vale	TOTAL
Tom Holford	24 April 1899	9 May 1922	5	1	5	11	6	9	19	**28**
Tommy Clare	22 March 1884	19 March 1898	0	1	0	6	19	22	4	**26**
Dick Smith	4 April 1914	9 May 1922	5	0	8	8	3	24	0	**24**
Billy Tempest	4 April 1914	7 September 1925	12	1	3	7	1	20	4	**24**
Billy Briscoe	21 April 1919	5 May 1930	13	0	1	7	1	0	22	**22**
Bob McGrory	9 May 1921	30 September 1935	14	1	0	6	1	22	0	**22**
Joey Jones	14 December 1914	13 March 1920	2	0	11	3	5	21	0	**21**
Joe Brough	28 March 1910	7 January 1922	4	1	5	6	3	0	19	**19**
Lewis Ballham	1 May 1886	18 April 1892	0	1	0	2	15	13	5	**18**
Billy Twemlow	30 September 1916	7 May 1923	4	1	8	2	3	14	4	**18**
Billy Elson	15 October 1887	27 March1894	0	1	0	2	14	0	17	**17**
George Price	19 March 1898	25 September 1905	0	0	0	12	5	0	17	**17**
Charlie Parker	4 April 1914	25 September 1920	1	0	8	5	3	17	0	**17**
Jack Maddock	6 October 1917	26 January 1929	11	0	2	3	1	6	11	**17**
Tom Page	25 September 1920	15 September 1928	12	1	0	4	0	0	17	**17**
John McCue	18 November 1944	26 October 1959	6	2	2	4	3	17	0	**17**
Alec Milne	20 April 1914	24 January 1925	5	1	1	7	2	16	0	**16**
Bob Connelly	24 September 1921	6 February 1932	12	1	0	3	0	0	16	**16**
Jimmy Ditchfield	5 February 1887	26 December 1891	0	0	0	1	14	0	15	**15**
Jim Beech	8 October 1894	21 April 1902	0	0	0	5	10	0	15	**15**
Billy Heames	8 October 1894	14 September 1903	0	0	0	8	7	1	14	**15**
Lucien Boullemier	26 April 1897	6 October 1902	0	0	0	7	8	1	14	**15**
Harry Croxton	22 September 1902	14 January 1911	0	0	4	11	0	0	15	**15**
Arty Watkin	4 April 1914	24 January 1925	7	1	0	7	0	15	0	**15**
Billy Herbert	29 March 1915	6 October 1919	0	0	10	0	5	15	0	**15**
Tommy Sale	18 April 1931	16 August 1945	3	0	6	3	3	15	0	**15**
Roy Sproson	1 October 1951	1 May 1970	6	0	0	5	4	0	15	**15**
George Bateman	9 December 1882	10 May 1890	0	1	0	3	10	3	11	**14**
George Shutt	9 December 1882	28 September 1891	0	1	0	3	10	13	1	**14**
Billy Rowley	1 May 1886	7 May 1892	0	1	0	3	10	13	1	**14**
Alf Underwood	15 October 1887	7 May 1892	0	1	0	3	10	14	0	**14**
Bob McCrindle	30 November 1889	27 March 1894	0	0	0	2	12	0	14	**14**
Davy Brodie	29 March 1890	8 February 1896	0	0	0	3	11	14	0	**14**
Alf Wood	30 October 1893	22 October 1900	0	0	0	4	10	9	5	**14**
Adrian Capes	15 April 1901	28 March 1910	0	0	1	11	2	0	14	**14**
Harry Oscroft	6 January 1951	24 April 1961	6	2	0	3	3	11	3	**14**
Billy Reynolds	9 December 1882	26 December 1891	0	1	0	3	9	0	13	**13**
Bob Ramsey	1 May 1886	27 March 1894	0	0	0	1	12	4	9	**13**

206

MOST APPEARANCES

PLAYER	FIRST DERBY	LAST DERBY	Football League	F.A. Cup/ English Cup	Other Leagues	Other Cups	Friendlies	Stoke	Vale	TOTAL
Davy Christie	29 March 1890	10 September 1894	0	0	0	2	11	13	0	**13**
Joe Schofield	27 April 1891	19 March 1898	0	0	0	4	9	13	0	**13**
Jimmy Bradley	24 April 1899	29 March 1915	0	0	0	7	6	13	0	**13**
George Clarke	21 April 1919	13 October 1923	7	1	1	4	0	13	0	**13**
Peter Pursell	6 October 1919	28 April 1924	6	1	0	5	1	0	13	**13**
Wilf Kirkham	28 April 1924	9 May 1932	9	0	0	4	0	2	11	**13**
Harry Sellars	28 April 1924	30 September 1935	10	0	0	2	1	13	0	**13**
Frank Bowyer	18 November 1944	26 October 1959	5	2	2	2	2	13	0	**13**
Frank Mountford	18 November 1944	29 April 1957	4	1	4	2	2	13	0	**13**
Neil Aspin	23 September 1989	12 October 1997	9	2	0	1	1	0	13	**13**
Billy Poulson	9 December 1882	20 December 1890	0	1	0	3	8	0	12	**12**
Alf Edge	1 May 1886	9 May 1891	0	1	0	3	8	12	0	**12**
Meshach Dean	30 March 1891	8 October 1894	0	0	0	2	10	0	12	**12**
Arthur Bridgett	22 September 1902	26 December 1917	0	0	6	3	3	12	0	**12**
Albert Pearson	25 January 1915	7 January 1922	1	1	6	1	3	0	12	**12**
Tom Lyons	13 January 1917	2 October 1920	4	0	7	1	0	0	12	**12**
Bob Whittingham	13 January 1917	13 March 1920	2	0	7	0	3	11	1	**12**
Harry Davies	7 May 1923	4 March 1933	9	0	0	3	0	12	0	**12**
Johnny Sellars	5 May 1945	29 April 1957	6	2	2	0	2	12	0	**12**
Johnny King	4 September 1954	24 April 1961	5	0	0	5	2	12	0	**12**
Andy Porter	21 March 1988 (sub)	1 March 1998	10	1	0	0(1)	1(2)	0	12(3)	**12(3)**
Dean Glover	23 September 1989	1 March 1998	8(1)	2	0	1	1	0	12(1)	**12(1)**

Top Goalscorers

PLAYER	FIRST DERBY GOAL	LAST DERBY GOAL	Football League	F.A. Cup/ English Cup	Other Leagues	Other Cups	Friendlies	Stoke	Vale	TOTAL
Bob Whittingham	13 January 1917	6 March 1920	1	0	10	0	2	13	0	**13**
Arty Watkin	20 April 1914	7 January 1922	1	3	0	6	0	10	0	**10**
Billy Herbert	21 April 1917	28 April 1919	0	0	8	0	2	10	0	**10**
Tommy Sale	26 September 1931	16 August 1945	1	0	5	1	3	10	0	**10**
George Mountford	17 February 1945	5 May 1945	0	0	9	0	0	9	0	**9**
Wilf Kirkham	24 January 1925	5 May 1930	7	0	0	1	0	1	7	**8**
Lewis Ballham	7 May 1887	26 December 1891	0	0	0	0	7	6	1	**7**
Willie Dickson	17 February 1894	8 February 1896	0	0	0	1	6	7	0	**7**
George Shutt	9 December 1882	5 February 1887	0	0	0	4	2	6	0	**6**
Mart Watkins	22 October 1900	6 October 1902	0	0	0	6	0	6	0	**6**
Aaron Lockett	1 April 1918	6 October 1919	0	0	3	0	3	3	3	**6**
Freddie Steele	27 April 1936	16 August 1945	0	0	4	0	2	6	0	**6**
Alf Edge	5 February 1887	29 March 1890	0	0	0	0	5	5	0	**5**
Joe Schofield	17 February 1894	8 February 1896	0	0	0	2	3	5	0	**5**
Alf Wood	27 March 1894	22 October 1900	0	0	0	3	2	4	1	**5**
Vic Horrocks	28 March 1910	14 January 1911	0	0	1	4	0	5	0	**5**
Billy Tempest	14 December 1914	24 January 1925	1	1	0	3	0	4	1	**5**
Billy Briscoe	21 April 1919	9 May 1921	1	0	1	2	1	0	5	**5**
Jimmy Broad	1 October 1921	13 October 1923	5	0	0	0	0	5	0	**5**
Harry Davies	7 May 1923	15 September 1928	1	0	0	4	0	5	0	**5**
Wattie Bussey	15 September 1928	26 September 1931	4	0	0	1	0	5	0	**5**
Stanley Matthews	9 May 1932	27 April 1936	1	0	0	2	2	5	0	**5**
Frank Bowyer	18 November 1944	25 April 1955	1	1	2	0	1	5	0	**5**
Stan Steele	29 April 1957	10 October 1960	1	0	0	2	2	0	5	**5**